The Philosophy of Nationalism

The Philosophy of Nationalism

Paul Gilbert

The University of Hull

Westview Press
A Member of the Perseus Books Group

Copyright © 1998 by Westview Press, a Member of the Perseus Books Group

Published in 1998 in the United States of America by Westview Press, 5500 Central Avenue, Boulder, Colorado 80301-2877, and in the United Kingdom by Westview Press, 12 Hid's Copse Road, Cumnor Hill, Oxford OX2 9JJ

Library of Congress Cataloging-in-Publication Data
Gilbert, Paul, 1942–
   The philosophy of nationalism / Paul Gilbert.
      p.   cm.
   Includes bibliographical references and index.
   ISBN 0-8133-3083-1 (hardcover). — ISBN 0-8133-3084-X (pbk.)
   1. Nationalism.   I. Title.
JC311.G557   1998
320.54—dc21   98-11322
                                                                                                          CIP

The paper used in this publication meets the requirements of the American National Standard for Permanence of Paper for Printed Library Materials Z39.48-1984.

10   9   8   7   6   5   4   3   2

Contents

Preface

This book originates in a paper given to the International Society for the Study of European Ideas conference in 1990 (published as "Criteria of Nationality and the Ethics of Self-Determination," *History of European Ideas* 16 [1993], pp. 515–520). While that paper provides the book's *leitmotiv*, it now strikes me as grossly oversimplified and, worse, absurdly overoptimistic. Recent events on the world stage have helped me to realize this, but I also have many colleagues at Hull and elsewhere to thank for enabling me to improve on what I wrote then—too many, I fear, to thank individually. For reading and criticizing the manuscript, however, I should like to express my special gratitude to Matthew Festenstein, Kathleen Lennon, Loretta Napoleoni, and an anonymous reader for Westview Press. My commissioning editor, Sue Miller, provided valuable encouragement at the start of the project, and toward the end my copy editor, Christine Arden, did her best to make my text accessible. My thanks to them and to my project editor, Melanie Stafford, as well as to Chris Glover, who turned my words into a typescript.

Paul Gilbert

Introduction

Nationalism, which for nearly fifty years had seemed of interest only to specialists in political science and of no interest at all in political philosophy, is now back in the mainstream of both subjects. An enormous literature on nationalism has developed in political science,[1] in addition to a small but growing one in philosophy.[2] The former concentrates on the explanation of nationalist movements, the latter on their moral justification. But the two concerns are seldom brought together. In this book I set out to do just that, by arguing that the explanation of different nationalist movements depends upon the different justifications they can offer for pursuing their goals. In particular, I maintain that different nationalisms differ in the accounts they give of what constitutes a nation. This difference, in turn, is determined by what kind of group is held to have a right to independent statehood. The proliferation of diverse accounts of what a nation is—ethnic, cultural, economic, political, and so on—is best explained by regarding the nation as a group of a kind that has a right to statehood. The different accounts follow from the different grounds that can be offered for such a right.

The main task of the book, therefore, is to attempt to classify the accounts of nationhood that can be given in terms of the kinds of argument for statehood they support. It also aims to locate these accounts within their intellectual backgrounds and to provide some philosophical assessment of their strengths and weaknesses. This effort, given the huge scope of the subject, is necessarily tentative and programmatic. But it does involve treating nationalist ideas seriously and eschewing the widespread view that nationalism "hardly counts as a principled way of thinking about things."[3] I have proceeded on the assumption that even when no explicit defense of nationalist positions is offered, one can often be reconstructed—and, indeed, I wrestle with some sample texts with the intention of eliciting such a defense. I do not, however, believe that simple philosophical theories can be detected in their pure forms in many actual nationalist movements. These movements involve, for the most part, sometimes unstable combinations of different intellectual elements, so the theories I discuss may be regarded as ideal types. Yet my intention is to throw light on the real world by means of them. This book may be compared, then, to an introductory chemistry text

1

that lists the elements, explains their principal compounds, includes sketches of blast furnaces and sulfur kilns, and mentions Lavoisier and Dalton. If it is of some use in explaining the complex phenomena of nationalism, the present work has achieved much of its purpose.

The book's aim may seem idealist in an objectionable sense, relying on ideas to explain historical phenomena rather than on material circumstances. But this charge is unjustified. There is still a place for explaining why a particular group which aspires to statehood adopts the account of the nation that it does, and it is not unduly cynical to suppose that this account will apply easily to the circumstances that the group finds itself in—a territorial account if it shares a territory, an ethnic one if it is of common descent, and so forth. These are material circumstances which it is the province of history or political science to uncover, along with the particular concerns which motivate urgent demands for statehood. It should be noted, however, that nationalism, as I understand it, is by no means restricted to such aspirant groups. Nationalism pervades the politics of established states as well,[4] so much so as to be nearly invisible. I accept the arguments recently offered[5] that questions in political theory about democracy or distribution within such states presuppose some idea of the nation which legitimizes them, and on this point I have nothing to add here. Indeed, it follows from the view of nations suggested that states may commonly legitimize themselves through assuming that they are nation-states. Whether they are in reality depends not only upon whether their citizens are what they take themselves to be but also upon whether their account of nationhood supports their claim to legitimacy. If it does not, then they do not represent a nation.

It is here that much in the book will ring strangely in its readers' ears. For the book does not take the existence of the nation for granted. Rather, it proposes that the nation's existence depends upon whether there is a kind of group which possesses a right to statehood and, if so, upon what kind it is. The first chapter defends this approach. It attacks, in particular, the nominalist assumption which many political scientists make, that a nation is just what its members call a nation. This, I believe, is the wrong reaction to the proliferation of diverse accounts of nationhood. Specifically, it fails to account for disputes as to what nations there are in a territory and, hence, what states there might be rightfully be there. In Chapter 2 I answer the question as to why nations have a right to statehood by appeal to the principle that the members of a nation have, or might appropriately have, national obligations which a state could enforce. A nation is determined by its membership, which in turn is decided on the basis of either the sort of people or the kind of community thought to constitute the nation. An answer to the previous question, then, depends upon which can explain national obligations.

Chapter 3 investigates the view that nations represent *natural* divisions of humankind. We can develop this view by seeing people either as sorted out ethnically or as forming family-like communities. Both versions are rejected, however, so we turn, in Chapter 4, to accounts of the nation in terms of its members' psychological attitudes. Here we look, in particular, at two forms of the voluntarist view that nations are constituted by their members' will to associate together; but neither is plausible, as we shall see. Voluntarism is often associated with political (or civic) nationalism, which is investigated in Chapter 5. In holding that the features that collect people into a nation can be identified only in terms of their actual or desired state, political nationalism overstates, I suggest, the connection between nationhood and statehood for which I am arguing. Nevertheless, statehood does impose conditions on the character of nations, most notably territorial ones. These are discussed in Chapter 6, which culminates in a more promising account of the nation—namely, an economic one.

Nationalism is frequently taken to involve the promotion or defense of a national culture. The concept warrants a more extended treatment than it usually receives; accordingly, the next three chapters are devoted to it. In Chapter 7 culture is discussed as a system of communication, such as that exemplified in a national language. Here, in contrast to the usual essentialist versions, a plausible social constructionist account of such a national culture is identified. Its plausibility depends, however, upon its tacit importation of certain values. Chapter 8 turns to a discussion of culture as a value system. It considers and rejects a wide range of arguments for national rights to statehood based upon distinctive national values, proposing instead a form of communitarianism which incorporates values arguably common to all nationalisms. Even if this ethical case for nationalism were accepted, however, it is doubtful that any contemporary groups would qualify as nations under it. But nations are thought to be historical entities which transcend such ephemeral circumstances. In Chapter 9, accordingly, I examine the notion of a national history, commonly lumped together with other aspects of national culture. This notion does not, I conclude, yield results which strengthen the case for nationalism.

In a brief conclusion I express skepticism at the prospects of success for the nationalist project. It may well be that nationalism continues to enjoy its pervasive political power only because it has not been given the serious scrutiny it deserves.

Chapter One

Nationalism, Nations, and Names

The Nature of Nationalism

No easy hope or lies
Shall bring us to our goal,
But iron sacrifice
Of body, will, and soul.
There is but one task for all—
One life for each to give.
What stands if Freedom fall?
Who dies if England live?[1]

These lines by Rudyard Kipling may seem the epitome of nationalism, with their appeal to personal sacrifice in pursuit of a common national task—the task of ensuring the survival and independence of the nation, which is of greater importance than the lives and interests of its individual members. However, in introducing the World War II anthology in which this poem was reprinted, Harold Nicolson uses the poem to illustrate his observation that "our patriotism"—the English kind, that is to say—"is not nationalistic."[2] English patriotism, he must have thought, does not peddle the "easy hope or lies" that nationalism, as he understood it, depends upon. "English pride" is not the complacency and self-satisfaction about the country that fosters them. How, then, are we to understand nationalism? What is it, and how should it be evaluated?

At least four sorts of answers have been suggested; so before trying to characterize nationalism in detail, we need to get clear what sort of phenomenon it is. Is it a sentiment or feeling? Is it a system of practices or rituals? Is it a policy or course of political action? Is it a set of beliefs or doctrine? Nationalism, it has been suggested,[3] is a certain type of sentiment, a feeling of loyalty to one's nation. In this suggested sense, nationalism is sometimes equated with patriotism[4] and sometimes, as it seems to be by Harold Nicolson, contrasted with it.[5] Which of the two pertains may de pend upon whether nationalism is thought well or ill of; for patriotism is generally allowed to be a virtue.[6] Nationalism, on the other hand, is often condemned either as a bad form of patriotism—like jingoism or chauvinism—or as a sentiment contrasted with it. However, while patriotism evidently is a sentiment, nationalism is not. At most, it gives rise to sentiments, perhaps to patriotic ones. Patriotism is love of one's country, whether one's country is thought of in nationalist terms or not. Nationalism, I shall suggest, involves, among other things, a belief about the proper object of patriotism—namely, one's nation. Putting this belief together with someone's belief as to what his nation is will naturally lead him to patriotism. It may be natural, therefore, to confuse the sentiment of patriotism to which nationalism gives rise with the belief that it consists in, but such a view would be mistaken. And similarly mistaken would be the view that nationalism is a sentiment of the same order as patriotism, but to be contrasted with it because it is the wrong sort of feeling or the right sort of feeling directed at the wrong sort of object.

One reason for thinking of nationalism as a sentiment of attachment to one's nation rather than as a belief that the nation is the proper object of such a sentiment may be the view that this attachment arises not from any belief but, rather, from a natural human disposition. Some nationalists, as we shall see, advance this view. But it is one thing to hold the view and therefore to espouse a form of nationalism, and quite another thing to have the supposedly natural sentiment it posits. Furthermore, though some nationalists may in fact have no good or adequate reason for their attachments, it does not necessarily follow that they hold no beliefs which they *count* as a reason. To suppose otherwise is to erect a crude dichotomy between reason, which cannot lead us astray, and passion, which often does. In this vein, patriotism is sometimes thought of as directed at the right sort of object, because it is one for which there is a reason, and nationalism as directed at the wrong sort, because there is only an irrational attachment to it.[7] But to follow this line of thought is to avoid engaging intellectually with the nationalists' system of beliefs which justify their choice of object.

A second sort of reason that might be offered for rejecting the view that nationalism consists in a set of beliefs, though not necessarily for thinking of it as a sentiment, is the observation that we may describe as a nationalist someone who simply takes pride in her nation and gives it her support. But vigorous flag waving at football matches, which may be taken as an expression of nationalism, does not, it may be concluded, imply the possession of beliefs about nations. Nationalism, on this account, is not so much a system of beliefs as a set of practices,[8] through which national loyalty is cultivated and nations are sustained. This is indeed nearer the mark than the view of nationalism as national sentiment, but it similarly confuses effects with causes or, more properly, acts with their justifications. Certainly not all nationalists could articulate the beliefs which, I shall argue, characterize their nationalism; but they take their support for a nation, even if they cannot produce the justification, to be justified. Perhaps the justificatory beliefs are articulated by nationalist intellectuals or perhaps their articulation may be the task of an observer, since it plays no part in the practices that the beliefs justify.[9] In either event the practices in which the nationalists engage are not to be thought of as contrasted with beliefs: They are the expressions of them. Much the same can be said of the suggestion that nationalism consists in the pursuit of certain policies—namely, those taken to favor a nation. Nationalism as a form of political action would be unintelligible unless the policies that such action supported were not founded on a set of beliefs. Again, whether or not individual nationalists consciously hold the beliefs, their actions still express them.

It is necessary to establish that nationalism is a set of beliefs or a doctrine if we are to have any hope of understanding and evaluating it in terms of the reasons there may be for and against it. Yet establishing that it is a doctrine only leads us into the difficulty of determining precisely what doctrine it is, because several very different doctrines all seem to count as nationalism. Indeed, the problem of definition routinely troubles observers.

Here the diverse doctrines that different nationalists seem to hold make an answer difficult. Consider only a few examples. In Ulster, Irish nationalists challenge the existence of the Northern Irish state while Ulster Unionists support it as part of the United Kingdom. Their disagreement is not simply a factual one as to whether, by certain agreed criteria, Northern Ireland satisfies the conditions for being part of Ireland or those for being part of the United Kingdom.[10] The criteria employed by the two sides in the dispute are different, and this difference reflects a disagreement in their doctrines, though even these conflicting doctrines are themselves not free of internal differences and complexities. On the Irish nationalist side a united Ireland is mainly dictated by the criterion of common occupancy of the national homeland. Irish nationalism is the doctrine that a certain territory—the island of Ireland—constitutes the national home and thereby warrants national statehood. Surely, it may seem, this doctrine is quite typical of nationalism generally.[11]

A moment's reflection will dispel the illusion. For, contrary to the impression created by nomenclature, we observe in Northern Ireland a contest not between nationalism and something else but between two forms of nationalism. Ulster Unionism is, of course, a type of British nationalism, attested by the Unionists' constant asseveration of British nationality. Their criterion has nothing to do with occupancy of a British homeland. While asserting their right to occupancy of Northern Ireland, they do not base their claim to British statehood on its being part of a British national home. Rather, they base their claim on an allegiance they take themselves to share with the people of Britain. That is what they believe constitutes them as part of a British nation and entitles them to live under the British state.

The two nationalisms are so different that it seems hard to see what they have in common apart from the vocabulary of nationhood employed in support of analogous but competing political claims. Yet both are undeniably forms of nationalism: Irish nationalism is paradigmatically so and a model for many other nationalist movements, whereas British nationalism is arguably the forerunner of nationalisms generally[12] and still retains its essential features.

Welsh nationalism,[13] by contrast with mainstream Irish nationalism, is founded on an assertion of the distinctiveness of Welsh culture from, in particular, that of England. Although Welsh nationalism has political goals, these may seem to be subordinate to its cultural ones, most notably the preservation of the Welsh language. This, too, seems a characteristic form of nationalism, to be found, for example, in Quebec and Hawaii. Indeed, many thinkers take a common culture to be essential to the nationalist conception of nations.[14] These nationalisms seem quite different, however, from the British, Canadian, and American nationalisms with which they compete. The last contrast is particularly acute. The American nation is, after all, ostensibly based on quite other principles than common culture or ethnicity or even a territorial homeland.

> *America is West and the wind blowing.*
> *America is a great word and the snow,*
> *A way, a white bird, the rain falling,*
> *A shining thing in the wind and the gull's call.*
> *America is neither a land nor a people. . . .*
> *Here we must live only as shadows.*
> *This is our race, we that have none, that have had*
> *Neither the old walls nor the voices around us.*
> *This is our land, this is our ancient ground.—*
> *The raw earth, the mixed bloods and the strangers. . . .* [15]

Quoting these lines by Archibald Macleish as the United States prepared to enter the war against fascism, Harold Nicolson countered the notion that American nationalism is "something comparatively artificial and unauthentic . . . not a pulsation of the blood but a deliberate form of be-lief,"[16] by observing that its basis in an idea, rather than in "generations of gradual growth," does not make it any the less genuine.[17]

The American "melting pot" absorbs a wide range of cultures and races, requiring of its members only commitment to its constitutional principles of individual liberty and formal equality. American nationalism conceives of the nation as a sovereign people whose national unity is forged by just such constitutional commitments. It is a form of nationalism that recurs in postrevolutionary France, whose example was followed by many. Some theorists regard this emphasis on the sovereignty of the people as paradig-matic of nationalism.[18] But American nationalism could scarcely be more different from cultural nationalism, or from the ethnic nationalism of, say, Chicano nationalism or black nationalism directed against it in the 1960s. For here we have a nationalism that celebrates ethnic origins and yet ex-cludes from the nation, whose interests it advocates, those who do not share these origins. In the minds of many, this has seemed the inevitable tendency of nationalism, and a deeply disturbing one, however under-standable it may have been in the cases just mentioned.

What, then, among all this diversity, is nationalism? After all, even the aims seem very different: territorial integration, freedom of political asso-ciation, cultural survival, popular sovereignty under a liberal and demo-cratic constitution, ethnic segregation. Just what core of common belief could lead to such differences remains quite unclear.[19] Yet it is evident that the differences spring from contrasting conceptions of what a *nation* is: the population of a territory, a voluntary association, a cultural com-munity, a sovereign people, an ethnic group. Depending on how the na-tion is conceived, the aims of its corresponding form of nationalism differ. The implication is that if there *is* any unity beneath the diversity of na-tionalisms, it is to be found in some common core of their conceptions of the nation.

The Concept of Nation

The word "nationalism" is a relatively recent coinage,[20] entering common currency as late as the nineteenth century, the era of the great spread of nationalism in Europe. "Nation" is a much older word; of Latin etymol-ogy, it was used in its original sense in the eighteenth century.[21] Vestiges of this earlier usage persist today. "Nation" meant, very roughly, what we sometimes mean by a people, when we are thinking of them as distinct from others, particularly in terms of birth or descent. It was thus applied most easily to strangers and, for this and other reasons, was readily used to refer to the Jewish people. Shakespeare, we may recall, had Shylock say about Antonio that "he hates our sacred nation."[22]

Nearly three hundred years later, George Eliot's Jewish hero, Daniel Deronda, took a different line: "[T]he idea that I am possessed with is that of restoring a political existence to my people, making them a nation again, giving them a national centre, such as the English have, though they too are scattered over the globe."[23]

It is not that Jews no longer constituted the kind of entity they did in Shakespeare's day but, rather, that a shift in the *concept* of nationhood had taken place. It is a shift that, notoriously, led many to make efforts to assimilate into nations instead of reconstructing their own. Thus, for example, Sean O'Faolain introduced Moll Wall, a twentieth-century "Irish speaking, Dublin born Jewess," as follows: "[H]er real name was not Moll. It was Miriam, but since in her excessive efforts to *nationalise* herself she always signed her name not only in Gaelic but in an outmoded script . . . , her fellow students called her Moira, or Maurya, or Maureen, until she ended up by being universally known as Moll."[24]

What led to this change, and what concept of the nation did it leave us with? Three developments, I believe, led to the change—and each determines a somewhat different concept of the nation. The first is the rise of the modern state with its claim to sole authority over all those who live within its borders. Such a state needs a notion of those who are subject to its authority in view of their membership of it. For the power of the state must be experienced by its members not simply as an external force, nor yet as the manifestation of personal feeling, but rather as the proper expression of the state's impersonal relation to its members. Their membership must be a clearly legal status, conferring certain rights and imposing certain duties. This status, I suggest, is what lies at the heart of the legal conception of nationality.[25] The aggregate of those who share their nationality in this sense is the nation, and in the same sense a single nation corresponds to every state.[26] The old sense of "nation" has been modified and made precise in a particular context—a context unavailable before the rise of the modern state. In this sense of the word, no general answer can be given to the question "What is a nation?" over and above providing the directions for discovering how the constitutional arrangements of a particular state determine what is the nation corresponding to it. These differ from state to state. French nationality is, roughly speaking, acquired by birth in the land of France, whereas German nationality depends upon German descent and is accorded even to those whose forbears have lived for generations outside of Germany. Different sorts of nationalists, however, may disagree as to which arrangement is correct in terms of *really* determining a nation.

It is immediately evident that this legal sense is *not* the sense of "nation" which nationalists employ. If it were, then it would be self-contradictory for a nationalist to press for independent statehood for a portion of an existing state, on the grounds that it constituted a separate nation. Simply by virtue of their membership of the existing state the inhabitants of that portion constitute part of the same nation, in the legal sense, as others, and not a separate nation. Yet a demand for independent statehood of this sort is just what typifies many nationalists. Even when they do not need to make this demand because they already have their own state, they commonly entertain the possibility of the demand in conjuring up the specter of foreign domination as something to be resisted in the name of independent statehood.

A second sense of "nation" is one that has been employed by anthropologists and others concerned with the scientific classification of social groups.[27] The growth of science in the seventeenth and eighteenth centuries was characterized by a demand to classify the objects of study more rigorously than in common speech. Birds, butterflies, and peoples, particularly the "primitive" peoples of the expanding European colonies, yielded themselves up to classification. The old imprecise notion of a nation could be pressed into service here. *How* things are classified depends on what theory we have as to what makes them the same or different. In biological classification, evolutionary theory plays this role. In anthropological classification of peoples, a theory is needed to determine what is to count as a nation. Throughout the nineteenth century it was commonplace to regard people as divided up into races according to their physical attributes. Nations could be conveniently regarded as subdivisions of races, largely on the spurious basis that, since their languages were related, then they were also. Language thus became a test for nationhood. With the passing of racial theories peoples came to be thought of as distinguished by their own perceptions of themselves as different—for example, in view of their different languages—such that language is still a test for nationhood, despite the very different conception of the nation that is involved. Thus, in this usage, Switzerland may be thought of as inhabited by people of different nations: French, German, Italian, and so on.

The anthropologist's term "nation" is an observer's term: It need have no parallel in the discourse of the people to whom it is applied. Our ordinary concept of nation is not of this kind, however: It figures ineliminably in nationalist discourse. It is a concept which we employ as political agents in a world of nation-states where this discourse is part of our ordinary unreflective talk. We should not, therefore, be seduced into adopting some loose version of the anthropological usage. We are not, for the most part, amateur anthropologists, because we are not scientists at all, not even amateur ones. We have no knowledge of, or interest in, the theories that determine anthropological classification. Our classificatory aims are quite other than those of scientific theorists, just as the countryman's traditional classification of birds and butterflies is differently motivated from that of the scientific ornithologist and entomologist. Nor, with certain exceptions to be discussed later, is the nationalist's interest in classifying nations an anthropological one. Most nationalists would not consider their claims about the existence of nations to be falsifiable by anthropologists' theories. Their claims, in the main, have a quite different kind of justification.

I insist on this point in order to indicate how misguided it is to sift through the definitions of the nation offered by social anthropologists, political scientists, and so on—in order to extract some common core of meaning as giving us a concept of the nation relevant to considering the claims of nationalists. Such a process is all too common among political theorists, many of whom are, in truth, not clear about what kind of activity they are engaged in—scientific, philosophical, historical, or whatever. But this process is quite misguided, since different definitions presuppose, if only implicitly, different theories and, as often as not, theories aiming to provide explanations of different phenomena.

The mistake, however, goes deeper. It lies in supposing that there is an account of the concept of nation to be offered independent of the context in which it figures. Such a supposition, I have argued, is not tenable. The legal concept is distinctive because of the context in which it figures, and so is the anthropological concept or concepts. Neither of these, though, is the context in which we ordinarily think of nations. That, I suggest, is an unavoidably *political* context. But my point here should scarcely be surprising, since we typically think of nations when thinking of nationalism. We think of them when we explicitly think about nationalists' demands for statehood and other political claims. We also think of them when, perhaps without realizing it, we accept some particular nationalist account of nations. But when we do that, we swallow the political doctrine in which it figures. For the different accounts of nations which make the giving of a unitary definition so problematic are different, I shall argue, precisely because of the political purposes in pursuit of which these accounts are put to use.

The third development which affects the old concept of the nation and provides it with a new context of application is, indeed, the development of nationalism itself. Nationalism is a doctrine that implies particular political goals which themselves presuppose the development of the modern state. Moreover, nationalism is a modern phenomenon,[28] and the concept of the nation it employs is a modern concept unintelligible outside of its modern political context. This fact, however, has a consequence unwelcome to those who think that we can grasp what nationalism is on the basis of an understanding of what nations are, anterior to and independent of nationalism. There is, I am suggesting, no such understanding. Nationalists are not simply utilizing in its agreed application a concept ready at hand. The use to which they put the concept they find changes it—specifically, in a way that undermines the agreement there is about its application.

The reason for this outcome is that the context in which the political concept of nation occurs is a context of *debate*, not, as with the legal and scientific concepts, a context of description. This debate includes debate about the application of the term "nation." The Irish nationalists and Ulster Unionists evidently do not agree on the application of the term. As mentioned earlier, there is no a straightforward disagreement about the facts on the basis of which a concept with agreed criteria is applied. Rather, it is a disagreement about those criteria themselves. Any satisfactory account of the political concept of the nation must allow for this latter disagreement. No synoptic descriptive account can do so.

Nominalism

Faced with this predicament, many theorists have given up the struggle to find a unitary account of nationhood. Instead they have concluded that there is no single concept of the nation but that a nation is just whatever people who take themselves to be a nation take themselves to be. A nation is, in a beguiling phrase, a *self-defining* political community.[29] One community will take itself to be defined by territory, another by language, a third by a common allegiance, and so forth. But there is no agreed kind of political community that they all take themselves to be, as would be the case if they shared a single conception of nationhood.

It is easy to see how this view of nations as self-defining escapes the problem of trying to characterize nationhood in a way that makes sense of competing claims to it. What *appear* to be substantive disputes over the identity of nations are really only disputes between claimants to rival statehoods or the like, who simply trick themselves out in national dress. There are only political problems to be dealt with, not intellectual and ethical ones to be debated. One national group cannot, for example, deny another's claim to statehood, since each *is* a nation if it defines itself as such. Yet, as we have just seen, it seems a genuine question whether Ulster Protestants are part of the Irish or the British nation.[30] Their self-definitions do not eradicate this issue. The self-definitional view of nation is thus a very pessimistic one. Its inevitable consequence is that, insofar as national demands are grounded on claims about national identity, they cannot be compared and assessed as such. Talk of national rights and the like makes no sense on the self-definitional view. Rather, national demands assume the character of power struggles, which, if they can be adjudicated upon at all, must be judged on the basis of quite other grounds.

This consequence may itself seem a *reductio absurdum* of the self-definitional view, but it faces other difficulties as well. What, on this view, does a political community define itself *as* when it counts as a nation through its self-definition? It cannot, contrary to appearances, be as a *nation*, since, on this view, nations are whatever their members take them to be, and so the idea of a nation would play no real part in determining what it is they define themselves as. The same difficulty affects the influential view[31] that "a nation exists when a significant number of people in a community consider themselves to form a nation." Again we can ask, What is the *content* of their belief? What is it that they consider themselves to form? But this suggestion, like the last, provides no possible answer. Its intelligibility presupposes that a common concept of nationhood enters people's thoughts about their national identity while simultaneously denying that there is such a concept. Another way of reaching this conclusion[32] is to notice that if people's belief that they are a nation is what makes them a nation, then *what* they believe when they believe they are a nation will be that they believe they are a nation. But the content of that belief will also be that they believe they are a nation, and so on *ad infinitum*. This infinite regress of beliefs is vicious, since it means that the content of a belief in nationhood is never determinate.

In fact, the only obvious way to make sense of the self-definitional view is to see it as holding that people constitute a nation when they style themselves as a "nation." It is not that they apply a determinate concept of nation to themselves but, rather, that they apply just the word "nation," or whatever word in their own language functions, for political purposes, in the same way as "nation" does in English. We could extend this condition a little by saying that they call themselves by the same name, and that the name functions in the same way as those that we call "names of nations." This interpretation of the self-definitional view of nations treats it as a form of *nominalism*—the doctrine that all the instances of a general word have in common is that they are referred to by that word. Thus the self-definitional view is a species of nominalist accounts of nations: Nations just are whatever are *called* nations. It is that species that makes what people call themselves definitive of what a nation is. In what follows I shall restrict my use of the term "nominalism" to refer only to this species.

Nominalism introduces a use of the word "nation" that, like the legal or scientific uses, is essentially an observer's rather than a participant's.[33] The nominalist account tells us not to bother whether peoples or states are right to call themselves nations, not to participate in their practice of it, but just to go along with their own descriptions. "Nation," for the nominalist, means *so-called nation* and, in terms of the self-definitional version of nominalism we are looking at, *self-styled nation*. The use of the word "nation" here might just as well be in scare quotes, for the nominalist declines to employ it *in propria persona*. There may sometimes be a justification for this implicitly scare-quoted usage of the word "nation" when we wish to report what nations people take themselves to be without committing ourselves to their criteria.[34] (Indeed, I shall often engage in this usage myself in order to avoid the long-winded periphrasis "supposed nation" or variations thereof.) But we must not forget that those who do use the term *in propria persona* take themselves to have a coherent use for it. It is a counsel of despair to assume that they are misguided in this assumption, for if we are to have any hope of understanding their discourse as they take themselves to understand it, then we must uncover some concept of nationhood common to the political disputants. Without that we shall have no grasp of nationalism from the viewpoint of the participants and no chance of evaluating it as a political doctrine.

Indeed, the matter is worse than this. If there is no coherent concept of the nation, then there is no set of beliefs which count as nationalism, for these apparent beliefs will either lack any content—there will be muddle and confusion where a concept ought to be—or they will have different contents depending on the kind of nationalism in question, with nothing linking them except a name. But this position is very implausible, for if either scenario prevailed it would be a mystery as to how rival nationalists could understand each other to the extent of continuing to engage in debate.

State and Nation

The great sociologist Max Weber appreciated the problems involved in trying to analyze the idea of nationhood: "[I]f the concept of 'nation' can in any way be defined unambiguously, it certainly cannot be stated in terms of empirical qualities common to those who count as members of the nation," because "the reasons for the belief that one represents a nation vary greatly."[35] Weber also suggested that "the concept means, above all, that one may exact from certain groups of men a specific sentiment of solidarity in the face of other groups."[36] But the sentiments of solidarity that bind people together into nations are, he observed, very various. The only way to identify them as *national* sentiments and hence to pick out the groups they delineate as nations is, he argued, to discuss them in terms of a political tendency: "If one believes that it is at all expedient to distinguish national sentiment as something homogeneous and specifically set apart, one can do so only by referring to a tendency towards an autonomous state."[37]

National sentiments are those that the members of a group possess in virtue of which the group has a tendency toward independent statehood. Thus Weber defined nations in terms of the results they tend to achieve.

Insofar as there is a common object lying behind the obviously ambiguous term "nation" it is apparently located in the field of politics. One might well define the concept of nation in the following way: a nation is a community of sentiment which would adequately manifest itself in a state of its own: hence a nation is a community which normally tends to produce a state of its own.[38]

In short, Weber regarded "nation" as signifying a dispositional concept, like that of a caterpillar. Caterpillars are grubs of a kind which have a disposition to turn, in appropriate circumstances, into butterflies. They are identified on the basis of appearance, but only because things with that appearance tend to become butterflies.

There is, I shall argue, a good deal that is right in this account. But there is also something that is wrong. Weber noticed that "nation" is applied on the basis of many different features, but he failed to grasp the implications of the widespread disagreement over what features should form the basis of its application. How would he have explained such disagreement? It would have to have been disagreement about which kinds of group *did* tend to acquire a state of their own. Yet this seems quite implausible. The dispute between Irish nationalists and Ulster Unionists does not look like a disagreement as to whether there *will* be a united Irish state or whether the Six Counties will continue to be part of the British state. It does not even seem to be a disagreement over the more general question of whether groups which identify themselves in terms of a shared territory are more or less likely to acquire statehood than groups which do so in terms of shared allegiance. These disagreements are the sort that exercise political sociologists. They are not the sort that concern those who participate in politics, those whose use of the concept of a nation we are here considering.

Described in this way, Weber's error is immediately obvious. The disagreements he had to interpret as about which groups *tend* to acquire statehood were in fact disagreements about which groups *should* acquire statehood. Weber's notion of an empirical tendency is unsatisfactory, and there are some hints of his own discomfort with it. He concluded from the fact that the concept implies "that one may exact from certain groups of men a specific sentiment of solidarity in the face of other groups" that "the concept belongs in the sphere of values."[39] He meant that the claim that we may exact a sentiment of solidarity from certain groups is a value judgment. Similarly, his characterization of a nation as a community which *normally* acquires statehood seems to imply a value judgment. For the notion of normality involved here typically has to do with what happens unless a nation is obstructed or interfered with. This is not an empirical notion. It implies value judgments about the treatment that members of a nation may expect. Perhaps it implies that a nation will usually acquire statehood if its rights are not interfered with. Again, Weber's definition of a nation as what would "adequately manifest itself" in an independent state embodies an evaluative notion of what is adequate for the nation. Maybe it embodies in part the idea of the nation exercising its right to recognition through statehood.

The foregoing suggests that, instead of following Weber's definition of a nation as what tends to independent statehood, we should think of it as a group of a kind that has, other things being equal, the *right* to statehood. Then disagreements about what nations there are will be disagreements over what sorts of groups have these rights—a conclusion which fits well with the sort of political disagreements over nationhood we have encountered.

This is an initial statement of the thesis which I shall develop in the remainder of this book. It relies upon what I shall refer to as the *constitutive principle of nationalism*—a normative principle governing our application of the concept of nation. The principle provides, I suggest, both a necessary and, with certain qualifications, a sufficient condition of nationhood. As a necessary condition it operates least controversially, holding that there is, other things being equal, a national right to independent statehood.[40] This is a corollary of the principle of national self-determination, for if a nation has a right to determine under what constitutional arrangements it should be governed, then it must, other things being equal, have a right to the various forms of government between which it must choose, and one of these will usually be thought of as independent statehood. If nationalists deny that a group is of a kind to possess this right, then they are committed to denying that it is a nation. Or more generally, if we wish to deny that the right of national self-determination exists at all, then, I maintain, we must deny that there *are* nations. This is one sense in which the principle is constitutive of nationhood. There is no general understanding of what a nation is, I also maintain, such that we can discuss whether or not on that understanding a nation has a right to self-determination. For any such understanding will either not reflect the political concept governed by the principle of nationalism or it will reflect the particular understanding offered by a species of nationalism, so that it is the claims of this species of nationalism that are being assessed, not the claims of nationalism in general.

So much for the principle of nationalism as providing a necessary condition for nationhood. Even if we accept that the application of the concept of nation is constrained by its entailing a presumptive right to independent statehood, it is going a good deal further to admit that possession of the right is a sufficient condition for nationhood, that a nation just *is* the kind of group that has a right to statehood by virtue of the kind of group it is. What could justify this claim? The answer is that nationalism as such does not specify *what* kinds of group have the right to statehood: It claims only that there *are* groups of such a kind. It claims, I suggest, only that there are nations, and all it tells us about nations is that they are the kind of group that has this right. Any further elaboration of the idea of a nation generates a specific type of nationalism, a particular theory about what nations are: It does not narrow down the concept of nation that all nationalisms share.

If this claim seems hard to swallow, I offer two palliatives. The first may help those who think that nations must be *more* than merely a kind of right holder. It is to commend the account of nationhood as a concept governed by the constitutive principle on *methodological* grounds. It is best, I advise, to regard nationalism as comprising those doctrines which have this idea of the nation at their core. It makes sense, most simply, of the great diversity of doctrines that can be described as nationalism, and it does not lead us to describe as nationalism doctrines we would not wish to. It makes sense of different nationalisms because it sees each of them as offering a distinctive conception of what a nation is, just because it can construct an argument as to why a nation under this conception should have a right to statehood. It enables us, then, to classify and evaluate nationalisms in terms of the different sorts of argument they produce for allowing groups this right. Whether nationalism in general is acceptable boils down to the question of whether any of these arguments are successful. If they are not, then nations do not have a right of self-determination: But that is because there are no nations, as I am treating them here. Employing the constitutive principle to delimit them thereby gives us a way of tackling the general question of nationalism's acceptability.

The second palliative may help those who think there are nations but who reject talk of rights of self-determination or of statehood as a national goal. It is to regard the constitutive principle of nationalism as susceptible to a variety of formulations, depending on the kind of nationalism in question, which cluster round the initial statement I gave in terms of a right to independent statehood by virtue of the kind of group a nation is. To start with, talk of *rights*[41] may sometimes be capable of being whittled down to talk of what is desirable for a national group or of what a group is apt for. A state which does not correspond to a nation would, except for special reasons to the contrary, lack legitimacy under the initial statement of the constitutive principle. Under this reformulation, such a state is morally or rationally indefensible: It exists not contrary to right but contrary to what is good or reasonable. Notice that though this principle can, for some nationalisms, be whittled down, it cannot in general be vamped up into the claim that "the political and national unit should be congruent."[42] The latter is much too strong and could be sustained only by nationalists who hold, for example, that *only* nations are apt for statehood. Other nationalists could assert that, while nations had a right to statehood, it was, for a variety of reasons, sometimes preferable not to exercise it—perhaps because a nation's particular goals would be better accommodated under some other political arrangement.

Next, then, we should be willing to allow that it need not be the right to or desirability of *statehood* as such that nationalists must argue for, by contrast to some other forms of political independence such as regional autonomy. The key point is that the nation should be politically organized in respect of those matters relating to its distinct nationhood independent of other groups. What this amounts to may differ from one type of nationalism to the next (and, again, it is an option whose exercise need not be demanded at any given time). The arguments in this book are mostly couched in terms of the strong form of the constitutive principle of nationalism, although they can often be modified in terms of a weaker one. Whether they can or not I leave as an exercise for the reader who thinks that they should be weakened. Notice, however, that it is *independent* governance that is in question, not necessarily *self*-government—that is, government of a group by itself. Whether autonomy, in *this* sense, is sought again depends upon the type of nationalism.[43]

The possible dilutions of the principle as initially stated exhibit, I suggest, a sufficient family resemblance to count as versions of the same idea. They all have in common one crucial element—namely, that the right (or whatever) being claimed is claimed on the basis of the *kind* of group it is claimed for. Two contrasts are of particular importance here. First, we need to distinguish a group's right to independent statehood by virtue of the kind of group it is from the right a group may have by virtue of the *circumstances* it is in. This contrast is particularly striking in the case of rights to secession, which may be argued for either on a national basis or on the grounds that the group is being subjected to injustice that only independent statehood could prevent.[44] Even if the injustice is being done to a national group, it arguably has a separate right to secede, not through being that kind of group but through being placed in circumstances of injustice that a non-national group might equally be placed in. Such a right deriving from injustice done will, I suggest, normally trump a national right. That is why the national right is a presumptive right only—a right which may lie in abeyance should a right to escape injustice conflict with it. Hence the *ceteris paribus* claim in the formulation of a right to a state as a necessary condition of nationhood.

The second contrast is between a right to statehood that a group has by virtue of being the kind of group it is and the right a group has by virtue of the way its constituent groups exercise their rights. The obvious case of the latter is a federation decided upon by its constituent nations. The group consisting of these nations would usually be conceded a right to its state, since it derives from their exercising their rights of self-determination. It does not follow—as it would if the sufficiency condition of nationhood was not qualified with a *ceteris paribus* clause—that these nations disappear, only to be replaced by a single nation corresponding to the federal state.[45] For here the right to a federal state does not trump national rights, which can survive federation and later lead, in some cases, to secession. If the account of nationhood in terms of the constitutive principle is accepted, it enables us to mount yet another attack on the influential self-definitional view and others which incorporate that view. It brings out the reason we might think of the world as divided into nations without significant overlap—a result the self-definitional view signally fails to accommodate. Because we regard states as forming a global system, those entities that have a right to statehood—namely, nations—must, with only minor exceptions, be capable of forming an analogous system. Radically different self-definitions would make such a system impossible. For then we would have no reason not to allow nations with overlapping memberships that resulted from conflicting self-definitions to have equal rights to statehood. But allowing this would lead to irresoluble conflicts of rights. In fact, claims to statehood are founded on particular conceptions of the nation which, in consistency, will disallow rival conceptions from generating equal claims. Such an outcome would ensure a system of nations precisely by virtue of the requirements of a system of states.

Summary

In this chapter I have argued for a principle which underlies the methodology of this book—the constitutive principle of nationalism. The principle states that a nation is a group which has, *ceteris paribus*, a right to independent statehood by virtue of being the kind of group it is. Different nationalisms should therefore be classified, I suggest, in accordance with the different sorts of argument they deploy in support of such a right. In subsequent chapters, different kinds of nationalism will indeed be identified and evaluated on this basis (though in political practice they are often combined). This approach, I claim, makes sense of the striking variations that are noticeable in different conceptions of the nation. These variations arise precisely because different sorts of nationalist arguments identify different kinds of groups as those that have a right to statehood. Unless we grasp that the idea of a nation has this essentially political character, we will be at a loss to discern any common element in different accounts, ending up in the nominalist impasse of regarding a nation as whatever those who take themselves to be a nation take themselves to be.

Chapter Two

Identity and Community

Nationality and National Loyalty

During the Easter Rising of 1916, an Irish Republic was proclaimed in these terms:

> We declare the right of the people of Ireland to the ownership of Ireland, and to the unfettered control of Irish destinies, to be sovereign and indefeasible. The long usurpation of that right by a foreign people and government has not extinguished the right, nor can it ever be extinguished except by the destruction of the Irish people. In every generation the Irish people have asserted their right to freedom and sovereignty. . . .
>
> The Irish Republic is entitled to, and hereby claims, the allegiance of every Irishman and Irishwoman. The Republic . . . declares its resolve to pursue the happiness and prosperity of the whole nation and of all its parts, cherishing all the children of the nation equally, and oblivious of the differences carefully fostered by an alien government, which have divided a minority from the majority in the past.[1]

Here an Irish declaration of national independence is linked to an appeal for national loyalty. An assertion that the nation is the proper focus of loyalty is often taken to be an essential part, perhaps *the* essential part, of nationalism.[2] Yet we can see in the proclamation of the Republic a crucial linkage between a nation's claim to independent statehood and its appeal for the loyalty due to it. For the legitimacy of the state depends upon its being entitled to that loyalty. There are not two independent principles at work here, as usually seems to be supposed—one, the constitutive principle, declaring a right to statehood, the other asserting the proper direction of loyalty. Rather, the right to statehood is argued for through an appeal to the existence or appropriateness of a national loyalty that could be offered to it. Most generally, I suggest, it is argued that since a rightfully constituted state is entitled to its citizens' loyalty, then a state whose right to exist consists in its being a national state must base that entitlement upon the loyalty that those citizens owe their nation.³

Put succinctly, we should answer the question "Why does a nation have a right to statehood?" by observing that a rightful state can impose political obligations on its members. Then a nation has a right to a state because its members have, or it is appropriate for them to have, national obligations which can be enforced as political obligations. The members of the nation are therefore those who have, or might appropriately have, such obligations. This principle is illustrated, I suggest, in the way that citizenship of a state is usually allocated. Citizenship is accorded only to those who can be expected to have a proper sense of their political obligations, and those who have this sense are limited in normal circumstances, or so it is assumed, to those who have the sort of obligations in common with other citizens which we regard as national obligations. Who these citizens will be depends upon what account is given of the nation that the state represents. Recent examples of controversies over citizenship which really concern the question of nationhood are provided by debates in the Baltic states as to whether Russians should share the citizenship of ethnic Balts. The question turns on whether they can have the same loyalties— loyalties that are not necessarily merely political.

We shall thus be looking repeatedly at accounts of obligations of national loyalty in examining the arguments which support claims to national statehood. It could, however, be argued that a state cannot be rightfully constituted upon a national basis precisely because national loyalties are morally undesirable and, hence, no suitable foundation for a morally acceptable state. National loyalties, it might be said, are exclusive and thus, at best, unjustifiably partial, at worst, aggressive and inhumane.⁴ This is an important objection. It cannot, however, be considered except in connection with particular conceptions of the nation and of national loyalty. For only then will we be in a position to assess the justifications that are offered for acting from national loyalties. National loyalties cannot be spelled out independent of describing the kind of nation to which they are supposedly owing. What national loyalties come to depends upon the type of nationalism that appeals to them. "Because our forbears have toiled and spilt their blood to build and defend the nation," it has been suggested, "we who are born into it inherit an obligation to continue their work."⁵ The implication is that it would be disloyal not to—but disloyal to our nation by failing to live up to our national *past*. Evidently it is only if a nation's history is conceived of as crucial to its identity that loyalty to it will exact such obligations. Under another conception, what "our forbears" did might be construed quite otherwise than as nation building—as, say, aggressive militarism from which the modern nation should dissociate itself.[6]

When people are forced to decide where their national loyalties lie, they often confront a conflict between two sorts of obligation, not both of which can be fulfilled. In Elizabeth Bowen's *The Last September*, set during the Irish War of Independence barely three years after the Easter Rising, an Anglo-Irish family, the Naylors, entertain some English officers, one of whom has captured the rebel son of their tenant.

> "Oh, I say, Uncle Richard, Lesworth has captured Peter Connor."
> "I'm sorry to hear that," said Sir Richard, flushing severely.
> "His mother is dying. However, I suppose you must do your duty. We must remember to send up now and enquire for Mrs. Michael Connor. We will send some grapes. The poor woman . . . it seems too bad." He went off sighing into the library.
> Gerald was horrified. His duty, so bright and abstract, had come suddenly under the shadowy claw of the personal. "I had no idea," he exclaimed to Laurence, "these people were friends of yours."[7]

Sir Richard Naylor has given his explicit allegiance to the British crown, and this requires that he assist its officers. However, he lives in Ireland and among its people, dependent upon them, and they upon him, for a livelihood. This situation gives him a loyalty to them which moves him to sympathy and support in times of trouble. What ensue are conflicts of putatively national loyalties. In such circumstances he cannot wholeheartedly display both. The different loyalties are expressed, though, in different ways depending upon the kind of nation they are supposedly owed to. Loyalty to Britain, as Elizabeth Bowen tells the story, is inseparable from loyalty to the British state and the public duties that this entails. Loyalty to Ireland, by contrast, is loyalty to people who share a land and its way of life, implying a more personal relationship.[8]

The foregoing is the barest sketch of positions which will be examined in detail later. My aim has been to bring out the different sorts of obligations that constitute national loyalty for different conceptions of the nation—that is, the different sorts of things that different kinds of supposedly national groups expect of their members. To *be* a member of a nation, to have a nationality, thus implies different things for different kinds of nationalists, for whom members have different relationships to the nation. Their having these obligations is justified and explained by what their membership consists in. In the example just mentioned, membership of the Irish nation consists in living a life in the island of Ireland. The obligations of membership are those that living such a life are taken to impose. But what determines which sorts of features confer membership for different nationalisms?

The dilemma of the Anglo-Irish in *The Last September* provides an illustration. If Sir Richard Naylor is British, then this is so because he has given his allegiance to Britain. It is, on this theory, the voluntary acts of individuals that confer upon them their national identities. If this in turn is so, then their national obligations result from these acts: In performing the acts that make them members of the nation, they undertake the obligations that go with membership of it. By contrast, if Sir Richard is Irish, then this is due to the fact that he lives in a certain social group and, because he does so, he is a member of that group's nation whether he likes it or not. The obligations he incurs likewise have nothing to do with his individual wishes. They derive from relationships to other people in which he already stands. There are many different factors involved in each of these stories about the origin of national obligations. I want to focus here on only one of them: the distinction between membership of a nation ascribed on the basis of the individual's social relations to other members and membership of a nation ascribed on the basis of individual features and nonsocial relations.

The distinction between what I shall term societal and nonsocietal (or aggregative) accounts of national identity is a pervasive one, though apparently overlooked by theorists. This may be because, as we shall see, it cuts through other more obvious distinctions, like that between cultural accounts and noncultural, statist ones. Or it may be because it collects together apparently diverse conceptions, such that the voluntaristic British-style nationalism just touched upon falls under the same nonsocietal head as, for example, an account of nationhood in terms of shared racial characteristics. Nonetheless, it is a crucial distinction between different treatments of the nation. On nonsocietal accounts, nations as such are aggregates of individuals.[9] What collects them together are properties they have by virtue of which they are similar, or shared relations they have, other than those that relate them socially to their compatriots. The social relations they have to their compatriots may well depend upon their mutual performance of their national obligations. But the *appropriateness* of their obligations is prior to the existence of these social relations.[10]

Societal accounts treat the nation as an entity identified, at least in part, by the network of social relationships that its members are involved in. It is participation in these relationships which makes people members, not their individual characteristics or other relations. The distinction between a mere aggregate of individuals and a social group is a graphic illustration of the contrast between the accounts. It enables us to appreciate an important point about many societal nationalisms—namely, that they can impose membership qualifications for entering the group. Only people with certain properties (or non-social relations) may be admitted to mem-

bership. Despite this, it remains true that membership is accounted for re-
lationally, even though the account is, in an obvious sense, a *mixed* one.
We can here distinguish membership from membership qualifications;
both need alluding to in specifying the nation. In the case of aggregative
nationalisms, however, this distinction collapses: To be qualified by the
relevant properties *is* to be a member.[11]

What the societal and nonsocietal accounts do is to offer different conceptions of what distinguishes one nation from another. Nonsocietal accounts do this by finding some feature of individual members of a group
which distinguishes them from the members of other groups; and societal
accounts, by finding some feature of the group as a whole. Toward this
end, societal accounts view the national group as constituted by the social
relationships which bind members together into it. Outside of these relationships there need be nothing to distinguish them, and, indeed, there is
nothing to distinguish them except where a mixed account is offered.[12] In
the unmixed cases the contrast between the accounts is very sharp and
marks a fundamental division over what nations are. For it marks a division over what it is for someone to be a compatriot or to be an alien.

What is more, the two accounts tend to generate different national
goals—though the matter is a complicated one. Basically, the national
right to independent statehood may be taken as a right to either separate
or shared statehood. If national obligations are imputed on the basis of
the individual properties of members of a nation, then what is supposedly wrong with its lacking independent statehood is that its members
are expected to associate politically with those to whom they have no
such obligations. The right whose enjoyment they lack is their right as individuals not to be governed together with members of other nations—
the right of separate statehood. But that all members of the nation should
be governed in the *same* state—that they have a right of shared statehood—is not immediately evident from these considerations.[13] If, by contrast, national obligations are ascribed on the basis of existing social relationships between members, then not only is there a corresponding
argument for separate statehood but there may also be an obvious one for
a *shared* state. For if members of a nation are split between states, then
they may form distinct political communities for which there is no foundation in their pattern of social relationships. If these relationships are
thought of as making the members a single community, then, as we shall
see, they are given an argument for shared statehood. This argument, in
turn, provides support for what I shall call *unitary* nationalism. Whether
nationalist movements are principally separatist or unificationist can depend in part, then, on whether they adopt aggregative or societal accounts of the nation.[14] The proclamation of the Irish Republic, with its
claim to a United Ireland, is a clear illustration of the latter.

National Identity

I'm Polish. I mean, I'm American. My family has been here, for four generations; that's a lot. My great grandfather came over here from near Cracow.
I've never been to Poland. I'll never go there. Why should I? It's in your
blood. It's in your background. But I live *here*. My wife is the same, Polish.[15]

Those who have arrived in a country, even some generations before,
may find it hard to say what their identity is. Living and working in a
community, they may nonetheless regard their identities as given by factors prior to their participation in it. What factors might they choose? People are similar or different in countless ways. Why should they identify
themselves in one way rather than another? The Polish-American quoted
earlier picks out three factors on the one side and two on the other: ancestral origins, "blood," and cultural background counting toward Polish
identity; family residence and personal domicile counting toward American identity. Despite the preponderance of factors on the first side, his
overall judgment seems to favor the other. The points of similarity with
the Americans he lives among outweigh, in importance for him, the
points of difference.

The process whereby people determine their own identity by attaching
significance to points of similarity and difference is replicated in the way
that identities can be determined by others. When the English began to
occupy parts of Ireland, it seemed to their rulers that they were in danger
of losing their English identity and, hence, of ceasing to serve English interests. In consequence, the Statute of Kilkenny was passed in 1367, for-
bidding them to use the Irish language, to assume Irish names, to inter-
marry with, foster, or stand godparent to the Irish, or even to ride a horse
in the Irish manner.[16] Again, culture and kinship are emphasized as distinguishing features; and self-identification too, as evidenced by the use
of personal names, is fostered as reinforcing them. It would perhaps be
anachronistic to see a *national* identity as being involved here; but the
process is analogous to those which help to form it, if national identity is
thought of in accordance with what I have termed nonsocietal accounts.
Certain features of individuals are taken as markers of their national
identity. What, on such accounts, makes an identity a *national* one?

The particular reply will vary from one kind of nationalism to another,
and we shall investigate in later chapters a wide variety of nonsocietal answers. Here, however, I want to ask a more general question: Why should
some feature not referring to social relations with compatriots be taken as
a marker of national identity? What function must such a feature perform
in order to be so taken? What it must do is to categorize the world into fellow members of the nation, on the one hand, and foreigners, on the other.

It must do that in a way that enables one to identify those who are to be governed together and those who are to be excluded from the scope of such government. So much follows from the constitutive principle of nationalism which locates nationhood in rights to independent government. But what, we may ask, is the harm that independent government prevents? Again, there may be many specific replies depending on what sort of nationalist is answering. There is, though, one general answer: *alien rule*. The obvious example is rule *by* foreigners, in accordance with laws and policies that are theirs rather than one's own. But less obviously one is under alien rule if governed in accordance with laws and policies that are adapted to others as well as to oneself. One is not then governed in accordance with laws and policies that are wholly one's own, as in the case of sharing statehood *with* foreigners.

What, to repeat, is the harm that independent government prevents? It may be possible to identify some actual or threatened oppression or injustice occasioned by alien rule. But this is to identify some reason for independent statehood on the basis of the circumstances one is in, not on the basis of the kind of group one is a member of. It is not, therefore, to back up a *national* claim to independence, as I have understood it. From a nationalist viewpoint there need be no *consequential* harm. But to be under alien rule is *in itself* harmful, other things being equal,[17] since it imposes upon people obligations to others not of their kind——obligations which are appropriately owed only to those of their own. The factors that mark out some as the same as ourselves and others as alien serve essentially to structure people for the political purposes of asserting or denying a right. What counts as the same or different is dependent upon a given assertion or denial, so that those who designate certain features as markers of national identity are those who seek to assert or deny the right. What aggregative nationalisms have in common is that they believe that people of the same *sort* should be governed together, whereby people count as the same sort by virtue of their individual properties and presocial relations. It is that its members are people of a certain sort that makes the nation a group of a certain kind. What *distinguishes* different aggregative nationalisms, however, is that they view different types of features as sorting people into nations.

Nonsocietal nationalisms are particularly ambitious in that they aim to demonstrate why individuals should be governed separately rather than together with others simply in terms of their possessing features which the others do not. To be governed together is one way of being brought into mutual social relationships. There are other ways, which may be taken to create social groups warranting political independence. But either way, nonsocietal accounts can be regarded as explaining or justifying the existence of social groups in terms of the properties or presocial relations of their members. Nonsocietal accounts, then, take explanation and justification a step further back than societal accounts, which presuppose the existence of the social group and argue for its independence from the properties such social groups have.

Abstract as the foregoing may be, it nonetheless sets some limits to the sorts of property that aggregative accounts can appeal to. They must be the sorts of property that could divide people up into separate states. The nature of the state will therefore impose limits upon such properties. Two factors are crucial here. First, the state is a *spatial* entity: It administers law and order over a defined area and, in consequence, seeks to maintain control of its borders. The nonsocietal properties that people must have to be members of the state must either be their residence within those borders or some features that could readily distinguish them from those across the border. Second, the state is a *temporal* entity: In order to secure the consistent administration of justice and the effective pursuit of policies in the interests of its inhabitants, the state must continue to exist over a relatively long time span, reproducing itself continuously over that period. The nonsocietal properties required for this outcome must, on the one hand, be correspondingly long-term properties of individuals and, on the other, properties that pick out people who could reproduce themselves as a continuing group.

More generally, we may refer to these properties as providing the *recognitional* and *reproduction* conditions required for a long-term social group. Recognitional properties are properties that could be fairly readily recognized and acted upon in the formation of social relationships, or in abstention from them. Reproduction properties are long-term properties that could bring people together and separate them from others in a continuing state of affairs where social relationships can exist. Putting these two conditions together, we find that the properties must set long-term social *boundaries*. Being a man or a woman satisfies the first condition, but not the second. The Amazons were, according to legend, a nation of women near the Black Sea. But they had to go to some lengths to maintain their distinctive nation in existence. In the absence of dramatic bio-technological developments, that would continue to be the case. The second condition, but not the first, is satisfied by those with a transmissible private attachment. The recent troubles in the north of Ireland put some old Anglo-Irish Protestants in the Republic in a difficult position, inasmuch as they continued to feel an attachment to Britain.

> They took from the walls of the hall the portrait of their father in the uniform of the Irish Guards because it seemed wrong to them that at this time it should hang there. They took down the crest of their family and the Cross of St. George, and from a vase on the drawing room mantelpiece they removed the small Union Jack that had been there since the Coronation of Queen Elizabeth II.[18]

In short, the *public* emblems of attachment are removed, for such things can count against acceptance into the group. What remains private cannot be a marker of national identity because it cannot be recognized as such: And this is still the case even if such shared private attachments are necessary for the solidarity of nationhood.

This second point, we may observe in passing, strikes yet another nail in the coffin of self-definitionalism, at least as it seems to be understood ordinarily. People cannot constitute a nation simply if they consider themselves to be so, so long as this sentiment remains a private one. Only some public demonstration of their sentiment—*calling* themselves by the name of the nation, for example—can serve.

What is important for many aggregative nationalisms is that they should be identities which could be recognized *pre-politically*—that is, identities which members of the nation have independent of their relations to a state that actually exists or is posited by nationalists.[19] In these cases a very strong justification for the pattern of statehood claimed by nationalists can be mounted—namely, that this patterning would correspond to a quite independently recognizable patterning of peoples. Not all nonsocietal accounts, however, are so ambitious. For some the pattern of states can be justified only in terms of whether it corresponds to people's political loyalties. In the former case, these loyalties might themselves be explained or justified through nonsocietal properties; in the latter, the loyalties are a brute fact about people's identities which cannot be attributed to other properties they have. Examples of both kinds of account will be investigated in detail; but are there any *general* criticisms which could be mounted against aggregative or nonsocietal species of nationalist philosophy?

National Stereotypes

It is one thing not to know what you are—English or Irish, say—but quite another not to know what the identity you might be consists in—what it is to be English or to be Irish. The latter question was raised in 1907 by the first performance in Dublin of J. M. Synge's *The Playboy of the Western World*. Although the play tells the story of life in the west of Ireland where Irish nationalists were wont to seek their identity, the nationalist audience rioted at its supposed immorality and blasphemy: "It's little you'll think my love's a poacher's, or an earl's itself, when you'll feel my two hands stretched around you, and I squeezing kisses on your puckered lips, till I'd feel a kind of pity for the Lord God is all ages sitting lonesome in His golden chair."[20]

Lines like these beautifully capture the lyricism and musicality of Irish folk idiom, but their content offended an audience who located their

Irishness in a Catholicism and Gaelicism that distinguished them from the Protestant English oppressor. The Irish Literary Revival of which Synge was a part located Irishness, by contrast, in a Hiberno-English language and culture accessible to Protestants, as most of its members were, as well as to Catholics. To accept this view of Irishness would be to concede also the relative unimportance of a Gaelic identity, contrary to those who followed Thomas Davis in thinking that "a people without a language is only half a nation"[21] and condemned Hiberno-English as a "hopeless half-way house."[22]

> When audiences in Ireland and in America hooted at "The Playboy" they told themselves that their national susceptibilities were outraged by the injustice of a libellous and immoral caricature. In fact they were shaken by the unaccustomed spectacle of truth. . . . [N]othing is more alarming to the sentimentalist than passion, nothing more disturbing than the lack of confusion between the one quality and the other, for sentimentality after all is but a mistaken identification for passion, and if there is not sentimentality in Synge it is simply that there is no confusion and no mistake.[23]

That is the verdict of one of Synge's editors: Synge's critics were simply wrong about what Irishness consisted in, deluded by a sentimental picture of it. Synge's unsentimental representation was an accurate one. By contrast, Flann O'Brien—himself no apologist for a Gaelic Catholic Ireland—lamented that "nothing in the whole galaxy of fake is comparable with Synge . . . and now the curse has come upon us because I have personally met in the streets of Ireland persons who are clearly out of Synge's plays. They talk and dress like that and damn the drink they'll swally but the mug of porter in the long nights."[24]

Synge's representation of Irishness is not truth but fabrication. It is, however, an effective fabrication, for the Irish came to resemble the representation. Flann O'Brien's move was to step outside the controversy over Irishness conducted between Synge and his critics. He would have had no kinder words for their alternative representations. Instead, he implied that this sort of representation which invites identification is necessarily no more than a fabrication, an invention: The more effective it is, the more of a fake.

O'Brien's point may suggest the conclusion that there *is* no such thing as Irishness, in the way it is conceived on accounts that treat it as a nonsocietal property of Irish people: There *is* no such property. One way of taking such a claim would be to see it as denying the possibility of a nonsocietal account of Irishness—that is, as accepting that possession of Irish national identity *can* be attributed, but denying that it is attributed on the basis of some nonsocietal property of individuals. There is just no such property to be found. Such a position would need a good deal of argument for each case of attributed national identity. It could scarcely be turned into a general argument against nonsocietalism. But this line of argument does not bring out the *fabricated* character of Irishness that O'Brien imputes to Synge's representation and perhaps to any other representation. O'Brien's imputation seems to imply acceptance of nonsocietalism as the way to characterize national identity, but also a denial that such accounts do describe one. What they do instead is to *construct* an identity, an identity which does not correspond to any real property. This position, then, would constitute a very general criticism of nonsocietalism.

The criticism involved here derives from the social constructionist view that certain concepts, like that of the nation, designate entities that are not identifiable independent of the particular social and historical contexts within which they play a part, and in which they are shaped for specific purposes by social agents through the production of discourses that designate them. It may seem that I am myself committed to this view through adopting the right to statehood as constitutive of nationalism. Such a stance, however, would go too far. All that the constitutive principle commits us to is a view about the concept of the nation; indeed, it would be inconceivable outside the appropriate political context. But this is not to suggest that the boundaries drawn by the concept would not be detectable without the concept, as social constructionism requires. They might be detectable through the use of other concepts, as those who argue that national identities correspond to preexisting ethnic ones would maintain.[25] The only thing the modern development of talk of nationhood would introduce, on this view, would be a new way of talking about what was already recognized as a special sort of group, even though not conceptualized as a nation. Are there any *general* arguments for ruling out such a view?

One argument is suggested by the controversy about Irishness described earlier. It is that the nation must be a social construction because of the diversity of ways in which nations have been identified. How could a concept which can pick out so many *different* kinds of entities pick out an independently identifiable *kind* at all? Surely its application is arbitrary with respect to independently identifiable kinds of things and explicable only in terms of specific political objectives. The imputation of arbitrariness needs to be disposed of first. If one is correct to take the application of "nation" to be governed by the constitutive principle, then the variety in its application is by no means arbitrary; it is not settled on simply to give rhetorical backing to an independently attractive political claim. Rather, this application of "nation" is adopted as picking out a group on the basis of features which provide them with a *reason* for the claim. If this fact is overlooked, then the distinctions between membership of a nation and nonmembership can indeed seem to be arbitrary

structurings of similarities and differences to draw boundaries which exclude "the Other," as many structuralists and poststructuralists have assumed they are.

None of this shows that social constructionism is false, for socially constructed concepts are not necessarily arbitrary. (Nor is social constructionism necessarily nominalistic; for the fact that the term "nation" needs to
be in use for groups to be recognized as nations does not imply that they
are simply what are so called: A social construction may involve much
tighter constraints, depending upon how the nation is constructed.) Establishing the social constructionist case requires us to show that a class
of people *could* not have been picked out as being of the same kind except
by means of the socially contextualized concept of nationhood. Flann
O'Brien's criticism of Synge suggests a way in which this might be done,
for his criticism is, of course, that Synge presents a stereotype—a conven-
tionalized representation whose capacity to stand for Irish people in general results not from Synge's having *observed* what is typical but from his
having *chosen* something to perform that function. The suggestion is that
we then identify members of the class only through their similarities to
the stereotype. Without the stereotype, no corresponding similarities between them would emerge.

This suggestion may well hold for Synge's attempt to represent Irishness in terms of a Hiberno-English language and culture, since what is
presented as typifying Irishness is surely the result of political choices. In
particular, it is the choice of a rural stereotype, selected in accordance
with an injunction by Yeats (Synge's literary associate), to Irish poets, to

> *Sing the peasantry and then*
> *Hard riding country gentlemen.*[26]

In a rural setting the Protestant Anglo-Irish gentry can plausibly be
viewed as part of the same Irish nation as their Catholic tenants. Yet it is
hard to see how to generalize an argument like this to *all* attempts to characterize nations in terms of pre-political nonsocietal features. In a later
chapter we shall note the importance of literary stereotypes in fashioning
nationalisms, but for the moment let us leave as an open question
whether all attempts of the sort under discussion must, as a matter of empirical fact, be only constructing the nations they aim to describe. Indeed,
in considering some particular nationalisms we shall see how the social
constructionist hypothesis bears on them, and how well it stands up.

Suppose, though, that all alleged nations *are* social constructions.
Would it follow from this that there are in reality *no* such properties as
those employed in the constructions? Would it follow, for example, as
Flann O'Brien seems to imply, that there can be no such thing as Irishness,

if its identification depended upon the use of stereotypes like Synge's? I do not see that it would. We use stereotypes all the time to recognize a great variety of things—breeds of cattle, styles in painting, fashions in dress, and so on. But our doing so does not show that there are no strawberry shorthorns, that cubism does not really exist, or that no one really looks passé. It may lead us to doubt the importance of the classifications (perhaps those of us who do look passé don't give a damn), but this is a very different matter. It may lead us to see that things could have been, and perhaps could still be, otherwise—a result that may be significant politically as well as philosophically. If things are as they are, it is because of social factors. This is the feature of social constructionism that may arouse the most suspicion at pre-politically nonsocietal accounts of nationhood. If such accounts seek to explain the formation of social groups in terms of properties of individuals, then those properties had better not be ones whose detection presupposes the societies they seek to explain. But, again, whether this criticism holds is decidable only through considering the relevant nationalisms case by case.

National Communities

Theorists frequently take it for granted that nations *are* social groups, or "communities" as they generally refer to them.[27] Weber himself did so, as we may recall from the passages quoted in Chapter 1: "[A] nation," he said, is "a community of sentiment."[28] But this stance overlooks the crucial difference between societal and aggregative accounts of nationhood. By societal accounts, I mean (as noted earlier) accounts which regard membership of the nation as constituted by the social relations in which the members stand to each other. So far this is a very abstract characterization. What the relevant social relations are is a question which, as we shall see, different societal nationalisms answer differently, though they must satisfy certain general conditions to which we shall return shortly. That it is these relations which constitute nationhood, and not properties (or other relations) of individuals, is the key feature of societal nationalism. The contrast it makes with aggregative or nonsocietal nationalism is not dimmed by the fact that people with national properties picked out nonsocietally often do live together in social groups, and that people in supposedly national groups often do have such common properties. It would be surprising if it were not so, since, on the one hand, it is likely to be an existing social group that makes a claim to statehood, and, on the other hand, members of such social groups are likely to have *some* features which distinguish them from others. Neither of these points affects the distinction between the kinds of reasons for their claims that societal and aggregative nationalisms make.

The distinction shows up not only in different sorts of secessionist claims and the like but also in the politics of established states. Consider, for example, racial discrimination—the failure to treat the members of some group within the state on equal terms with those of others on account of their race. Why do we consider this wrong? There are many possible answers, but one is that members of the group discriminated against are members of our community, contributing to it equally with others. They are therefore entitled to equal treatment. To deny it to them is unjust. Their "race" is irrelevant to their rights. Now, consider that the same answer can be given a national twist. The group discriminated against is part of the nation by virtue of its being part of the community: The members of this group are not foreigners who cannot claim the same entitlements as compatriots, but to discriminate against them is to treat them like foreigners. Co-nationals must be treated equally in respects relevant to their national membership. This requirement follows directly from the nation's claim to statehood, since citizenship of the state must be, in those respects that make it membership of the state, formally equal. To present an argument of this sort is to presuppose a societal account of the nation. This account contrasts sharply with a nonsocietal one, which can admit that members of the group discriminated against are members of the community but denies that they are members of the nation on the grounds of their racial difference.

One example of this contrast is provided by the way that black nationalists in the United States of the 1960s and 1970s turned the societal argument against discrimination back on itself and opposed to it an aggregative nationalism. In the words of the black nationalist Eldridge Cleaver:

> As an ideological tenet, integration embodies the dream of the mother-country which sees America as a huge melting pot. It seeks to pull the black colonial subjects into America and citizenize them.
>
> . . . Integration represents an attempt by the white mother country to forestall the drive for national liberation by its colonial subjects. . . . France, England and Portugal have all failed in their attempts to hold on to their colonial possessions by trying to get the colonial subjects themselves to stop short of taking complete sovereignty in their drive for a better life. And so is America doomed to failure in this respect. In fact, America's failure is even more obscene and contemptible because, as often happens to exploiters, it has believed its own propaganda, its own lies, and it has taken all its perverted descriptions for reality . . .
>
> Oppressed because of the color of their skin, Black people are reacting on that basis. A nationalist consciousness has at last awakened among the Black masses of Afro-America.[29]

Cleaver's contention is that black Americans will inevitably be treated differently within a predominantly white country. The claim that the

United States is a nation through forming a single political community is therefore false. The conception that seemed to make it possible for someone to have the nonsocietal properties of a Pole yet to be an American does not work for blacks.[30] The conclusion to draw is that black people in America constitute a separate nation.

Cleaver's argument exemplifies a common type of criticism that can be leveled against societal nationalisms. But it should first lead us to ask what are the general characteristics of a social group that might in principle be a nation. First, the group must be closed[31] in the sense that the relationships which constitute it must not be indefinitely extensible but, rather, must be bounded in their scope. This I shall call the *closure* condition. Second, there must be a fairly clear sense of who is included in the relationships and who excluded. This constitutes what I referred to earlier as a *recognitional* condition on national membership. Third, the relationships must be long term and of a sort such that the group they form could reproduce itself without losing its group identity. This is the *reproduction* condition. The recognitional and reproduction conditions are derived, as explained earlier, from the nature of the state to which the social group lays claim.

Putting the closure condition together with the recognitional and reproduction ones yields, I suggest, a further condition on which social groups could in principle constitute nations. It is what I shall term the *obligation* condition: National groups must be "communities of obligation"[32] in the sense that their constitutive relationships have an obligatory character. What this obligatory character amounts to varies between accounts. The relationships may be formed through the undertaking of obligation, or obligations may arise from relationships of interdependency. In any event, it must be the case that conformity to the rules governing the relationships expresses the performance of an obligation: It cannot be fully optional. The reason is that the relationships which include some and exclude others must have the sort of stability that comes only from the performance of obligations to some and not others, and which cannot be maintained in a public long-term way on the basis of fluctuating individual interests. What is more, given the reproduction condition, the relationships must be transmitted across changes of membership (e.g., over generations), requiring that the imposition of obligations continues in the same way upon new members.[33] What sorts of general argument could there be for groups conceived in accordance with these conditions to have a right to statehood? The fundamental argument is that a group under this conception has a right to statehood because it has a right to those institutions which can enforce the obligations which regulate its constitutive relationships.[34] The state is precisely such an institution,[35] inasmuch as the state claims a monopoly on the use of force,[36] for the purpose of ensuring the performance of its citizens' obligations. If members of a social group recognize certain mutual obligations, then widespread nonperformance will result in social discord, producing precisely that disorder which it is the function of the state to prevent. So far this is an argument only for *some* state to enforce group members' obligations—a task which could be performed by a colonial regime, for instance.[37] What makes it an argument for a *separate* state? It is that within the state, at least in its modern form,[38] all citizens must be under the same obligations; otherwise, they will lack the formal equality of citizenship. But this must be equality under the law across the state. The implication is that different national obligations cannot properly be enforced within the same state (unless the separate nations involved agree to an arrangement which derogates from the normal conditions for formal equality).

What are we to make of this argument? We are considering it as a perfectly general one, not dependent upon any special conceptions of the national group apart from those set out in the stated conditions for a societal account. (Those versions of it that may depend upon these special conceptions will be discussed later.) Basically the argument depends upon the assertion that a national group has a right to have its obligations enforced. If that assertion is not granted, then it can be no part of a state's job to enforce these obligations. But why should a national group under the general conception be in a position to make the demand that it does? There seem to be three possible answers.[39] First, it is in the nature of a national group that its obligations should be enforceable. But either this claim must be spelled out in terms of some specific conception, or it simply comes down to the claim that the group is national through its right to enforcing institutions and so can be no argument for the right. Second, a national group under the general conception is intrinsically worthwhile and so has a right to the enforcement of the obligations which maintain it. But, again, while a case for this claim might be made out under some more specific conception, it is hard to see how a general case can be sustained. Hitler's *Volksgemeinschaft* satisfied the required conditions, but we scarcely want to agree that it was worthwhile at all—not just worthwhile insofar as it satisfied those conditions but abhorrent in its details. Indeed, the fact that the relationships that formed it satisfied the conditions made it worse, not better. The third argument is instrumental—namely, that it is good upon the whole that there should be national groups under the general conception because the obligations involved in them provide a useful way of getting people to bring about good results overall rather than bad ones. On the instrumental view, different special conceptions of the national group will be argued for on the grounds that one kind of group is better at achieving these good results than another. Indeed, some specific arguments may be plausible. Yet the general claim is hard to evaluate.

The misery caused by supposedly national groups, particularly those already organized into states, is not obviously outweighed by the good they do.

Fortunately we do not need to pursue the question here, for any attempt to derive a right to statehood from the general conditions in relation to societal nationalism must be unsuccessful. Any such attempt would simply create *too many* nations, thus failing to be of use in resolving many disputes between conflicting nationalisms. Because the general conception does not specify what type or scope of relationships should be constitutive of national groups, it is so far quite conceivable that people could simultaneously be members of smaller and larger ones—Euskadi and Spain, say, or Padania and Italy.[40] In the first case, cultural relationships could be enclosed within wider political ones; and in the second, economic relationships within cultural and political ones. But these are the sorts of dual membership that nationalism cannot permit since they lead to a conflict of rights to statehood. The general argument for statehood can function, then, only as a *form* that more specific arguments may take. As an argument in its own right it is self defeating.

To put the point in a different way: Communities could be very different sorts of things, and to claim to constitute a nation because of constituting a community is, so far, to say very little. Such vagueness may suit the turn of nationalists in certain situations. It is a useful rhetorical device, of the sort that Eldridge Cleaver exposes, for responding to the complaints of those who feel they are discriminated against by others differing from them in some significant nonsocietal way. But this vague appeal to community does little to advance the arguments for statehood that nationalists need to mount. The nonsocietalist claim that "people of the same sort should be governed together" invites the immediate riposte, "What sort?" The societalist claim that "people in the same community should be governed together" does not arouse the same suspicion. "What sort of community?" we should ask, and in the ensuing chapters we shall.

Summary

Here I have begun the task of classifying nationalisms and their associated conceptions of nationhood by asking how we might phrase an argument for a group of a certain kind having a right to statehood. Most important, such an argument needs to establish that the group is of a sort that can provide its state with the loyalty of its members, thereby legitimating that state. This idea immediately generates a distinction between two types of accounts of the nation, which I call societal and nonsocietal. Societal accounts regard a nation as a group characterized by social relations between its members, by virtue of which they have obligations of loyalty to each other—that is, as a community of a certain sort. And nonsocietal accounts view a nation as characterized by the properties (and nonsocietal relations) of its individual members—properties which put them under, or make it appropriate for them to have, the relevant obligations.

More generally, to qualify as nations, groups must be of a sort that could form states. In particular, they must satisfy recognitional and reproduction conditions; in other words, their membership must be clearly identifiable and must be transmissible across generations, so that long-term social boundaries are created corresponding to those of a possible state. Arguments for statehood, however, must identify not just the kinds of groups which *can* form states but also ones which *should*. Thus the groups are required to have properties which make statehood for them desirable in general, not just in particular instances.

Chapter Three

"The Most Natural State"

Lines of Descent

"God," wrote the nineteenth-century Italian patriot Giuseppe Mazzini, "divided Humanity into distinct groups upon the face of our globe and thus planted the seeds of nations. Bad governments have disfigured the design of God. . . . Natural divisions, the innate spontaneous tendencies of the peoples[,] will replace the arbitrary divisions sanctioned by bad governments. The map of Europe will be remade,"[1] and it was. But whether the resulting map corresponded to the "natural divisions" of nations is doubtful, not least because there is some question as to whether nations can be regarded as marking out *any* natural divisions. The idea that they do, however, has been and still continues to be a potent one. It purports to provide a justification for statehood, as Mazzini implied, on the grounds that only natural groupings of people can make for good government, to which people have a right. Just how such an argument is to be articulated cannot become clearer until we know what sort of natural grouping is involved.

"Race" seems to have been one property which Mazzini regarded as distinguishing nations.[2] But what might race be, and how could it divide people into nations? Like "nation," the word "race" has shifted in meaning over the years. We see the older senses of both words in Daniel Defoe's famous diatribe against "The True Born Englishman."[3] England is, he said, possessed by *Ingratitude*:

> *He made her, First-born Race to be so rude,*
> *And suffer'd her to be so oft subdu'd:*
> *By several Crowds of Wandring Thieves o're-run,*
> *Often unpeopl'd, and as oft undone.*
> *While ev'ry Nation that her Pow'rs reduc'd*
> *Their Languages and Manners introduc'd.*

From Whose mixed Relicks our compounded Breed
By Spurious Generation does succeed;
Making a Race uncertain and unev'n,
Deriv'd from all the Nations under Heav'n. . . .
These are the Heroes who despise the Dutch,
And rail at new-come Foreigners so much;
Forgetting that themselves are all deriv'd,
From the most Scoundrel Race that ever liv'd.

Little changes, one may think, on reading what may seem to be an early anti-racist tract. But the dominant notion of *race* has changed, for in Defoe's poem it is not that different races—Celtic, Teutonic, and so on—are mixed into a single English nation, which is what we might expect. Quite the reverse, nations, qua peoples, are mixed into a single, though "Scoundrel," race. We do not recognize the Englishman by some supposedly racial characteristics he shares with his compatriots. All he shares with them is a common descent, "compounded" though it is. A race, in this sense, is a descent group.[4] Might nations, in the modern, political sense, be races as so understood, such that being a member of a nation consists in the nonsocietal property of belonging to such a group?

The first difficulty is that this notion does not provide a way of ruling out nesting or intersecting nationhoods and, hence, of settling competing claims to statehood. Identities conceived in terms of descent can be wide or narrow. For example, in early twentieth-century South Africa, black people's "identities were not necessarily exclusive and they were often fluid. People could conceive of themselves as clan member, Zulu, and African"; and, indeed, this was possible because "the people of pre-colonial chiefdoms intermarried, treated, and traded, absorbed or conquered one another."[5] This is precisely the sort of situation Defoe described as having produced "Your *Roman-Saxon-Danish-Norman* English." What is usually required to prevent such fluidity is endogamy, which is lacking in the aforementioned cases; and it is endogamy which is needed to make the group an ethnic group as traditionally conceived.

But this observation gives rise to a second difficulty. For if the nation conceived of as a descent group must be endogamous, is it any longer *natural?* Or is it, *pace* Mazzini, arbitrary? Rules about permitted or preferred reproductive unions (and, indeed, rules about the membership of the issue of such unions) are *conventional:* They are fixed by a social group and cannot be derived from facts about its existing membership. If this is doubted, if it is thought that some unions are within the race and others are miscegenative, then the presupposition is that we have a way of identifying the race so that we can distinguish "true-born" members of it from others. Defoe's poem shatters that illusion. But the situation is even worse than this. If to make membership of a descent group usable for demarcating nations we have to concede that it does not pick out a natural property, we also have to concede that it no longer picks out a property which could explain or justify social groups, since its conventional element presupposes them. A nation can be a descent group only on pain of circularity and confusion, for the supposedly nonsocietal descent group can be identified only through a societal nation, since the relationships which the conventional element in descent depends upon are social ones.

Forgetting these objections, could we still argue that a descent group as originally postulated could have a claim to statehood and thus satisfy the condition for being a nation? What would be claimed here would be a right based on some *natural* property associated with common descent. At this point I should like to distinguish between two kinds of consideration concerning a putative nation invoked in arguments for its statehood. One is what I shall call an *aptness* reason—a consideration which supposedly makes the nation apt for, well adapted to, independent statehood. Weber's suggestion that a nation has "a tendency towards an autonomous state" by virtue of being "a community of sentiment"[6] is a case in point. It is a consideration which would apparently make such a group better suited to statehood than one which lacked the tendency. Indeed, the criticism of some ex-colonial states is precisely that they do lack the required sentiments. The other type of consideration I term an *entitlement* reason—one which purportedly entitles, or helps to entitle, the nation to statehood. That the members of a group collectively owned a large territory might provide an entitlement reason in the context of an argument that they thereby had the right to political control over it. The two types of consideration are quite different, though sometimes it might be unclear which role a reason is playing. A well-functioning separate community may be viewed as either apt for statehood or entitled to it. In the case of an aptness consideration, some further normative premise will, of course, be needed to establish the right. We may also allow, however, that a group lacks a right if it is constitutionally inapt for exercising it, so that what makes it apt may need to be teased out. It is therefore commonly in the context of establishing such necessary conditions that aptness considerations are brought into play. The present case is no exception: Kinship, it can be argued, is what makes people apt for shared government. Why should it do so?

The most plausible answer is derived from sociobiology. Sociobiologists argue that the unit of evolution by natural selection is the gene. It follows that organisms which behave in such a way as to maximize the chances of replicating their genes will be selected. But organisms that share the same genes will do this best through cooperation rather than competition, for they will thereby be practicing "kin selection." Conversely, organisms carrying different genes will be selected to compete with each other. Thus we may expect organisms, including humans, who are related by kinship to cooperate better than those that are not. Cooperation and common loyalty clearly favor common government; conflict does not. Taking a nation to be an ethnic group that claims a right to statehood, then, we find that "the nation-state is legitimated by kin selection—the most fundamental basis of animal sociality."[7] Let us assume that the science involved here is true. Does it establish its ambitious conclusion? I do not see that it does. Scientists allow that the natural processes of kin selection described can directly explain only the behavior of groups much smaller than those we might think of as nations. In these larger groups, "any common kinship that they may share is highly diluted."[8] In consequence, mechanisms must be invoked to mediate between the propensity toward kin selection that is favored evolutionarily and its extension to "fictive" kin.

In fact, the markers we employ to recognize our compatriots are mostly cultural, like language. To rely on these mechanisms would be to abandon any attempt at a naturalistic explanation of nationhood.[9] The only credibly noncultural markers are such things as color of skin and hair, bodily build, and physiognomy. Actually it is quite impossible to recognize one's compatriots reliably on this basis—and, in any case, those who *look* similar can often have a very different genetic makeup. But suppose this were not so. It would also need to be shown that we favored those who look like us, over those who do not, as a result of some *natural* predisposition. The difficulty in showing this involves ruling out factors which might explain any such preferences in terms of cultural reasons—that is, ruling out any *beliefs* that people have about who should be given preferential treatment. There seems to be no way to do this. Indeed, it seems much more likely that people's culturally determined beliefs, rather than their natural predispositions, are what explain discrimination. For people do not need to *detect* any genuine physical differences in order to believe that they exist, and *see* them in those they discriminate against. Nazi Germany is ample evidence of this fact. It is not an example of the workings of kin selection.

Racial Types and National Characters

Nazi racism employs a quite different notion of races from the archaic one we have been looking at. It is a notion of races as distinguished from one another by the distinct and uniform characteristics inherited by their members, with membership of a race determined by the possession of such characteristics. On this account, "race" is a classificatory term which picks out a *type* of people.[10] According to the eighteenth-century theory which gave rise to this notion, the natural world is divided up into a great many unvarying types of plant and animal, and a race is just another natural division within it. This shift in the meaning of "race" is, on the one hand, a reflection of the scientific taxonomy that fosters the picture. On the other, it mirrored the increasing interest in what distinguishes peoples that paralleled the expansion of colonial empires and the corresponding imperative to allot subject peoples to appropriate social roles. Thus race, it has been suggested, is "irreducibly a *political* category."[11] With this in mind, one must ask, Could nations, another political category on my account, consist of races or some subdivisions of them?

The argument would be that nations consist of peoples who have similar characteristics by *nature*. That they are similar for biological reasons is shown by the fact that their similarities remain constant from one generation to another and are therefore presumably inherited. This is just what it is for these similarities to mark out racial types. That they are naturally similar is what gives such races a right to independent statehood, for one or both of two reasons. First, an aptness consideration might suggest that their innate similarities render them well adapted to common governance and inapt for government with others. Second, an entitlement consideration might be proposed that independent government would preserve their racial purity, which might otherwise be lost by a commingling with others over which they have no control. Notice that the racial-type theory of nationalism, though only an aggregative nationalism, generates an argument for shared as well as for separate nationhood. A single state is supposedly needed to preserve a single race, rather as a single bloodstock agency is thought necessary to preserve the purity of a breed. These arguments, which we can, not unfairly, label *racist*,[12] may sometimes arise from the attempt to bolster up a common descent group's claim to statehood. For since this claim appeals to kinship, and since kin may well have similarities presumed to be inherited, these similarities may be invoked to justify separate government.

What are we to make of these arguments? Before going further we must note that this notion of race as a fixed type has been scientifically discredited. There are no races as so envisaged. In the first place, anthropological observation has shown that there are no clear-cut racial divisions: Rather, "a racial or ethnic type, as it is sometimes called, is simply a combination of averages, an abstraction, and very few individuals in a population are very similar to the type."[13] If it is thought that this situation is the result of originally "pure" races having merged by interbreeding, it should be pointed out that, insofar as there are geographically identifiable differences, they exist because certain distinctive features have been evolutionarily selected for in populations that have been subjected to the same environmental factors over a long period. But natural *variety* in a population is necessary for there to be selection at all. These Darwinian considerations totally undermine the science on which the original theory of racial types depends.

It is necessary to rehearse these facts, partly because the now-discredited theory of racial types had considerable influence on many of the nineteenth-century nationalisms by which the map of Europe was remade, and partly because it continues to exercise a hold on the thinking of racist nationalists today. But rehearsing them is not enough to neutralize their arguments. More sophisticated racists could concede the Darwinian account and still hold that a nation is a racial type in the less objectionable sense of a "combination of averages" (and that is how we shall now continue to think of it). They might go on to observe that the evolutionary story of adaptation to environments actually helps their case, showing that immigrants are unlikely to be constitutionally suited to their new homes and thereby unqualified for membership. I shall waste little time on this contention except to observe that nothing can be inferred about one's ability to adapt to new environments from facts about one's evolutionary history. The only demonstrable cases of maladaptedness are those that have to do with lack of immunity to disease linked to climate and the like. Darwin provided no support for racists.

However, the racist argument for statehood must be returned to, since the aptness considerations it proposes are so influential. Why might the sort of dissimilarities describable as racial, on a post-Darwinian understanding, render people unfit for common government, as is the racists' assumption? Remember that these racial dissimilarities are purely phenotypical; they have to do only with observable characteristics like skin and hair color, head and body shape, and so on. Why should *such* dissimilarities render people inapt to share a state? The only conceivable answer is that they do so because they elicit adverse reactions, which have evolved as responses to phenotypical differences which usually signify genetic difference. This answer is a slightly extended version of the sociobiological argument encountered and criticized in the preceding section, and commonly appealed to by nationalists on the Right: "Any fool knows (though some fools would rather not know) that the process that Darwin called natural selection means that, on the whole, people prefer their 'ain folk'—their own ethnic stock. It's in our genes. It is part of every person's nature, black or white."[14] So wrote a commentator in the *Daily Star* in the mid–1980s. One need not be a fool to think this. Indeed, a Conservative philosopher, invoking a mechanism rather more obscure than the Darwinian, can write that there are "sentiments which seem to arise inevitably from social consciousness: they involve natural prejudice, and a desire for the company of one's own kind. That is hardly sufficient ground to condemn them as 'racist.'"[15]

This argument is based on the observation that many people dislike or distrust those who look different. What distinguishes the racist's claim is that he believes the adverse reactions are *natural*. The theory to back up this contention is, as I tried to show, unproven and implausible. There are, furthermore, innumerable instances in which it is disconfirmed in practice. People *can* get on with those who look very different from them. What stops them has much to do with the organization of, and within, states—and nothing to do with nature. But in that case dislike of those who look different cannot be used to justify the organization of states.

Racism often relies on even less defensible claims. It is not appearance but innate *character* that is most often appealed to as definitive of a nation. It is the shared national character that gives people a right to independent statehood in accordance with the foregoing aptness and entitlement considerations. A naturalistic argument of this form does not need to be couched in terms of race. As we shall see in Chapter 6, it can rely on the view that the national character of a people is natural because it arises from the environmental conditions of the land in which they live. The two versions are lumped together in a typical example of nineteenth-century thinking about national character—the English character, as eulogized by an American, Ralph Waldo Emerson:

> [I]t is in the deep traits of race that the fortunes of nations are written, and however derived, whether a happier tribe or mixture of tribes, the air, or whatever circumstance, that mixed for them the golden mean of temperament—here exists the best stock in the world, broad-fronted, broad-bottomed, best for depth, range, and equability, men of aplomb and reserves, great range and many moods, strong instincts, yet apt for culture . . . abysmal temperament, hiding wells of wrath, and glooms on which no sunshine settles; alternated with a common sense and humanity which hold them fast to every piece of cheerful duty.[16]

Indeed, Emerson assembled an astonishingly detailed character sketch of the English, in which he constantly contrasted them with other nationalities—among whom the Irish t~r.d to come off worst. He explicitly took on Defoe: "Defoe said in his wrath, 'the Englishman was the mud of all races.' I incline to the belief, that, as water, lime, and sand make mortar, so certain temperaments marry well, and, by well-managed contrarieties, develop as drastic a character as the English. . . . [C]ertain temperaments suit the sky and soil of England . . . whilst all the unadapted temperaments die out."[17]

Suppose that we accept for the sake of argument that people of the same character are specially apt for common government. Is it remotely conceivable that we should be able to distinguish nations by their national characters in the way that Emerson assumed and that only some naturalistic story could possibly suggest? Surely it is not. Characters are even more variable than appearances; and even if there were some limited plausibility in constructing a classification of racial types in terms of a "combination of averages," there is none whatever for an analogous classification of characters. This truth was succinctly expressed by Somerset Maugham:

> Every nation forms for itself a type to which it accords its admiration, and though individuals are rarely found who correspond with it a consideration of it may be instructive and amusing. This type changes with the circumstances of the time. It is an ideal to which writers of fiction seek to give body and substance. The characteristics which they ascribe to this figment of their fancy are those which the nation at a given moment aspires to, and presently simple men, fascinated by these creatures of fiction, take them as their model and actually transform themselves, so that you may recognise in real life a type which you have seen described in novels.[18]

Stereotypes are what serve to determine which characters count as national. Nations cannot, therefore, be distinguished naturalistically by the national character of their members.

I can think of no better proof of this than the following striking fact. There are significant differences between the views that people have of their own supposed national character and the views that others, from other countries, have of it. For example, a recent study of such comparisons[19] reported that only one out of six national characteristics ascribed to the French matched their "auto-stereotype"—namely, independence. While there was some measure of agreement on three characteristics, two that were ascribed to the French—being individualistic but not scientifically minded—were denied by them. It is worth adding that the attitudes of people from different countries also differ significantly: The Danes and the English apparently view the French as competitive and egoistical, whereas the Dutch, Belgians, and Germans do not. While it might be argued that differences of the last sort are due to differences in opportunities for observation, this contention could scarcely explain the difference between auto-stereotypes and others' perceptions. If these views really did reflect the observed facts of national character, then we would expect them to be the same. If, on the other hand, they are socially constructed stereotypes, then we would expect to find such differences, since the political purposes for which images of others are constructed differ from those for which images of one's own are.

The naturalistic entitlement reason for statehood goes the same way as the aptness one: If there are no natural national characters, then there can be no pure type of character which could be "diluted" or "contaminated" by an admixture of other peoples. The real fear masked by this discourse is, it might be suggested, that other peoples would come to have a hand in the construction of national stereotypes and influence them in ways that the dominant group would not wish. The naturalizing discourse is, it could be continued, an ideological one which redescribes contingent relationships of power as inevitable, biologically determined ones, whereby nothing needs to be justified because nothing can be changed. One way, then, to view the naturalistic, nonsocietal accounts of nationhood we have been considering is as elaborate ways of *avoiding* the task of justifying claims to statehood. The state (or proto-state) does not, for example, need to justify its demands for loyalty: It merely claims to receive loyalty naturally from all those who are members, such that those who do not give it reveal their nonmembership. And this goes for loyalty to the national cricket team as much as to anything else.[20]

Extended Families

"The most natural state is . . . *one* nation, an extended family with one national character. . . . For a nation is as natural a plant as a family, only with more branches. Nothing, therefore, is more manifestly contrary to the purposes of political government than the unnatural enlargement of states, the wild mixing of various races and nationalities under one sceptre."[21] So wrote the German philosopher Johann Gottfried von Herder, toward the end of the eighteenth century. The passage can be read as presenting not one but two kinds of claims about what sort of group should enjoy statehood, and both claims are naturalistically based. One is the claim we have just been discussing, that a state is natural and therefore to be promoted if it corresponds with natural divisions between people marked by their relevant nonsocietal properties, by what they are like as individuals. Possession of a certain sort of character is such a property. The other is a societal argument. It holds that a people make up a state that corresponds to natural divisions if they form a social group like a family, but with more widely extended relationships. The existence of social groups of this sort, like that of families, is to be explained by facts of nature, not by facts about what "patched-up contraptions, fragile machines"[22] are devised by governments. Being a member of the nation is, on this argument, a societal property. A nation is not just an aggregate of individuals of the same sort. It is a social group constituted by their relationships, which are literally familial ones, not just metaphorically so.

This societal model differs profoundly from the nonsocietal ones just considered, despite its identical underpinnings in kinship and character.[23] The nonsocietal models hold that people are members of a nation independent of any actual social relationships with fellow members. Descent or racial similarity suffices, and it suffices in part because these properties give rise to, or are correlated with, a *disposition* to show loyalty to one's fellows. All that is needed is the opportunity to display it for a national community to begin to take shape. The societal model, by contrast, holds that the community must be there, and the loyalties must be operative, for a nation to exist; and, whatever their qualifications, that people are not members of the nation unless they are related by such loyalties. This difference has obvious political implications. In particular, the nonsocietal models (if they can mount an argument for unitary nationalism) license the repatriation of nationals or the extension of frontiers to include them. The societal one does not. It purports to *explain* the workings of a national community, but it can as easily tolerate *different* nations with people of the same stock and character as we can allow for different families who are closely related but in different households.

At first sight we may doubt that it really was Herder's intention to set out a societal argument. For might he not have been thinking of a family simply as a descent group and, hence, as not necessarily a group formed by social relationships? Of course he believed that biological relationships and a common character are necessary to the family-like group he was thinking of. Yet a nation, he said, is a "plant" rather than a "machine"— not just an aggregate of biologically related elements but an entity in which they are connected through functional relationships. In the natural state, he added, this connection is accomplished through "bonds of sentiment." It is evident that he had certain social relationships in mind here— specifically, relationships which contrast with the "mechanical contrivances" of the artificial state. They are relationships, Herder went on to say, which represent "the natural order," whereby "mutual assistance and protection are the principal ends of all human association." In a passage that Mazzini may have been echoing, Herder remarked that "as soon as the monarch wants to usurp the position of the Creator and bring into being by his own arbitrary will or passion what God had not intended, he becomes the father of misrule and inevitable ruin."[24]

Herder's notion that nature is *orderly,* so that "inevitable ruin" is somehow an indication of interference in the order of nature, could not survive Charles Darwin. Herbert Spencer, the nineteenth-century philosopher heavily influenced by Darwin, had no doubt that "government is begotten of aggression and by aggression. . . . [T]he coercive power of the chief . . . becomes great in proportion as conquest becomes habitual and the union of subdued nations extensive."[25] The enlargement of states is not here viewed as unnatural. On the contrary, it is the inevitable result of the aggression involved in the evolutionary battle for survival of the fittest. It would be futile to join such a debate. If political organization *is* to be explained naturalistically, then empires must, as Spencer intended, be explained in addition to supposed nation-states. But the question remains:

Are there any biological mechanisms to explain the latter other than those that explain the former?

Herder's answer depends upon the assumption that the family, of which the nation is an extended form, is natural. Yet the validity of this assumption is far from obvious. For what biological reason should groups of people live together for sex, procreation, and child rearing? We can concede that there are biological drives explaining *each* of these activities without conceding that there should be relatively stable social groups to fulfill them all. There is no biological imperative, for example, that males involved in sex should be concerned with child rearing or the protection of mother and young. If there were, they would not shirk their responsibilities as readily as they do. Even anthropologists who wish to explain human social organization along evolutionary lines would allow this. "The human nuclear family," writes one, "was formed when the total group created the reciprocal marriage rule, making such marriages not occasional (as they must have been for simple short-term individually expedient purposes), but regular between themselves and one or more other groups."[26] In other words, the family is not the natural unit of society; it is a creature of it.

Nevertheless, the familial model continues to be influential. Both fascism and the New Right draw heavily upon its resources. Fascism embraces forms of it in repudiating the liberal view that our political relationships, like others in the public sphere, are determined by contracts which individuals enter, thereby incurring the obligations that they do. (We shall discuss this liberal view in detail later.) Fascism sees all worthwhile social relationships as somehow springing from human nature, whether the latter is conceived biologically or mystically: The relationships which bind people into nations are just an example, though a cardinally important one. The New Right, of course, utterly rejects this view, holding that as large a space as possible must be left open for the exercise of human freedom in the contractual relationships of the marketplace, so that only a minimal state can be legitimate. The New Right needs a naturalistic account of the nation, however, to justify both the national boundaries of such a state and the loyalty it commands. If market freedoms operated in the choice of states, then all would do as rich men do: attach themselves to whichever was economically most advantageous. To prevent this outcome and marry nationalism to liberalism in accordance with the New Right prescription, membership of a properly constituted state must be determined naturalistically, and the obligations incumbent upon members follow from this determination. The familial model of the nation satisfies these requirements.[27]

If the family is not natural, then no argument will work which claims that the nation is natural because it is an extension of the family. One might concede this point, yet still mount an argument that rooted the nation in biology. For instance, one could claim that the family, though not biologically inevitable, nonetheless serves a biological function and is to be understood in these terms. The nation, one might continue, is an extension of the family in that it too serves the related biological functions of providing for the security and continuity of a group of people. No doubt, however, many different extensions to the family could provide the same—septs, clans, and so forth. The one that counts as the nation, according to the constitutive principle, will be that which can claim a right to statehood. Is there an argument for some particular extension of the family to have a right to statehood? Such an argument would have to derive from the claim that the ties of loyalty which bind people into a family are also what constitute the more extended group. The limits of these loyalties are the limits of the nation. People have a right to a state which does not go beyond these limits because such a state would impose loyalties on them beyond those they already have. These they could perform only mechanically, not as an expression of what Herder calls the nation's "inner life."[28] But this imposition, it could be argued, is oppressive and beyond what a legitimately constituted government has a right to do. Furthermore, it could be claimed, people who are bound into a family-like group by ties of mutual loyalty are also loyal to the family as an entity. Hence they have a right to a unitary state within which this common loyalty can be expressed. Any other arrangement would be one of Herder's "mechanical contrivances" in which the citizens' loyalties are inappropriately focused. The "natural state," by contrast, is, like a family, a natural corporation with a collective purpose determined by the natural function of such a group to serve its members needs, all and only theirs.

These arguments, which capture, I hope, some of Herder's assumptions, depend entirely upon the claim that certain loyalties are simply *given*. Like many others, I find myself in relationships whose observance is an expression of loyalty. Only these "bonds of sentiment" can properly link people in a state, as in a family. The alternative is "forced unions."[29] How, though, do these considerations cope with the problems posed by the overlaps in our loyalties which give rise to competing claims to nationhood? The model starts out, after all, from loyalties to one's family. Why should it not be these loyalties that give rise to separate government, as in tribal organizations, rather than the much more extended loyalties required by the model state? Even if there is a cutoff point beyond which I feel no loyalty—and this is doubtful—are there not many gradations in the strength of my loyalties before it is reached? Where should the borders of a state be drawn in this morass of feeling? The only obvious answer is that they should be drawn along the lines where our *supreme* loyalties lie. Family, this answer claims, takes second place to nation in, for example, decisions as to whether to stay at home or join the army to defend one's country. All naturalistic nationalisms claim that the nation is the object of its members' supreme loyalty.[30] That this notion solves the overlap problem is, perhaps, the reason they do so. For while it should be easy to show where someone's supreme loyalties *actually* lie, it could also, in principle, be shown where their *disposition* to repose supreme loyalty lies, thus possibly helping out nonsocietal nationalists confronted with the overlap problem.

The objection to this line of thought is surely that it is extremely implausible to hold that members of a nation do, or even should, give it their supreme loyalty. We do not expect this even of those who think of their membership in nationalist terms. W. B. Yeats defined a nationalist as "one who is ready to give up a great deal that he may preserve to his country whatever part of her possessions he is best fitted to guard."[31] He was immediately attacked by Arthur Griffith, one of Sinn Fein's founders, who said: "[U]nless he is prepared to give up all I do not deem him a Nationalist";[32] but then he was rehabilitated by Patrick Pearse, who remarked, "Our love of disputation . . . sometimes makes us ridiculous, as when we prove by mathematical formula that the poet who has most finely voiced Irish nationalism in our time is no Nationalist."[33] Naturalistic nationalists need the supreme loyalty of their compatriots to mark out a state and a nation, but they are not entitled to it. They need the "mathematical formula" to delimit the nation, implausible as such a formula may be.

The alleged *naturalness* of relationships in family and nation can be regarded as providing an explanation of their *givenness*. "Instinct" is often appealed to as an explanation of what we just *do*, as here by Bertrand Russell:

> Love of home and love of family both have an instinctive basis, and together they form the foundation of love of country, considered as a sentiment. . . . A nation, unlike a class, has a definition which is not economic. It is, we may say, a geographical group possessed of a sentiment of solidarity. Psychologically it is analogous to a school of porpoises, a flock of crows or a herd of cattle.[34]

But how can *love* of home and family be purely instinctive? To be truly loved, they must have a *value* set upon them. Yet speaking of them simply as the objects of instinctive feeling leaves no room for value. Any valuation or none is compatible with such a feeling. The same is true of the "gregarious instinct" that Russell invoked to characterize nationhood.[35] It is inadequate to account for the value people place on "mutual assistance and protection," as Herder dubs it. But this valuation is precisely what their "sentiment of solidarity" evinces. In the case of home and family, at any rate, this valuation is something given, something we find ourselves making. We cannot continue both to make it, however, and to entertain the possibility that our reaction is simply instinctive. Entertaining this possibility must lead us to suspend the valuation, since it brings us to question whether we can regard ourselves as having a *reason* for the acts our sentiment explains.

There is a gap in the argument for a familial nation's enjoyment of statehood. It is that the argument does not provide a reason why its members' family-like loyalties should be enforced by a state at all, since it does not indicate why they should be valued. "Mutual assistance and protection" might seem to provide an answer, until we wonder why mutuality of this particular *scope* is valued. It may be conceded in reply that there is no reason for valuing mutuality of this scope rather than some other, but mutuality of this scope is what we *can* engage in;[36] for these are the relationships we *do* have, and any such relationships are better than none. The individual would be badly off without them.

Perhaps this is true. But the reply fails to capture the role that the family plays in the argument. For we do not value relationships in the family just because they make for mutual assistance and support in what is, perhaps, the only way accessible to us. We value relationships with these particular people, and we do so even when the relationships are moderately dysfunctional. We value them for their own sake, not just instrumentally. The same is supposedly true of our relationships within nations. What is oppressive about "forced unions" is not just that *effort* would be required to make them work at all.[37] It is that we can see no value in the relationships involved, corresponding to the value of the relationships we are already in. If our rights are infringed through the denial of independent statehood, it is our right not to have to do what we can find no value in doing. This is how Herder's argument would need to be developed. Of course, it raises the question as to whether we value relationships at the national level in the same way as family relationships.

"A Haven in a Heartless World"

To echo the title of an influential defense of "family values"[38] is to suggest those features of the family which, extended across a nation, give it its supposed value and thereby justify institutionalizing its loyalties. They fall, I suggest, under two headings. One is the *givenness* of relationships within the family group, which I have already stressed. Though I can opt out of such relationships, I cannot enter them at will. Their value lies, then, in the escape they provide from the world of contractual relationships and conditional allegiances. In a word, it lies in *security*, but security intelligible only in terms of a human need for the *social* goods of support and loyalty—goods that cannot logically be enjoyed outside relationships, and not therefore intelligible simply in terms of what allows people to pursue their individual purposes in safety and confidence.

The second heading under which the goods of familial groups suppos-edly lie is the fact of their *particularity*. Their constitutive relationships are relations to particular people. Two contrasts are pertinent here. First, I am not a member of the nation by virtue of some role that I perform and which could in principle be played by someone else, even though as a member of the family I will perform such a role—that of father, for exam-ple. In this sense the nation differs from the state, where membership and the role of citizen are identical. Second, it is because of who I am, not the properties I have, by virtue of which I am taken into familial relation-ships. The relationships are *rigid*,[39] in the sense that I am included in the relationship regardless of my personal traits or any changes in them. In this respect, racism is a perversion of the familial model. It fails to provide at the national level for the fact that if I am *treated* as a member of the fa-milial group, then I *am* a member, whatever my genetic credentials—even if there was a mix-up at the maternity hospital. In general, though, who I am in terms of biological relatedness will correspond to the social identity that the familial group confers upon me. My continuing identity, despite changes in roles and traits, depends upon my being a member of the group. The value of the particularized relationships that constitute it is that of *continuity*.[40]

These are the sort of stories we might tell about the values to be found in families. But can they plausibly be held to be detectable in nations? Showing that there are analogies between the membership of families and of nations which would make it *possible* to find the same values in both does not show that we actually do so.[41] Still less does it show that we find values to such a degree in the nation that it is the nation which com-mands our *supreme* loyalties. One response would be simply to assert that we *do*, that our doing so is evinced in our behavior, and that intellectual skepticism disappears when action is called for, especially in time of war. This argument develops the claim that national relationships are simply *given*. But few would feel comfortable with it, preferring to seek specific explanations for particular instances of mass action rather than a general one in terms of national loyalty. Another response develops the particu-larity claim. It ambitiously asserts that one is defined by relationships that are valued for their own sake, as in the family.[42] National membership simply defines one and must therefore partake of such values. One can-not deny these values without changing one's identity. This argument could be given a naturalistic twist. I am fundamentally what nature makes me, for this fact cannot be undone. Relationships in family and na-tion are the natural relationships which make me what I am; and there-fore, because I cannot change my natural identity, I cannot deny their value. We have already had reason to dispute the naturalistic premise here. But, shorn of it, the argument lacks a defense of its claim that the nation shapes my identity. Whereas society in some general sense might do so, I cannot as yet see a reason why more specifically the *nation* should. Even if it does, there is no obvious reason why the nation gives me an identity that should not be changed. Surely that depends upon the identity in question.

A third reason for thinking the nation might enshrine familial values and even lay claim to my supreme loyalties is this: The larger relationships constitutive of the nation are what make possible, it could be claimed, the family ones. The family need not be viewed as a basic natural unit of society but as a social creation designed for biological ends. It is, nonetheless, held dear as the site of my first loyalties. Thus I have a superior obligation to protect the wider social relations within which it is embedded, for without them the narrower ones of the family would not be possible. While something like this argument is, I think, commonly presupposed in claims about what is due to the nation, it is surely a very weak one. If my first and original loyalties are to my family, it seems hard to see how these could be overridden by loyalties to anything that makes it possible, even if in virtue of my family obligations I have some obligation to what sustains it. And, even if wider social relations are required to preserve the family, it would need to be established that these were just the ones constitutive of nations; but it is hard to see how this could be done. I conclude that no good case can be made for assimilating the value of nations to that of families.

The discussion of the family model in this section applies for the most part as much to the nation conceived as a *metaphorical* family[43] as to its more literal exposition in Herder's work. It applies, too, to the nation thought of in terms of *imagined* kinship, as described by Edmund Burke.[44] Indeed, even if the nation is not thought of as really and literally an extended family, its social bonds can still be regarded as natural, as somehow deriving from human nature as essentially social. The difference between the two versions roughly correlates with a difference between Right and Left, between an emphasis on ancestral connection, real or imagined, and one on current relationships. The latter difference is often marked by an emphasis on what is due to our "forebears," on the one hand, and to our "brothers," on the other. The metaphorical, left-wing version may be less obviously prone to social conservatism and exclusivism than the literal, right-wing one. But the Left's talk of community can draw on socially conservative models of family, particularly in the area of gender,[45] while sections of the Left are just as likely as the Right to oppose such supranational institutions as the European Union, on the grounds of the damage it may do to the national community.[46]

Nonetheless, conservatism and exclusivism are, it will be allowed, characteristic features of right-wing nationalism. But there they can spring from a different model of the nation which, like the family, can be treated either literally and naturalistically or metaphorically and, in this latter case, mystically. There is an intimation of this different model in the rich passage of Herder with which I started the preceding section. The nation is "a plant," he said, with an "inner life";[47] or, as one might put it more generally and less pictorially, it is an *organic whole*. Some philosophers believe this view of a society—that is, of a nation—to be a necessary part of conservatism, explaining that

> organicism . . . takes a society to be a unitary, natural growth, an organised living whole, not a mechanical aggregate. It is not composed of bare abstract individuals but of social beings, related to one another within a texture of inherited customs and institutions which endow them with their specific social nature. The institutions of society are thus not external, disposable devices of interest to men only by reason of the individual purposes they serve; they are, rather, constitutive of the social identity of men.[48]

It is easy to see how the model described here fosters conservative policies, since any "artificial" change endangers the life of the organism. It tends toward exclusivism, for any graft threatens to overwhelm the original stock.

This model has a long history in the form of an analogy between society and the body. It resurfaces in its literal, naturalistic form in the biologism of thinkers like Herbert Spencer, who discerned four points of comparison between societies and individual organisms:

> That they gradually increase in mass; that they become little by little more complex; that at the same time their parts grow more mutually dependent; and that they continue to live and grow as wholes, while successive generations of their units appear and disappear; are broad peculiarities which bodies-politic display in common with all living bodies; and in which they and living bodies differ from everything else.[49]

Spencer argued for the organic view of societies by drawing on a wide variety of such "wonderfully close parallelisms" as that "blood vessels acquire distinct walls; roads are fenced and gravelled."[50] Such analogies, which find an evolutionary role even for railways, will not convince unbelievers that societies are natural growths. Yet even if they did, Spencer's social organism would not do the conflict-settling job required of it by nationalists. To possess clear individuating conditions, societies would presumably have to have "specific external forms." Spencer admitted that they do not, their forms being "in part determined by surrounding physical circumstances,"[51]—though this, he maintained, is the condition of most organisms, particularly plants. Such physical circumstances, however, do not seem to prevent some surprising increases "in mass":

"[A]long with the growth of a central power, the demarcations of . . . local communities become relatively unimportant, and their separate organisations merge into the general organisation. The like is seen on a larger scale in the fusion of England, Wales, Scotland, and Ireland."[52] Why a *single* nation should be discerned in the result and whether the process of "fusion" might continue are questions the model cannot answer.

Even if it could, in either its literal or metaphorical form, it is not clear why a group individuated as an organic whole *should* have a right to statehood. No doubt the sort of aptness considerations examined earlier would be adduced. Again, they would not suffice. Would a state corresponding to a single social organism be worthwhile? Would it be the sort of thing to which a people could have a right? Many on the Right as well as on the Left have disputed it. Karl Popper takes the organic view to apply not to societies in general but, rather, to a particular type of society, which he calls a closed society.

> The so-called organic or biological theory of the state can be applied to it to a considerable extent. A closed society resembles a herd or a tribe in being a semi-organic unit whose members are held together by semi-biological ties, kinship, living together, sharing common efforts, common designs, common joys and common distresses. It is still a concrete group of concrete individuals, related to one another not merely by such abstract social relationships as division of labour and exchange of commodities, but by concrete physical relationships.[53]

"Most attempts to apply the organic theory to our society," he continues, are "veiled forms of propaganda for a return to tribalism." Tribalism, he believes, lays "emphasis on the supreme importance of the tribe without which the individual is nothing at all."[54] In the closed society of the tribe, he suggests, no distinction can be made between natural regularities and unchanging social roles. This view of nationalism as a "resurrection of tribalism,"[55] as the form in which *primitive* psychosocial tendencies find their current expression, is itself, though, dependent upon an inadequately grounded naturalism. There is no reason to think of some forms of social organization as representing a more primitive, and thus more "natural," way of life than others; and still less reason to see nationalism as a revival of them.[56]

However, we do not need to follow Popper in his questionable anthropology or in his economic liberalism to accept the point he is making. The haven that organicism offers from the heartless world of abstract individuals is bought at too high a price. The organicist's state has no tendency to do what one considers it the task of any state to do—to ensure the formal equality of citizens and to regulate social relationships in their interests and with respect for their individual freedoms. No body of people, it may be argued, could have a right to a political organization that did not at least set out to do this.

Summary

This chapter has introduced the first substantive class of nationalisms which we shall consider. They are naturalist, since they regard nations as natural divisions of humanity and generate arguments for their independent statehood on the basis of some specific elaboration of this premise. I distinguish between two nonsocietal forms of naturalism, one treating nations as descent groups, the other as races, in the sense of collections of individuals with biological similarities. Neither withstands scrutiny. The most popular societal form of naturalism views nations as analogous to families, construed as a type of social organization natural to human beings. Another form sees them as analogous to organisms. Again, however, the empirical underpinnings of these positions are unsound, and, like naturalism generally, they fail to explain why it is *desirable* to construct states in accordance with such natural divisions, even were they to exist.

Chapter Four

The Nation as
Will and Idea

An Idea of the Nation

A nation as conceived by naturalists can exist even if its members do not think that it exists or do not have an idea of it.[1] Its members need only have the characteristics or the relationships whereby nature collects them into a nation. They do not need to have any idea of what these characteristics or relationships are. All that is necessary for them to form a nation is that by virtue of these characteristics or relations they should have the appropriate dispositions to treat fellow members differently from outsiders, or should actually be so treating them. It may seem to follow that they need to have an idea of who they are. No doubt they often do, and, as we saw earlier, it is thus difficult to establish that a *natural* disposition explains their behavior. But under naturalism this conception is not necessary. Just as we do not have to credit animals with concepts under which they bring members of their own kind in order to attribute to them the corresponding recognitional capacities, we do not have to do so with human beings who fall into national groupings.

In contrast to the *objectivism* which naturalism exemplifies, we can discern several sorts of nationalism which are *subjectivist* in the sense that they require the nation to be a collection of people who share a common idea of what kind of group they are, by virtue of being which they believe they form or ought to form a nation. What this means in terms of the constitutive principle of nationalism is that they have a conception of themselves by virtue of which they could claim, *ceteris paribus*, a right to independent statehood. W. B. Yeats, for example, asserted that a nation could not exist without "a model of it in the mind of the people."[2] That, as we have seen, was what Anglo-Irish Literary Revivalists like Yeats and Synge

aimed to construct, and to construct differently from their Catholic Gaeli-
cizing rivals. It is not our intention to continue that discussion here. Instead, we must ask why such a model is thought necessary to a nation.

Certainly people can do without it. One commentator remarked on the
difference between the rural Irish depicted by Synge and the Irish they
were a model for: "[T]his is the great burden of post-colonial national
elites: that, unlike the islanders of the Great Blasket or Inishmaan, they
must have an *idea* of Ireland."[3] Synge's audience was part of a people
seeking independence, and in order to seek it they had to have a conception of who it was they were seeking independence for. If a nation was a
group *claiming* independence, then it would follow straightaway that it
needed an idea of itself as that for which independence was claimed. But,
I have suggested, it is not a *claim* that characterizes nations in nationalist
discourse but, rather, a *right*. It cannot, as noted, be a claim, inasmuch as
competing claims would yield overlapping nations, when it is precisely
the defense of a claim that it represents a right to statehood and the competing claim does not. In general, to have a right is one thing, whereas to
claim it—which requires both knowing about it and considering it worth
exercising—is another. What reason can there be for thinking it necessary
for their having a right to statehood that a people should have an idea of
themselves as a group of a kind that has the right?

We should not necessarily expect a single answer rather than a number
of different answers about what generates the right, each of which implies the subjectivist conception. Nevertheless, there is, I believe, a general dissatisfaction with objectivism underlying them[4]—namely, the suspicion that it cannot establish a *right* on the basis of facts of human
similarity or social organization. At most, objectivism can make out a
case, as Weber did, for the existence of a tendency toward statehood. For
it misses the point that whether one is governed in an independent state
is not just a fact of political organization. It is a matter of whether one enjoys a certain good or suffers a certain evil, of whether one is free or in
subjection. The right to independent statehood is a right to a certain sort
of freedom. But to be in subjection, it may be argued, does not just consist
in being a member of a group governed by members of a different group.
It consists in recognizing one's situation as lacking what one would have
if one were governed by one's own. It is insofar as people think of their
situation in this way that they have a right to independent statehood, a
thought process that in turn, of course, requires them to have a conception of that which is lacking—namely, freedom for such and such a group.
They need to have a national consciousness.

Individuals may be oppressed under a colonial regime, for example.
This circumstance may give them a right to statehood of the sort that I
contrasted with a national right, inasmuch as such oppression does not

yet make of them a certain kind of group. For this to happen they would typically see themselves as oppressed because of what they are in the eyes of the colonialist. Consider how Frantz Fanon explains pan-African nationalism:

> For colonialism, this vast continent was the haunt of savages, a country riddled with superstition and fanaticism, destined for contempt, weighed down by the curse of God, a country of cannibals—in short, the Negro's country. Colonialism's condemnation is continental in scope. . . . The efforts of the native to rehabilitate himself and to escape from the claws of colonialism are logically inscribed from the same point of view as that of colonialism. . . . Colonialism did not dream of wasting its time in denying the existence of one national culture after another. Therefore, the reply of the colonised peoples will be straight away continental in its breadth.[5]

To be in subjection as a national group, they need to be aware of the scope of colonial oppression in Africa. If they are not, then it will just be as individuals or as members of this tribe or the other that they are oppressed. What right they have to the independence that can in principle prevent oppression depends, on this account, on how they think of themselves as victims of oppression. If they think of themselves as oppressed *qua* black Africans, then it is as these that they have a right of independence. There is no way of specifying what right of independence they have without drawing upon their self-conception.

Whereas under naturalism people just *are* prone to display loyalty to certain categories of their fellows, it is quite a different matter for people who have a conception of who they are and of how others differ from them. Armed with this conception, they will have to rely not only on their own inclinations but also on opinions about what is owed to different categories. They will be able to display national loyalty in a quite different way—that is, loyalty to people by virtue of their fellow membership of the nation, not just to people who are in fact members of it. Thus national *sentiments* for subjectivists are quite different from what they are for naturalists. The idea that a nation is a "community of sentiment"[6] is, as it stands, ambiguous in terms of whether the sentiment requires a conception of the nation—is, as I shall say, *reflective*—or whether it does not—is *unreflective*. The difference between reflective and unreflective sentiments is not simply that between conscious and unconscious ones. There is no reason to believe that the sentiments of, say, solidarity that I may feel with people because I recognize them as compatriots represent the coming to consciousness of feelings that I would have had anyway. This assumption lies at the root of the nationalist argument that "preexisting sentiments" are the source of the "large-scale solidarity, such that people feel themselves to be members of an overarching community."[7] But it also seems to embody a false view of feeling as consisting of visceral and intellectual components, the former giving necessary substance to the latter. In fact, recognizing someone as my compatriot and having the appropriate belief as to what my attitude to her should be can generate the sentiment. It does not need to preexist the recognition and belief in some inchoate form.

A community of reflective sentiment is a different thing from a community of unreflective sentiment. But the mere possession of either sort of sentiment is not sufficient for a community, in the sense required for a societal account of the nation. As we have seen, people may have sentiments toward each other, yet not thereby enter into social relationships. Entering into such relationships requires, in Herder's phrase, "bonds of sentiment."[8] It requires the observance of acknowledged rules governing the sentiments to be felt and expressed, not just the regular occurrence of the same sentiments. A grasp of whether people are displaying the right or the wrong sentiments does not require a conception of what sentiments they should be feeling. Indeed, in personal relationships we often have a sense that the rules are being subtly broken without any explicit conception of what social emotion is correct. But such a conception does facilitate the regulation of relationships and, in the national case, demands that the sentiments regulated be reflective ones. Only in this way can we set out what is expected of members of the nation.

Furthermore, the existence of these reflective sentiments makes possible a quite new species of sentiment—namely, one directed not just at members of the nation but at the nation itself. It is because I recognize these members as English, say, that I can regard them as constituting a nation, the English. There are, so far as I can see, no prereflective reactions to the totality which can generate an unreflective version of this sentiment. It is what we tend to think of *as* national sentiment:

> *England, with all thy faults I love thee still—*
> *My country! And, while yet a nook is left*
> *Where English minds and manners may be found,*
> *Shall be constrained to love thee.*[9]

This is the love of country which goes with national *pride;* in fact, it has even been suggested that "national identity is fundamentally a matter of dignity. It gives people reasons to be proud."[10] Yet just how this sentiment relates to its predecessor, how feeling part of a nation relates to feeling solidarity with its members, is unclear. Indeed, that it even requires solidarity is unclear, as demonstrated in Byron's parody of Cowper:

England! with all thy faults I love thee still,
I said at Calais, and I have not forgot it. . . .
Our standing army, and disbanded seamen,
Poor's rate, Reform, my own, the nation's debt,
Our little riots just to show we are free men,
Our trifling bankruptcies in the Gazette.[11]

The official patriotism that Byron lampoons is quite compatible with a breakdown in the social relationships which supposedly justify it. This love of nation is not constitutive of national community.

Nor do the ambiguities of national sentiment stop here. Is it necessarily a *feeling* at all, as a patriotic sentiment must be, or simply an *opinion* as to one's nationality? In the following passage an analogous ambiguity appears with respect to a people's *sense* of what they are:

> Nationality is the sense of community which, under the historical conditions of a particular social epoch, has possessed or still seeks expression through the unity of a state. Various as are the conditions on which it rests, the sense of nationality is itself definite and strong and moving . . . so that men are aroused by its name and thought to deep stirrings of devotion, sacrifice, and even worship. There are many spiritual unities, and nationality is but one. Why has it been in modern history so decisive as against the others? Why has the "soul unity" of the English squire and coster, corporation-lawyer and coal miner, counted for so much . . . ? Why is it that men . . . poles apart . . . nevertheless because they belong to the same nation, feel a oneness that in the hour of crisis supersedes all obvious differences?[12]

Like the "large-scale solidarity, such that people feel themselves to be members of an overarching community," this "sense of community" oscillates between a belief that justifies a feeling, on the one hand, and the feeling which gives rise to the belief, on the other. If it is a belief that certain people belong together, then it needs some grounds. If it is a feeling, then the question arises as to whether it is appropriate, whether it is the right feeling to have. But while the justification of belief rests on the facts, the appropriateness of feeling depends in part upon the value of the relationships it is necessary to.

These two readings of "sense" and "sentiment" point in quite different directions in the defense of claims to statehood. People's beliefs as to what nations they belong to settle the matter only on certain accounts of nationhood. They do not do so on naturalistic ones, where members are in no better position than others to determine what group they fall into. Yet if a particular group is determined, in whole or in part, by its members' conception, then they may well be in a better position to identify it. This would be especially true on accounts like the one just quoted. For if "[n]ationality is the sense of community which . . . seeks expression through the unity of a state," then those possessed of this sense are presumably in a better position than others to report on it. It may be for this reason that their feelings of community, and their beliefs that they form one, are apt to be conflated on such accounts. Yet here it is the common feelings which must be appealed to in defending a claim to statehood, not the beliefs. And this is true in general. It is the factors which ground a belief, not the belief itself, which can justify statehood. But if people's feelings of solidarity are what justify it, then, as we shall see in the next section, this is because what they *want* is, other things being equal, allowed to establish their right to it.

"Think of It Always"

In 1875 the French impressionist painter Edgar Degas painted a picture of the *Place de la Concorde*.[13] In the background of the painting is a series of statues which viewers would have recognized as the personifications of French cities. But one is both the focal point of the composition and yet totally obscured by the black hat of its principal figure. It is the statue of Strasburg, the capital of Alsace taken by the Prussians in the Franco-Prussian War four years earlier, veiled in black crêpe until the city's return to France in 1918. "N'en parlez jamais, y pensez toujours," advised the French statesman, Léon-Michel Gambetta.[14] That is exactly what Degas did in this picture. But what is the point, we may wonder, of *thinking* about a lost portion of one's nation?

"If I should cease to think, perhaps I should cease to be," meditated Descartes,[15] since his essential nature lay, he thought, in being a thinking thing. There is a correspondingly Cartesian view of the essence of the nation: A nation's existence consists in its entertaining a conception of itself.[16] The most celebrated elaboration of this thought is attributed to another Frenchman, Ernest Renan: "A nation implies a past; which, as regards the present, it is all contained in one tangible fact, viz., the agreement and clearly expressed desire to continue a life in common. The existence of a nation is (if you will forgive me the metaphor) a daily plebiscite, just as that of the individual is a continual affirmation of life."[17]

The thought that maintains the nation in existence is a thought of it as something desired by its members. Wanting to live together with a certain group of people, in the way that statehood institutionalizes: This is the thought that must be repeated in order for the nation to continue. If the desire evaporates, so that the members' conception of who they are no longer motivates them, then the nation perishes. It is this that Gambetta's dictum implies. No longer to think of Alsace Lorraine as part of the national community one wants to live in is for the nation that included it no longer to exist. Loss of desire accomplishes what force of arms could not.

Renan's account of the nation is a *voluntarist* one. What makes people a nation is something they *will*. In Renan's version, what makes them a nation is that their desires to associate politically coincide.[18] It collects them together into a nation, he thought, precisely because their coincident desires confer on them a right to statehood. It does so because people have a right to associate politically as they desire. In holding this, Renan explicitly attacked naturalistic alternatives, as in the view that "[r]ace is what remains stable and fixed; and *this* it is that constitutes a right and lawful title. The Germanic race, for example, according to this theory, has the right to retake the scattered members of the Germanic family, even when these members do not ask for reunion."[19]

Renan's ironic objection to such views was that "lest we put too great a strain upon Science, let us excuse the lady from giving an opinion on problems in which so many interests are involved. . . . [L]et us ask her just to tell the truth."[20] Indeed, national rights cannot be founded on scientifically discoverable facts, for such facts might reveal groupings which their members have no wish to be institutionalized in states. It would be contrary to the right of people to have their wishes respected in these matters to impose a political organization upon them on this basis. But such an imposition was precisely what had happened to the people of Alsace Lorraine. At the National Assembly, which agreed to peace with Prussia, their delegates declared their "immutable will to remain French" and argued that "a compact which disposes of us without our consent is null and void."[21] "Against their will we shall restore them to their true selves," commented the German historian Heinrich von Treitschke.[22]

Renan's brand of voluntarist nationalism was committed to a more radical rejection of the idea that there is a truth about what nations there are than to the idea involved in rejecting scientific truths about it or talk of "true selves." It was committed to *anti-realism* about what nations there are—that is, to rejecting the idea that there is a truth of the matter about it in principle discoverable by any observer. The contrasting *realist* doctrine is, of course, implied by scientific naturalism, as well as by many other theories. It is also threatened by subjectivism, however, and falls before Renan's version. For Renan made the continued existence of the nation logically dependent upon the continuance of people's willing it—as expressed, for example, in a plebiscite (though no formal plebiscite is needed). When members of a nation enter the polling booth one by one, the question they ask themselves is, "What is my nationality?" But their answer is an expression of their will to be of a certain nationality. The question as to whether together they constitute a nation is determined by their practical conclusion as to whether to do so. This is not a procedure for *discovering* whether they do. It is a procedure for *deciding* whether to do so, such that whether they constitute a nation consists in nothing more than the outcome of the procedure. It is not a fact independent of such a procedure, as the facts uncovered by procedures of discovery are. Hence the anti-realism of Renan's account. For the members of the nation, though not for others, whether their nation exists is not a discoverable fact about them. It is something they can make and unmake at will. They may, of course, discover from a plebiscite what others will, but that such knowledge can affect the direction of their own willing demonstrates that it does not settle the question of their national membership, in the way that discoverable facts would have to do.

Renan's conception of a plebiscite is totally different from that of an opinion poll held to discover, along realist lines, what nationality people *believe* they are on the basis of discoverable facts. However, if discoverable facts do not determine what nationality they are and this depends, even in part, on what conception they have of themselves, as under subjectivism generally, then again the poll takes on an anti-realist aspect. For those being polled will now have to decide under what conception to think of themselves. They may make that decision for a number of reasons apart from simply considering with whom they wish to associate. They may feel, for example, that there is something fantastical in claiming some long-suppressed nationality, however much they would welcome an independent state. But whatever the grounds of the decision, its existence as part of the response procedure means that the poll is, properly speaking, no longer a canvass of *opinions*. It becomes, as in Renan's account, an anti-realistically conceived plebiscite. I shall spend no more time, however, on this general subjectivist case.

What we need to look at now is the logically voluntarist version. How, in more detail, might this version generate a right to statehood? Writing somewhat earlier than Renan, John Stuart Mill expressed a similar view.

> A portion of mankind may be said to constitute a nationality if they are united among themselves by common sympathies, which do not exist between them and any others—which make them co-operate with each other more willingly than with other people, desire to be under the same government, and desire that they should be governed by themselves or portions of themselves, exclusively. . . .
>
> Where the sentiment of nationality exists in any force, there is a prima facie case for uniting all the members of the nationality under the same government, and a government to themselves apart. This is merely saying the question of government ought to be decided by the governed. One hardly knows what any division of the human race should be free to do, if not to determine, with which of the various collective bodies of human beings they choose to associate themselves.[23]

There are several different arguments here for the national right to independent statehood (and indeed to unitary statehood), but they all have some things in common. First, the right of the nation derives from the rights of its individual members to determine their associations and government. It is not the right of a group which is irreducible to the rights of its members as in the case of racist theory, say, whereby the supposed right of a racial group to its own government does not derive from its individual members' rights but, rather, applies only to a group constituted by their supposed racial similarities.[24] I shall call this Millian doctrine *political individualism*. Second, the right of the nation derives from the rights of individuals *qua* human beings, not from individuals as already possessing properties over and above those possessed by all human beings, or at least all sane adult ones. This contrasts, for instance, with the view that one has a right to associate with others by virtue of one's similarities to them, though it is up to individuals to choose which similarities to make the basis of association. The view that Mill and Renan appear to share here I call *humanism*.

Two points follow from the foregoing arguments—namely, that the right to statehood cannot derive from the reasons people have for wanting to exercise it, only from the fact that they want to; and that the right cannot derive from anything they have in common apart from the fact that they have a common desire. These points enable us to clear up a possible confusion in Mill's account. Taken *au pied de la lettre*, Mill seems to regard "common sympathies" as prior to and explicative of shared desires and will, though it is the latter which generate the right. But if this is so, then no such facts as that people with these sympathies would be apt for shared statehood can be invoked to justify it. They must have the right, whatever it is that explains the way they choose to exercise it and even if they are totally wrong in the reasons they have for their choices. Mill appears to have overlooked this point in arguing that people's common sympathies are necessary in order for them to enjoy "free institutions,"[25] the opportunity for which he seems to have treated as justifying shared statehood.

However, at least two arguments, unaffected by this possible confusion, can be discerned in Mill's account of national rights, both of which are paralleled in Renan's. The first is that people have a right to independent statehood because they have a right to freedom of association. This is simply an example of the general liberal right to be free to do as one wishes, so long as it does not interfere with the freedom of others. If in the national case people wish to "co-operate with each other," as Mill put it, or to "continue a life in common," as Renan did, then no obstacles should be placed in their way. One kind of association desired might be a political one (i.e., it might have the political goals of statehood); or it may be that the kind of association desired—for example, just to "continue a life in common"—is made possible only by statehood. In either case, the freedom of association argument is held to generate the right to statehood.

The second argument, often confused with the first,[26] is more specifically focused on what can justify the scope of a government, rather than the scope of an association which requires government. Again, it exemplifies a more general principle—in this case, that people should be governed only with their consent. This principle can be employed in a number of ways—for example, to argue for a democratic system as the only sort that will ensure government by consent.[27] It can be founded on different bases, too. One is that the power of government derives from that of the people, so that only if people consent to a certain use of their power by government is it legitimate. This, of course, is the classic doctrine of popular sovereignty.[28] Another, however, is the more abstract point that government differs from mere coercion, precisely in that it requires the consent, or at least the acquiescence, of the governed. But government is less likely to be an interference with freedom than coercion, such that the general liberal right to individual freedom can again be invoked—this time, to ground consent theory. The theory is then used in the nationalist case to argue that the wish for government of a certain scope generates a right to it, since any other government will lack the legitimacy that stems from consent.

It is evident that any voluntarist nationalism based on these arguments can be used to justify the secession of a people from their existing state if they desire it. This is the case even where the state previously reflected its people's desire to associate. But, as Renan allowed, "[H]uman wishes change"[29] and, with them, the constitution of nations. Furthermore, liberals must prefer a strong version of consent theory which permits the withdrawal of consent to a weak one which does not, since the former restricts freedom to a lesser degree than the latter.[30] The only arguable limitations on a right of secession under voluntarism are practical ones, having to do with the viability of a secessionist state or of whatever state would remain after secession. It is quite impermissible, on voluntarist principles, to qualify that right, as Mill notoriously went on to do, by claiming:

> Nobody can suppose that it is not more beneficial to a Breton, or a Basque of French Navarre, to be brought into the current of ideas and feelings of a highly civilised and cultivated people—to be a member of the French nationality, admitted on equal terms to all the privileges of French citizenship, sharing the advantages of French protection, and the dignity and prestige of French power—than to sulk on his own rocks, the half-savage relic of past times, revolving in his own little mental orbit, without participation or interest in the general movement of the world.[31]

His justification seems to have been that "the half-savage" is not in a position to exercise his right to freedom of association rationally, though contact with civilization will lead him to be able to do so. Needless to say, a more thoroughgoing liberalism can have nothing to do with Mill's stance on this matter.

Nonetheless, Mill's qualifications highlight an important feature of voluntarist nationalism—namely, its grounding in what are seen as rational principles of human social action and political organization, principles that any rational person can give assent to. The contrast here is with those nationalisms that are seen as irrational, as relying on instinctual affections rather than on a conscious choice of association which inevitably has a conscious objective in view. But it should not be thought that these voluntarist principles are *opposed* to nationalism,[32] favoring instead some form of cosmopolitanism. As should be clear from Mill and Renan, they are opposed only to what are seen as false—and dangerous—conceptions of the nation. The reason is that Mill and Renan insisted on rights of freedom of association and government by consent, which they did not believe would be exercised in a cosmopolitan manner, desirable as this might be.

It is beyond our present scope to investigate the liberal principles on which these rights are founded. How, though, should we assess their application here? Taking the freedom of association argument first, we should note, as earlier indicated, that it does not necessarily presume that political association is what is wished. There are both political[33] and nonpolitical forms of voluntarist nationalism. Whereas the former would lead directly to a claim for statehood, the latter would do so only via supplementary arguments to the need of statehood for the association desired. I shall postpone consideration of some of them. But note that even where a political association is not what is directly desired, what makes the association that *is* desired a nation is, by the constitutive principle, the right of such an association to independent statehood. Can the right to statehood be justified as maximizing freedom of association?

Political association is of its essence exclusionary. It designates a class of people together with whom one does not wish to be governed. But the state which governs together those who so wish it is a territorial body: It governs all who occupy a certain territory. It follows that, with occasional exceptions, all those with whom its citizens do not wish to be governed must be excluded from occupation of its territory. The effect of this exclusion is not only to prevent *political* association with them; it is also to prevent a whole range of other associations which require a common life—in particular, work and family relationships. Many of these are effectively blocked by the controls on immigration which preserve the political association. But now what must be asked is whether the freedom to associate politically has been bought at too high a price in terms of people's other freedoms to associate.

It seems doubtful that the balance comes down on the side of maximizing individual freedom to associate by authorizing the freedom of *political* association, by contrast, say, with a cosmopolitan system. It does so only if we can rely upon the assumption that people's desires to associate with others in nonpolitical relationships run on all fours with their preparedness to associate politically. The Millian theory assumes, in other words, what it can in no way defend: that the desire to associate is largely homogeneous, political association being but one aspect of a deeper fellowship. Do people's desires to associate give them a right to statehood even if this assumption of homogeneity of association can be made? So far we have tacitly assumed that people should enjoy freedom of association only when their desire to associate is reciprocated. This is an important aspect of the freedom in question, for it implies a right to associate with whom I like and not to associate with whom I do not like. I must not have to put up with unwanted attentions. Yet it is far from clear that this freedom gives me the right to deny others the *opportunity* to associate with me. Freedom of association, in a wider sense, implies the provision of just such opportunities. Yet it is these that political association in a state inevitably denies.

Thus far, of course, we have questioned only the *ethics* of the freedom of association argument. Metaphysically logical voluntarism runs into other problems. There will commonly be *no* nations, as logical voluntarism conceives them, because there will be no complete coincidence of wills as to whom to associate with politically or otherwise. No wonder the French were exhorted to think of Alsace always, for if a significant number had acquiesced in the German occupation of Alsace Lorraine, the existence of the French nation itself would, on voluntarist principles, have come into question. This problem is closely allied to one which besets consent theory when applied to the determination of statehood: "[O]n the surface it seemed reasonable: let the people decide. It was in fact ridiculous because the people cannot decide until somebody decides who the people are."[34] It is fanciful to suppose that people will fall easily into disjoint groups, each unanimous in its choice of statehood. If they do not, how does consent theory determine what states there should rightfully be and, hence, by the constitutive principle, what nations there are? The answer it usually returns is that this should be determined democratically—that is, by taking a majority vote. But how does consent theory determine *what* population will decide its political destiny by a majority vote? It matters a good deal, for example, whether this should be the population of the whole island of Ireland, or just the population of the Six Counties of Ulster. One ingenious suggestion[35] is that the majority principle should be applied recursively, so that a group wishing to secede can determine the population to be polled, other groups within it can determine a population to be polled on whether to secede from the secessionist state, and so on. On this principle, while it was right that Ulster Protestants had the opportunity to secede from a predominantly Catholic Ireland, Catholic areas in the north should be permitted the opportunity of seceding from the predominantly Protestant state thus formed, and so on. Such a process minimizes the chances that people will be governed without their consent, and it is thus the logical conclusion of consent theory.

I do not propose to consider whether the groups determined on this basis *would* have a right to statehood, only whether they would have it by virtue of being groups of a certain *kind*, and thereby have it as a *national* right. Certainly some withdrawals of consent might be motivated by the kinds of oppression which could, as I allowed earlier, give rise to a right to the self-protection that only independent statehood might provide. This, I suggested, contrasts sharply with a national right. Indeed, consent could be motivated in many ways different from a *mere* desire to associate with others. If it is plausible to view such a desire as giving rise to a national right, then it does so because it is a desire to associate with others on account of something they are taken to have in common,[36] rather than because they are in a shared situation where association is expedient. The distinction may not always be a sharp one on some accounts of nationhood—as when nationhood is rooted in shared interests. But it must at least require that the intention of the association is long term, because the basis of association is presumed to be so. There must be that about the group, in other words, which allows it to fulfill the reproduction condition of nationhood. If consent theory is carried to its logical conclusion, then it lacks the resources to satisfy this condition. The groups it permits cannot be nations.

Whereas the freedom of association argument may be elaborated in a way that is congenial to nationalism, consent theory, if rigorously carried through, cannot be. Perhaps the people of Alsace did eventually give their consent to German government, but they may still have wished to associate with their French fellows. Consent and will to associate can come apart, and when they do it is the latter which is the more plausible indicator of nationality—precisely because it gathers people together as a group of a certain kind, rather than simply as individuals in a common predicament. But can just wanting make it so? Is a coincidence of wills itself too indefinite and unstable to make people a nation, even if a right to statehood could be derived from it?

Social Contract

There is a big difference between wanting to associate with others, even when that desire is reciprocated, and actually associating with them. The version of a subjectivist voluntarism that we have been looking at is nonsocietal.[37] By contrast, an account of the nation as an actual association would be a societal one. There is one version of this kind of account which is closely related to, and even confused with, the freedom of association and consent theory accounts, themselves commonly conflated. It is that national societies are associations formed by a *contract* between their members. A classic statement of the view was made by Anthony Ashley Cooper, Earl of Shaftesbury, contrasting a group held together by force, as under an alien government, with one that comes together by mutual agreement:

> A multitude held together by force, though under one and the same head, is not properly united. Nor does such a body make a people. 'Tis the social league, confederacy, and mutual consent founded in some common good or interest, which joins the members of a community and makes a people one. Absolute power annuls the public. And where there is no public or constitution there is in reality no mother country or nation.[38]

There is a great deal going on in this passage which cannot detain us here. Two points are of immediate importance: first, that a nation is formed through a "social league" or "confederacy," grounded in mutual consent to some arrangements, or "constitution," for its operation; second, that the motive for accepting these arrangements is "some common good or interest." What makes a nation are actual social relationships, but these relationships are the result of deliberate individual choices about how to be "united" with others. These choices are an exercise of individual rights to freedom of association in pursuit of mutual benefits.

Contractual nationalism of this sort neatly combines societal nationalism, whereby the right to statehood supposedly derives from the existence of social relations, with elements it shares with nonsocietal voluntarism. Under it, a people have this right because their social group has a collective right to determine its government. But the latter arises wholly through the exercise of individual rights of freedom of association in the making of the contract. Thus, indirectly, the right to statehood is the result of the exercise of individual rights. On this model, which is essentially that of John Locke, people "join and unite into a community for their comfortable, safe, and peaceable living, one amongst another, in a secure enjoyment of their properties, and a greater security against any that are not of it."[39] These are individual ends, but ones that are shared by all members and hence constitute a "common good or interest." Although pursuing this "common good or interest" may in fact require a state, it is not, as such, a political objective, in the same way that being governed under the same laws is: Rather, government under the same laws is a method of bringing about the objective. We can describe such an association as a *civil* association, rather than a directly political one. It is a form of civil society—that is, a society held together principally by the economic exchanges which make a common life possible. These are conducted in the interests of individual members, through arrangements mutually agreed upon. This is a very different model of community from the family one we looked at earlier.

In a civil association, relationships are constituted by the reciprocation of obligations. Such obligations are entered into through the contract which sets up the association. Another liberal principle is involved in this claim—namely, that one is under an obligation only through having voluntarily undertaken it. Yet that is not to say that one can voluntarily renounce it. To enter into a contract to do something is not just to have an intention to do it: It is to incur penalties for nonperformance. The logical voluntarism we looked at in the last section makes no room for this fact, if people can cease to be a nation simply through losing their inclination to associate. But under contractual nationalism they are stuck with their national society so long as the arrangements for ensuring performance of their obligations persist. What are these obligations? They are compliance in the arrangements necessary for social life and, most important, the enforcement of these arrangements where necessary and the defense of a territory within which they can be relied upon. These last are national obligations which, within the framework of a state, will constitute *political* obligations. Indeed, they are political obligations precisely because they are, first of all, national ones.

Here, then, is a further justification for independent statehood. The state exists to enforce the obligations necessary to social life. In the civil association these are created by a contract between members of a certain group which thereby becomes a nation. The group has a right to enforce its constitutive obligations which derives from its members' voluntarily undertaking them. It has a right to the institutions of state required for that. But if the state was one which also enforced the obligations of others, it would impose political obligations upon some of its members which they had not undertaken and would thereby act without right.[40] Therefore, the state required must be an independent state. To this may be added the aptness consideration that its character as a civil association makes the group suitable for statehood: The obligations the state might seek to impose are already accepted by the nation. Again, we see in this account an intricate weave of societal argument and liberal principles locating rights in individual acts. The right to statehood again depends upon the existence of a society, but that in turn exists as a result of individual voluntary undertakings.

The existence of a civil association whose continuance is ensured by the constant undertaking and reciprocation of obligations satisfies the reproduction condition of nationhood that the existence of a group constituted by mere consent cannot satisfy, and that even one constituted by the wish for a long-term association cannot be guaranteed to satisfy, since, as lovers' vows amply illustrate, the wish for a long-term association is not necessarily a long-term wish. The long-term existence of the contractual nation is the result of the fact that it is not constituted by a wish but, rather, is brought about by a contract. Although contractual nationalism is a form of voluntarism, since people's desires to associate are what make them a nation, it is *causal* rather than logical voluntarism; for their desires to associate, as expressed in the contract, cause the nation to exist. The upshot is that contractual nationalism is realist. There is a discoverable truth of the matter as to whether there is a nation, because there is a truth as to whether there is a continuing contract. At the point at which they enter the contract, members have to ask not whether there is but whether there should be a nation and, thereafter, only if there is one.

Furthermore, the existence of the contract allows this form of nationalism to escape the indefiniteness that vitiates the logically voluntarist nation. On that account, I suggested, there will be many cases where no nations exist because people's wills to associate fail to coincide. A contract, however, ensures that they do, for people must know with whom they are contracting and who is excluded from the contract. Yet this requirement brings out graphically how unreal contractual nationalism is. For the fact that many mainland Britons *deny* that the Northern Irish are British—which most claim to be—seems to imply that these mainlanders do not think of themselves as having any national obligations toward them. Others are of a different persuasion. Yet if there *were* a contract which constituted people into a British nation, this uncertainty as to its scope could not exist.

The objection to contractual theories generally is, of course, that they depend upon a fiction. Except in special cases where a nation is supposedly set up through an explicit political act—as through the American Declaration of Independence, say—there is no explicit contract that people have entered into. This objection is predictably countered by the claim that members of a society give it their *tacit* consent through the acceptance of its benefits. They grasp that doing so puts them under obligations and voluntarily accept their position. There are many things to question about this matter, not least that citizens may see their position as different from the one described and thus decline to consent, despite appearances. Several regimes in the Soviet bloc were surprised to discover this truth. My purpose, though, is merely to investigate how the presumption of tacit consent impacts upon contractual nationalism. What sort of nation would the nation of a tacitly agreed association be?

It is, we can notice straightaway, the kind of nation that established states characteristically depict themselves as being. Without any special doctrine of the kind of nation theirs is—racial, cultural, or whatever—established states can claim that their citizens constitute a single civil association through their tacit consent to the social arrangements which the state enforces. Even separatist movements can, on this basis, be condemned as lacking popular support, simply on the basis of a state's presumption of its citizens' consent. This response, while credible against relatively recent, weak, or small scale secessionist groups, becomes increasingly implausible as they gain in strength and demonstrations of support. One motive for such movements having an electoral wing is indeed to demonstrate the falsity of any presumption of consent to the constitutional status quo. The employment of this presumption by states is, however, ultimately self-defeating. For if the mere existence of a functioning state is taken to be evidence of consent to the contractual arrangements which justify its existence, then it will lack any *independent* evidence of the national right on which it is supposedly founded. The mere current existence of a state can do nothing to establish its right to a continued existence.

Tacit consent, furthermore, undermines the supposed benefits of an actual contract over a mere wish to associate, in at least two ways. First, it fails to secure the relative permanence of the state since, while it implies acceptance of the current status quo, it cannot imply any intention not to change it. An express contract to form a civil association will be entered into only by those who wish for a long-term arrangement between certain people, for those who enter it have the power to negotiate its terms and must have considered such an arrangement beneficial. Those who are presumed to consent to an ongoing contractual arrangement are allowed no such power, and no such wish can therefore be imputed to them. Membership may suit them now, but so long as they fulfill their current obligations, nothing need hold them to it. They may withdraw their loyalty and either leave individually or secede collectively. Second, tacit consent may fail to secure the definiteness of an express and therefore explicit contract. Those who are presumed to consent to social arrangements may lack a clear grasp of their scope and limits. The upshot of this last point is that subjectivism itself is threatened if nations are taken to be constituted by merely tacit consent. For how does merely tacit consent ensure that people share a common conception of the kind of group they are, by virtue of which they have a right to statehood? Indeed, tacit consent does not ensure that they have a *conception* at all. All they need do is play their part in the civil association that is supposedly a nation; they do not have to possess any conception of that association.

The foregoing suggests, in fact, an account of civil society quite different from the subjectivist one. For it suggests that people may engage voluntarily in relationships with others of a sort that constitute a civil society, yet be quite unreflective about the character of their voluntary involvement. They may, indeed, willingly associate with others; but if they are asked whether they wish to associate with them under some description—racial, cultural, or whatever—they may deny it. People may just be *wrong* about whom they are willing to associate with under some description. The proof of whether they are or not is in behavior that need not involve this descriptive conception of their potential fellows. But this kind of error is a possibility for which subjectivism can find no room. It delivers us back to a form of objectivism in which a nation could exist and none of its members have any conception of it. Yet this form would not be of the naturalist sort with which subjectivism typically contrasts itself, for it is not, as naturalism is, *involuntarist:* The members' desires to associate coincide, but not under some shared conception of nation. A civil society so structured is a very different thing from the civil association of a reflective contractual voluntarism, for although there will be voluntary relationships within it, its overall character will appear not as that of a voluntary association but, rather, as a society within which people find themselves and participate by custom rather than by intent. We shall return to such a view of the nation later, but meanwhile we must look more closely at the role the state plays in some kinds of nationalism.

Summary

Here I have contrasted subjectivist nationalisms with the objectivism which naturalistic nationalism exemplifies. Subjectivism regards a nation as a collection of people with a shared idea of what kind of group they constitute, by virtue of which they could claim a right to statehood. The preferred basis for this claim is a voluntarist one; in its simplest form, people have a right to statehood, and thereby form a nation, just because they have a common will which statehood would institutionalize. But such logical voluntarism, as I call it, differs from the causal voluntarism under which people's entering into a social contract makes them a nation. This form of subjectivism, unlike the preceding one, is societal rather than nonsocietal, since it views the nation as an actual association, not just a collection of individuals wishing to associate. These forms of voluntarism, however, encounter serious difficulties in determining the boundaries of the states they are intended to justify, since there simply are no suitably disjoint groups of people, each with a clear and distinct idea of their shared nationality.

Chapter Five

The Nation-State

"Unity of Government . . . One People"

Completing his second term of office as President of the United States, George Washington delivered a farewell address to its citizens. He commended to them "some sentiments" which he thought important to their "felicity as a people." The first was "the love of liberty," the next:

> The unity of government, which constitutes you as one people, is also now dear to you. It is justly so; for it is a main pillar in the edifice of your real independence, the support of your tranquillity at home, your peace abroad; of your safety; of your prosperity; of that very liberty you so highly prize. . . . [I]t is of infinite moment, that you should properly estimate the immense value of your national union to your collective and individual happiness . . . indignantly frowning upon the first dawning of every attempt to alienate any portion of our country from the rest. . . . For this you have every inducement of sympathy and interest. Citizens, by birth or choice, of a common country, that country has a right to concentrate your affections. The name of "American," which belongs to you, in your national capacity, must always exalt the just pride of patriotism, more than any appellation derived from local discriminations.[1]

This is a succinct statement of what we can call *political* (or civic) nationalism. In fact, we have already encountered some forms of it in the preceding chapter, when considering voluntarism. Yet, as I stressed, despite a common assumption to the contrary, voluntarist nationalism is not necessarily political. An association, the desire for which supposedly confers a right to statehood, need not be, as such, a political one—even if, in one respect, it becomes so with statehood. Nor need the contract which allegedly creates the nation be a contract to enter a single state. John Locke rather uncertainly distinguished the *social* contract, properly speaking, which creates a society, from the political agreement to a government which creates a state.[2] We need, then, to characterize those nationalisms for which the nation is necessarily a political group.

I suggest that we think of political nationalism as holding that the features by virtue of which people constitute a nation can be identified only by reference to an actual or desired state.[3] It is the membership or intended membership of this state which makes them members of the nation. Thus Washington's fellow citizens were, on his account, formed into a nation through membership of the Union. The political approach contrasts sharply with the pre-political ones exemplified by all naturalisms—for no state is natural—and with many other theories of the nation which appeal to an independently identifiable group in order to justify the state it claims a right to.

One motive for adopting a political approach to nationalism is evidenced in George Washington's words. It is a view easily confused with political nationalism itself,[4] and one which, for convenience, we can call *statism*. Statism holds that there can be no group constituted by social relationships of the sort that is a candidate for nationhood on societal accounts—a community, for short—*unless* its members are united under a state. There are, for statism, no pre-political communities, only political ones. We shall return to the case for statism in a moment. For now, though, we can see why statism might lead to political nationalism, and this in two possible ways. First, a societal conception of the nation, combined with a statist view of society, immediately yields a form of political nationalism—namely, one in which, while there may be states without nations,[5] there are no nations without states. Washington's account of the American nation fits this pattern. It is an account, however, of obviously limited applicability, failing to identify as nations any groups aspiring to independent statehood, unless, that is, they already have some state-like structures such as provincial political organizations. Evidently such an account will fail to fit very many groups claiming rights of secession, for example, on national grounds. Second, therefore, a statist view of society might be combined with a nonsocietal conception of the nation which picks it out as a group aspiring to become a community through statehood. This kind of account has, I think, been implicit in the programs of many anti-colonial movements which see the nation as existing so far as its materials, so to speak, are concerned, but needing to be *built*. Yet the structuring of such materials is taken, on statist principles, to be possible only within a state. George Washington's America provides, perhaps, a precursory intimation of this attitude.

Another motive for political nationalism is voluntarism of a sort that espouses freedom of political association, so that the nation is identified by the state, actual or intended, that its members want. We touched on this kind of nationalism in the last chapter. There we saw that, if it is carried through consistently, it requires a strong version of voluntarism whereby withdrawal of consent terminates association in the nation. We can now see, however, how political voluntarism of this sort seems to be actually incompatible with statism. For suppose that we allow an unrestricted right of secession on voluntarist grounds. Then we would have to allow that a group could leave the state to pursue its own sectional interests. But what is wished for in desiring a state for one's people? If statism is correct, then what is wished for are institutions through which they form a single community. Yet what is wanted is then precisely that people give up their pursuit of sectional interests in subordination to the state, for if they pursue them the community will break down. If this is what is wanted in desiring a state, then the right to secede from it at will must be denied. And if it is denied to others, it cannot consistently be claimed by secessionists either. For if they pursue their cause and allow that others among them may do the same, then their own projected state will lack the secure basis needed for it to make itself a community. In short, voluntarism will "lead naturally to an indefinite disintegration of political societies,"[6] and secure communal relations will prove impossible.[7]

Again, the appropriate response to the problems of a strong political voluntarism is to look for a contract that ties people into a state and thus, on statist principles, ensures the stability of their community. This, of course, was the position of statism's founder, Thomas Hobbes. Unlike Locke, Hobbes discerned but one contract: that between people, which inaugurates the state. Each person says: "I Authorise and give up my Right of Governing myselfe, to this Man, or to this Assembly of men, on this condition, that thou give up thy Right to him, and Authorise all his Actions in like manner."[8] Such a contract is made to escape the "time of Warre, where every man is Enemy to every man"[9]—a situation which Hobbes notoriously thought to exist in the state of nature. The very same apprehensions create a motive to agree to a state that is imposed by conquest, and here there is the additional motive of fear of what the conqueror will do if one does not consent. Only a state which enforces laws binding on all can create social relationships between people in which they are secure from the consequences of irresoluble conflict.

Two features of Hobbes's account are of importance in considering its relevance to nationalism. First, there are no nations in the state of nature. Hobbes allowed that, in this condition—a largely mythical one, he believed, beyond "the savage people in many places of *America*"[10]—there could be harmony within families but not outside of them. He would have been committed to denying, therefore, any naturalistic societal accounts of nationhood. But he was also committed to denying nonsocietal naturalisms; for these impute a natural motive for association over and above what might motivate anyone placed in the same circumstances, this being the only motivation that Hobbes allowed. Second, then, Hobbes allowed no reason for maintaining a society separate from others. After conquest, separate societies are joined together; but because all have the same interest in security, this amalgamation cannot provide a reason to withhold consent. Nationalisms based on the idea of distinct civil associations grounded in divergent interests must, on these principles, be rejected. Yet while Hobbes's opposition to naturalism cannot easily be modified, this last type of anti-nationalism may seem to be. There seems no reason in principle why the range of motives for agreeing to a government should not be extended. If one can be assured that security will be preserved through secession, then one might support it as better able to serve the interests of members of one's group. And the necessary assurance will be forthcoming if one justifiably believes that the new contract is better able to do this than the old one that one wishes to dissolve. This, surely, was the position of the American colonists seeking independence. Whatever right to independent statehood people have on the basis of a political contract must be derived from their right to further their interests.

On Hobbes's account, the right to a state derives from the right of individuals to seek their own survival. In the state of nature they can do this only in ways that bring them into conflict with others. But within a state of government they can do it through cooperative relationships. States have analogous rights. Hobbes specifically compared the rights of a sovereign to procure her people's safety to that of an individual to procure his, since "[t]he Office of the Soveraign (be it a Monarch or an Assembly) consisteth in the end, for which he was trusted with the Soveraign's Power, namely the procuration of *the safety of the people*."[11] However, since there is no international authority which stands in the same relation to states as that in which they stand to their individual members,[12] Hobbes believed that states can stand to each other only in "a posture of War."[13] Their rights to uphold the interests of their members, that is, are precisely analogous to those of individuals in the state of nature. While we may grant Hobbes that in neither case is there anything to prevent the pursuit of self-interest at the expense of others, and even that such a pursuit is rational in the absence of any reciprocation of altruism, we may nonetheless balk at the idea that self-interest is thereby pursued by *right* rather than simply by might. If we do, then we would doubt whether there is a right to pursue one's shared interest with others through an independent state. We would also need additional arguments as to why this is desirable and in what sort of states it may be so.

Before continuing this discussion, we need to look at a further feature of the idea that unity of government can serve to constitute one people, and it is this: None of the pre-political approaches we have considered (with the possible exception of the family model) provide any obvious resources for regarding the nation as a corporate *body*, in which many people become *one* people.[14] Yet unless the nation is such an entity, we may claim, it will be incapable of possessing the collective properties we wish to attribute to a nation. It will be incapable of performing collective actions, of bearing collective responsibility, of claiming collective rights. The last mentioned is crucial if we are to follow through the constitutive principle and view a nation as what has a right to statehood. For if this is a collective right, in the sense that it cannot be reduced to the rights of individuals, then a nation must be a body corporate. Now, it may be continued, the only way that people can become a body corporate of the relevant kind is through incorporation into a state or state-like organization. Whether by contract or otherwise, they must be put into a position where their individual rights are given up in favor of the state. Only an organization of this sort can subsequently act on their behalf and thereby make them a single national entity.

I describe this perspective as one from which we view the nation as *politically corporate*.[15] It was evidently a feature of George Washington's thinking in his farewell address, over and above his general adoption of a political approach to nationalism and his implied statism. Yet while statism seems to entail this perspective, the latter does not entail statism, for it can allow that communities could exist which were not corporations. Furthermore, the politically corporate view of nations tends toward a rejection of a specifically Hobbesian statism. For Hobbes required citizens to surrender their power of acting to the sovereign. It is, he believed,[16] only the sovereign who, properly speaking, can act, not the multitude she represents. But in that case the corporation is in reality fictitious and not the subject of collective properties. The politically corporate view, however, regards the nation as a really existing body corporate which acts, even if its actions are performed through the person of its sovereign or other agents. Indeed, something like this idea seems to lie at the bottom of the obscure doctrine of popular sovereignty, which many theorists believe to be necessary to nationalism.[17] It is the people that act, and whatever authority a state has it possesses only when the people act through it. The right to a state is, on this account, the right to institutions which make possible collective action.[18]

The difficulty, though, is immediately apparent. If a nation must already have some state-like organization to *be* a corporate body, and hence to have collective rights and responsibilities, then it cannot have an antecedent right to such an organization. The best that could be claimed is that nations so incorporated have a right to exist, which can be asserted against separatists or imperialists, and a corresponding right to institutions strong enough to secure their continued existence, which a provincial government, say, may not be. Such a position would not be congenial to very many nationalists. Yet is the only possible way of thinking of nations as corporate, and hence capable of collective action, to think of them as politically corporate in the sense under discussion?

I do not see that it is. Two options seem to be open. One takes a necessarily political approach to the nation; the other does not. First, then, a people without a state might be incorporated through an organization which does not seek to govern them as a community, and hence cannot make of them a community, in accordance with statist principles. The people in question might or might not already be a community, but they claim a right to statehood on the basis of some political features. Their organization is aimed precisely at achieving this objective. It speaks and acts for them in pursuit of it, so that they can act collectively through it. This is the situation of many nationalist movements that claim to act on behalf of a people.[19] Whether they succeed in doing so because they organize the people into a body corporate depends on many factors—support, control, an appropriate structure, and so forth. What is surely not in doubt is that there *could* be a body corporate organized for such a limited purpose, and this is all we need. It may not be just because a people are such a body corporate that they have a right to statehood; but, so long as they are, then if this right is a collective one it can sensibly be attributed to them, whatever the grounds may be for their claim to it. The second possibility is that a people are incorporated into a single body as a pre-political group through institutions which allow them to act collectively—to trade, for example, as a group of producers or whatever; the details are unimportant. The point is that what incorporates them may be different from what brings them under government. If it is, and if several such groups are brought under the same government, then any of them will in principle be able to claim a collective right to independent government. Their right can therefore be argued for either pre-politically, because of the kind of group they are, or politically, because their group decides collectively to seek its political independence. I conclude from this brief consideration of such cases that nations need not be *politically* corporate in order to be corporate.

Statehood, however, bestows a power of acting that lesser corporations may be denied. Throughout this book we are asking what kinds of group might plausibly enjoy the enormous powers of statehood and thereby count as nations. Here we ask in particular what kinds of politically identified group might do so. We have already investigated the claims and difficulties of political association in the last chapter, both specifically and with respect to a civil association's putative rights to statehood. The discussion of the latter carries through to the former. A direct wish to associate politically can add nothing to an argument for statehood mediated by the wish for civil association. What other political approaches to national statehood are there?

"Republican Liberty"

George Washington placed "the love of liberty" at the forefront of the sentiments he commended to Americans. Unity of government he saw as "a main pillar in the edifice of your real independence" and thereby "the support . . . of that very liberty you so highly prize." Continuing the metaphor, he advised "that your union ought to be considered as a main prop of your liberty, and that the love of the one ought to endear to you the preservation of the other."[20] Thus the preservation of "Republican liberty" will persuade "every reflecting and virtuous mind" of the benefits of the Union "as a primary object of patriotic desire."[21] This is a different message from the appeal to an interest in security and prosperity upon which Washington also relied. Indeed, the difference, though perhaps unrecognized by Washington himself, is so great that it has led some to *contrast* this republican sentiment with those of nationalism:

> The problem with nationalism in the eyes of the civic republican is that it confuses selfishness with public virtue and offers a false resolution of the two. . . . [N]ationalist doctrine cannot allow that there might be a tension between private and public good, which classes it, in civic republican terms, as a form of idealism . . . but, beneath the idealism, as a doctrine by which selfish aspects of a collective persona invade the public realm and are given a false legitimacy.[22]

The contrast in question is between an appeal to interest and an appeal to value. The "republican liberty" which Washington celebrated is essentially a *value*, which is why reflection and virtue are required to discern it. But liberal nationalism, which superficially seems similar to this kind of republican nationalism, as we shall term it, is in fact quite different. For the liberal, freedom is not intrinsically valuable. Rather, it is a condition of achieving what is of value—that is, the condition of noninterference in individual efforts to attain what is deemed worthwhile. In Hobbes's famous phrase, freedom is "the silence of the law."[23] It is this conception of freedom which is at work in the claims to rights of freedom of association and of government only by consent or contract upon which liberal nationalisms are founded. "Republican liberty" is more obscure and contentious. The details of this debate need not detain us.[24] Suffice to say that republican liberty is thought of as itself a prerequisite of human flourishing, something to be desired and valued for its own sake, as well as for the other goods that it facilitates. The difference between pursuit of a common interest and commitment to a common value as bases for claims to statehood is, then, one aspect of the contrast between liberal nationalism and republicanism.

Thus we come to a crucial point—namely, that for republicans the group cherishing or seeking shared statehood must be doing something *good.* It was precisely our doubt as to whether groups with common interests could be seen as necessarily doing something desirable that figured among our criticisms of the liberal case. The liberal may respond, of course, with the Millian claim that "the sole evidence that anything is desirable is that people do actually desire it."[25] Yet without further argument we may still fail to see much of value in the self-interested communities that such liberals posit. And this exemplifies the general problem with many of the nationalisms that we have considered up to now. In order to have a moral right to statehood, a group needs to appeal to something other than mere empirical facts about itself. For merely empirical facts cannot disclose the desirability of a particular state of affairs. As we noticed, it could not be the fact of some ethnic grouping, only the desirability of it, which could generate a right to statehood. What goes for the fact that people have some ethnic similarity (or whatever) goes for the fact that they have some common interests or desires. Republicanism can be a species of those nationalisms—*value culture nationalisms* as I shall call them—which tackle this problem head on, by holding that a right to statehood derives only from the living of a good life.

What, however, of the view that republicanism is to be *contrasted* with nationalism, rather than regarded as a species of it? This view is, I believe, mistaken. Republicanism need not be nationalist, but it can be; and in the traditions of the American and French Revolutions, it is. It is not nationalist if it denies that there are *kinds* of groups which have a right to statehood and limits itself to asserting that a certain state has a right to exist if and only if it fosters republican values. But it need not so limit itself. A republican can hold that the people of a republican state have a right to its continuance through their pursuit of republican values, as do people who lack one if they are committed to that pursuit and capable of achieving it together in a particular state. In either case, a republican form of nation has been at least partially characterized. To suppose otherwise is to adopt an overly restrictive conception of the nation, which is more accurately thought of simply in terms of what satisfies the constitutive principle.

How, though, are we to answer the charge that "nationalist doctrine cannot allow that there might be a tension between private and public good"? This introduces a rather different consideration into the discussion, and it is one which marks republicanism out from some other value culture nationalisms, but not, I suggest, from nationalism *tout court.* It is republicanism's stress on the *public* and, in particular, political character of the values it endorses. What ties people together into a political community is that they work together through their public roles to realize certain values. These require only public performance for their instantiation, which is constitutive of a certain kind of polity, not merely incidental to it, and hence constitutive of a certain sort of life not possible outside it. The republican argument for independent government turns, then, on the idea that such a life is good, and independent government is implied by it. This argument contrasts in two related ways with certain other value culture nationalisms. First, the values are public ones, not private ones which in theory can be enjoyed by individuals alone or with their families and friends. They require membership in a larger group, not just instrumentally but in principle. Second, an appropriately functioning group just *is* a polity, not something, as some religious groups say, which may or may not have a political aspect. Thus the republican case for statehood, unlike that of value culture nationalism, generally does not need to argue either that a state is *in fact* necessary for the values to be realized or that the values are something worth realizing over and above the desirability of a certain sort of state. It is simply the desirability of this state that bears the burden of the republican argument. How does this argument fare?

That must depend upon the values promoted. Liberty, as we have seen, is at the forefront, and may be regarded as fully representative.[26] English nationalism, often seen as the first on the field, is historically associated with "the love of liberty" which its colonists carried to America. Despite its uneasy relations with monarchy, it contained recurrently vigorous elements of republicanism, as quite explicitly expressed in Shelley's rewriting of the National Anthem:

> *God prosper, speed, and save,*
> *God raise from England's grave*
> *Her murdered Queen!*
> *Pave with swift victory*
> *The steps of Liberty,*
> *Whom Britons own to be*
> *Immortal Queen.*[27]

Elsewhere Shelley lists the "graves, from which a glorious Phantom"— Liberty—"may Burst," including

> *Rulers who neither see, nor feel, nor know,*
> *But leech-like to their fainting country cling,*
> *Till they drop, blind in blood, without a blow,—*
> *A people starved and stabbed in the untilled field,—*
> *An army, which liberticide and prey*
> *Makes as a two-edged sword to all who wield.*[28]

These deformations of the polity give us an indication of what republican liberty is and does. It is freedom from the oppression of sectional and especially governmental self-interest, which is not only damaging to people's interests but destructive of reciprocal human relationships on both sides. It is a right relation to land and resources, such that "everyone . . . may live in freedom by their labours."[29] It is collective control of the coercive powers of the state. Indeed, without being too precise about how it works, republicans see liberty as an antidote to a variety of social and political ills. Let us grant that it is. Can we recognize in the fact that a people are committed to and capable of republican liberty that they have a right to statehood? Or is this *only* to say that those who do or can participate in a desirable state have a right to one, which seems too vague to enable one to discriminate groups of people as nations?

What is needed is a much more specific characterization of how republican virtues work in practice. Love of liberty alone will not deliver this characterization. We need to see how it is realized through the state becoming, in George Washington's words, "a primary object of patriotic desire." In other words, we need an account of republican patriotism as that through which republican values are pursued. What is crucial to republican patriotism is that love of one's country is love of one's fellow citizens.[30] To be a patriot is to be actuated by a concern for the common good—that is, the good of citizens as fellow members of the state. To engage in one's public duties as a citizen from such a motive is therefore to express this love, or civic friendship as it has been called.[31] A republican nation is thus a group held together by national obligations whose performance is motivated in a particular way—namely, by a concern for the welfare of fellow members and a common republican conception of what that welfare consists in. This characterization, it may be argued, is sufficiently precise to enable us to identify some groups as nations and to exclude others. Though only fully realizable in a functioning republic, the propensity to form such relationships within some state is detectable outside it, particularly among those involved in a struggle for political independence.

It is a beguiling picture, but nonetheless a problematic one. Membership of a nation, by contrast with citizenship, is not itself the occupancy of a role, for nations, unlike states, do not have determinate functions. National obligations cannot, therefore, arise from such roles, though they can be fulfilled in them. But because they do not arise from political roles, national obligations cannot be restricted by them. The restriction to public and political performance which republicans place on what is required by the nation must be justified instead by the republican values that the nation-state instantiates—liberty and the like. It is not easy to see how this is to be done—that is, how patriotism is to be confined to its proper ethical role. The problem surfaces most acutely when we ask what civic friendship should consist in. If it is simply an exchange of civic duties, then there are doubts as to whether it is really *friendship*, for friendship demands a readiness to go beyond the call of duty. Yet if it is not so limited and, instead, is a wider-ranging bond antecedent to and necessary to motivate the performance of national obligations, then a strictly republican account of nationhood has been abandoned; the declared ethical motive has been supplanted by a more obscure affection—indeed, perhaps by a more visceral one, with all the attendant difficulties in grounding claims to statehood already noted in our discussion of naturalism. In fact, with it we have moved away from political nationalism altogether, since a group united by sentiments such as these could in principle be identified without reference to an actual or intended state.

There is also an ethical objection to republican nationalism to be considered before we move on, though it is one we must leave for fuller discussion until we investigate value culture nationalisms generally. It is that the republican requirement upon members of the nation to pursue certain values is oppressive and illiberal.[32] Individuals, so the argument goes, have different values and it is not the job of the state to impose any particular ones upon them. Rather, a liberal state should create conditions in which a wide variety of different value systems can flourish. Indeed, the argument continues in an *ad hominem* spirit, if liberty means anything it means at least the freedom to pursue such values. There are two republican responses to this. The first, as we have noted, is that national values are *public* values, requiring only performance rather than belief, and hence are compatible with a range of individual ideals.[33] What is forbidden is that these individual ideals, which cannot recommend themselves to others simply *qua* citizens, should be given a political expression, for this is indeed to confuse the private with the public good. Thus, after the French Revolution the Jews were emancipated in accordance with the formula: "[O]ne must refuse everything to the Jews as a nation, and give everything to the Jews as individuals."[34] They were incorporated into the Republic, and their separate political corporations were abolished. The difficulty pertaining to this republican response is to prevent it from collapsing into the Hobbesian position which gives sovereigns authority in all "men's external actions, both in Policy, and in Religion."[35] "And for their *Faith*, it is internall, and invisible; they have the licence that Naaman had, and need not put themselves into danger for it. But if they do, they ought to expect their reward in Heaven, and not complain of their Lawfull Soveraign; much less make warre upon him."[36]

The second republican response does something, though perhaps not enough, to counter this unappealing picture. It makes a virtue out of the nonspecificity which we have noticed in republican values such as liberty. This nonspecificity stems, it may be held, from the fact that the substance of such values needs to be determined through collective decisions. What counts as liberty is determined by the members of the nation responding to their particular circumstances and drawing on their specific history. The results, though binding on members, cannot be regarded as oppressive or illiberal since they spring from the members' own participation as fellow nationals. We shall return to this sort of story in the next section. For now, however, we should note that it already imposes a conception of national membership which some may find itself oppressive. It requires—indeed, it is of the essence of republicanism to require—participation of the sort exemplified by active citizenship and subordination to its results. If this is what being a member of a nation requires, some may reply "I want no part in it. So long as the state has mechanisms to preserve individual freedoms and the like, civic virtue is a burden that I can do without."[37] It is, in any case perhaps, already in short supply.

"Down with the State"

Republican nationalism often has a revolutionary application; that is, it seeks constitutional changes on the grounds that the present arrangements are of their nature oppressive. A revolution is obviously not necessarily a national one—not even, as we have seen, if it involves secession. But a revolution need not be secessionist, or irredentist, to be a national revolution. All that is required is that the oppression which the revolution aims to end should be viewed as the oppression of people *as a nation*. This is as possible in a territory bounded by the borders of an established state as in some other. The French Revolution—regarded by many theorists[38] as the origin of modern nationalism—is an example. When the Abbé Sieyès asked "What is the Third Estate?" he had to answer that it was the French nation, since it was the common people of France whom he viewed as oppressed by the First and Second Estates, the clergy and nobility. As a result of their oppressive acts they placed themselves outside the nation, even affecting a different ethnicity which Sieyès turned against them, asking rhetorically why the Third Estate should not "repatriate to the Franconian forests all those families who preserved the crazy pretensions of descending from the race of the conquerors and of having inherited their rights of conquest?"[39]

An argument for independent statehood from the need to escape oppression may seem a good one. What, though, is it for people to be oppressed *as a nation*, rather than as a collection of individuals? Sieyès had an essentially political conception, derived from contract theory, of a nation as "a body of associates living under a common law and represented by the same legislative assembly."[40] Yet he developed it into a form of political voluntarism which contrasts with the individualistic type thus far discussed. The point of the legislature is to arrive at a common national will, suggesting a rather different account of the nation—namely, as a people picked out by their *collective* will. This is a political account of nationhood if the collective will could be identified only through the mention of a state, either because it is made possible only through some state or, perhaps, because, though articulated through some other collective organ, it is a will to have, and to realize itself in, some particular state. The argument for a right to statehood in such collective voluntarism is that people with a collective will which requires or aims at statehood thereby have a right to it. The argument for national oppression can then be that without it their collective will is thwarted, and that is for them to be oppressed.

This sort of view leads an influential if shadowy existence in many nationalisms, most notoriously in such sentiments as Mussolini's "the fascist State is an embodied will to power."[41] We shall shortly see how it might eventuate as such. But more immediately we can see how it derives quite naturally, and so far perhaps unexceptionably, from the aspect of republican nationalism which we noticed at the end of the last section. The goals of the nation are, on republican principles, to be determined collectively by the citizen body, and they are to be determined not by consulting one's sectional interests but by discovering the common good which embodies republican values. It is this idea that Jean Jacques Rousseau developed into his doctrine of the general will—that is, the will an assembly of citizens would have if they were engaging in its determination appropriately, just *as* citizens and nothing else. Such a will is to be distinguished from "the will of all" which results from "the sum of individual wills"[42] articulating their own rather than the common interest. The will of all could be wrong, but the general will cannot err. The assumption that there *is* a common good for a society leads quite naturally to the idea that this is what the society wills. To obstruct this will is *obviously* to oppress the society, since it is to deny it its common good.

So far so good, perhaps. The general will of a nation is an abstraction; but so long as all members are seriously trying to determine it, what they come up with is, in an obvious sense, a collective will. A state which produces such an approximation to the general will may seem to be tolerably well constituted, and one's only compunction might be that the good of others also should be considered not its good alone. But Rousseau does not stop here, and neither does all revolutionary nationalism:

> Whoso would undertake to give institutions to a People must work with full consciousness that he has set himself to change, as it were, the very stuff of human nature; to transform each individual who, in isolation, is a complete but solitary whole, into a part of something greater than himself, from which, in a sense, he derives his life and his being; to substitute a communal and moral existence for the purely physical and independent life with which we are all of us endowed by nature.[43]

In order to make collective decisions match the general will, members of the nation must themselves be changed. Their membership of the nation should be part of their identity, so that their motivations stem not from any calculation of interest but from the pursuit of the common good.

Three things seem to be happening here, all of them questionable. First, the common good of the nation is being uncoupled from the interests of its individual members. It thus becomes hard to see in what it does consist. Second, national membership is taken to constitute the primary identity of the nation's members. Indeed, this is why their individual interests *cannot* be aggregated into its common good; for their motivation to pursue that good is itself part of their identity, not something which individuals with independently specifiable identities and interests might have or lack. Third, what counts as a moral motivation is measured by whether it originates from one's national identity. This in turn explains the constitution of identity by the nation, for one's identity is a moral rather than a merely appetitive and selfish one, and cannot be brought about except through socialization in the pursuit of national rather than individual goals. I shall refer to these three claims as, respectively, the nondistributivity of the national good, the national constitution of identity, and the national relativity of morals.[44] They can create a lethal mixture. They add to the political principle of a right to statehood two features of a kind which many have thought basic to all nationalism: the "cultural ideal" that the nation provides people with "their primary form of belonging" and the "moral ideal of heroic sacrifice justifying the use of violence in the defence of one's nation against enemies, internal or external."[45]

The nondistributivity of the national good is a plausible consequence of a societal account of nationhood of the sort under consideration. As on the family model, there are social goods to be derived from collective action which do not reduce to the satisfaction of antecedent individual interests, as Rousseau's contrast between solitary and communal existence implies. These goods are, on the present account, moral ones, concerned not just with the existence of certain sorts of relationship—of fraternity, say—also but with the right conduct of them—in terms of equality, to take an example important for Rousseau's own conception. The national constitution of identity is much more problematic. The family model again provides an example of such identity constituting nationalisms. But there it is the naturalism of the account that provides whatever plausibility it can muster to the notion that one's *primary* identity derives from one's kin relations. National identity is explicitly *contrasted* by Rousseau with natural identity: It is the product of a substitution of natural motivations by moral ones. We may grant that one's identity is the result of socialization through which certain values assume a critical importance in one's life, and even that the influence of one's national background is large and inescapable. But other factors are at work too, and one is a member of other collective bodies with their own common goods, for all that Rousseau sought to abolish them. There seems so far no reason to think that the nation should provide one with one's primary identity, in the sense of something embodying one's overriding values. Indeed, this would be to go further even than the doctrine discussed earlier: that the nation furnishes one's supreme obligations and loyalties.

One way of getting to the conclusion required by the national constitution of identity doctrine is to assert the national relativity of morals—to assert, in other words, that to the extent one does *not* give overriding importance to one's national values, one is not acting as a moral being. This is to risk falling headlong into fascism: "The fascist conception of the State is all embracing; outside of it no human or spiritual values can exist, much less have value. Thus understood fascism is totalitarian, and the fascist State—a synthesis and a unit inclusive of all values—interprets, develops and potentiates the whole life of a people."[46]

But this is a welter of confusion. Let us agree that something counts as a moral value only because of its place in a certain social life. Let us even grant the statism which Mussolini assumed. Still, this position does not rule out even the possibility of other collective sources of moral value within society, though perhaps we could make it do so by viewing their values as insufficiently general to pass as moral. But what follows? Only that being moral requires one to be part of a society which determines its values collectively. What does not follow is that there is a well-defined set of such values, deviation from which is immoral. Nor that it is the duty of the state to proclaim such values, even if, on statist principles, there would be no society without the state. The most that follows from this is that the state should enforce the pursuit of those values necessary to the continuation of society (though fascism has in fact been singularly inept at enforcing such socially necessary values as peace and harmony). This still leaves room for much moral variety of a sort not tolerated by totalitarianism.

Indeed, if my moral being derives from my national membership, how am I to make a distinction between what is good for the nation and what is good *tout court*? From this standpoint alone it is hard to see any answer, for there is as yet nothing in my identity whereby I can be touched by what affects others. Again, it must be pointed out that we do not occupy this standpoint alone. We do have other social identities in which we can be affected. It is only statism of the sort that runs through the preceding quotation, and a strong version of statism at that, which could deny it. For if our social relationships depend upon our membership of the state, then, it could be argued, each of these relationships is in effect only an aspect of our relationships within the state and not a possible independent source of social identity. But such a conclusion is grossly implausible. There are a range of relationships unpatrolled by most states that might be a source of identity—in particular, personal relationships. It was to these that E. M. Forster famously turned in order to counter the influence of fascism at the outbreak of World War II:

> [I]f I had to chose between betraying my country and betraying my friend, I hope I should have the guts to betray my country. Such a choice may scandalise the modern reader, and he may stretch out his patriotic hand to the telephone at once and ring up the police. . . . Love and loyalty to an individual can run counter to the claims of the State. When they do—down with the State, say I, which means the state would down me.[47]

The danger of republican nationalism is that it substitutes, as sources of moral value, political relationships for the ordinary human ones Forster speaks of. Yet surely our political relationships within a state are to be justified by our human relationships, and not vice versa.

Summary

In this chapter I identify a class of political nationalisms, in the sense of doctrines which hold that a people form a nation by virtue of their membership or intended membership of an actual or desired state. One example is a type of voluntarism (as considered and criticized in general terms in the previous chapter) which views a nation as a group of people wishing to associate *in the same state*. But this view is distinct from regarding a nation as, whether by contract or otherwise, a body corporate, so that its right to statehood is a collective right rather than one derived from the rights of individuals to associate as they wish. Logical or causal voluntarisms can exemplify liberal political nationalism. Liberalism, however, contrasts with republican nationalism, which sees nations as constituted by the common pursuit of political *values* (in particular, liberty), not simply as groups of people exploiting the freedom to pursue their individual *interests*. Republican nationalism delivers a richer account of the nation as a body corporate, through its collective determination of what these political values come to in practice. But it is also fraught with profound dangers, not least that of sliding into fascism through the subordinating of human values to political ones. Hence there is some question as to why it is desirable for the supposed republican nation to have its own state. (Nationalism founded on a shared pursuit of values more generally will be considered in Chapter 8.)

Chapter Six

Geography and Economics

Territory

Many groups of people have political organizations to regulate the life of their communities. Among the traveling Roma, for example, the *Kris romana* brings elders together to decide cases brought against members and administer fines or periods of banishment.[1] But these are a people on the move ranging over wide areas and intermingling with other peoples. Their organization could not be that of a *state*. For a state exercises political authority over a defined territory. Indeed, it is this fact that brings the Roma and other travelers up against the state in which they live or through which they move. It administers over them laws that are not their own, as often as not enforcing a sedentary pattern of residence which fails to respect their kinship-based associations.[2] It used to be thought that the travelers' form of political organization was once universal. Thus Sir Henry Maine detected a revolutionary social change from tribalism to the territorial organization of the state.[3] Contemporary anthropologists reject this view, however.[4] Some peoples always and everywhere have claimed territory as their own, and their doing so is a necessary condition for claiming a state.[5]

Let us put this more precisely: To claim a right to statehood is to claim a right to *some* territory over which the state can exercise political control. But this is a different thing from claiming a right to some *specific* territory. The distinction is well illustrated by disputes in the late nineteenth century between religious Zionists who sought a Jewish state in Palestine and secular ones who merely claimed the right to some state for Jews to live in together, rather than among others and exposed to repeated pogroms. A scheme that was mooted to settle Jews in Uganda appealed to many who wanted to inaugurate a socialist state and "believed that any new territory would do."[6] But even if a specific territory is claimed, we can distinguish between those claims to it which are based on the same factors that are used to base a claim to statehood, and those which are not. In the case of national rights, the former kind of claim is that what makes people a nation is what gives them a right to a specific territory too. It seems unlikely that the religious Zionists' claim falls into this category. It *would* if Jews identified themselves as the descendants of people who had lived in the land of Zion, such that their claims to statehood as a nation and to the restoration of Zion were similarly based. In actuality, however, religious Zionism regards Jews as identified not by a relationship to a place but by a relationship to God: They are the people with whom God made a covenant at Sinai. Their claim to the restoration of Zion thus rests on the fact, only contingently related to their national identity, that they once lived there and were dispossessed. Nationalisms that answer to the stronger condition I shall call *essentially* territorial.

Among nationalisms that are not essentially territorial, we can distinguish, as indicated earlier, territorially specific from territorially nonspecific ones. All nationalisms, however, must be able to make out a case for some territory—and territory suitable for statehood, at that. This territory must usually be, for all intents and purposes, continuous and compact,[7] so that it may be governed as a single polity. Its borders must be well defined, so that its inhabitants are clearly identifiable and their security can be provided for. In this respect the modern state differs from older ones where frontiers were "porous and indistinct,"[8] since no question arose as to whether people had rights entitling them to some particular statehood. The territory must also, at a minimum, be a habitable area, where the life of a community can be sustained. But why, we might ask, should anyone have a right to this? Why should they not be content with the sort of government that nomadic peoples have, without the sort of territory required by states and state-like organizations? Why should any peoples have a right to some territory? The question is an important one, for if they do not, then, by an easy inference from the constitutive principle, they will not be nations.

It is not, I think, at all easy to answer this question in general terms. Rather, we shall see how different nationalisms seek to answer it differently; essentially territorial nationalists, for example, do so by deriving the right to some territory from the right to a particular territory involved in their national identity. We can, however, do something to uncover the assumptions on which the general nationalist claim to territory rests. First, as we have already seen, it assumes that I should not be regularly subjected to government other than that of my own nation. This is just the claim to independent government. But, second, it assumes that people engaged in day-to-day transactions with one another should be subjected to the same government. If they were not, it is supposed, their transactions could not be conducted on the basis of common rules, conformity to which both parties could rely upon; and this basis is surely something on which people do have a right to rely. Yet, put together with the first assumption, the second one yields the conclusion that our day-to-day transactions should be conducted with fellow nationals—in other words, that members of different nations should not regularly commingle within the same territory. The claim to some territory is thus the claim to exclusive occupancy for the purposes of everyday life. This presupposes, of course, a usually sedentary life. It is not easy to see how it can be sustained against the claims of nomadic peoples to be governed through their own laws and yet within the ambit of other peoples. The second assumption on which it rests, though, is open to question. For we would be able to rely upon transactions with other peoples if we were satisfied that the rules under which they were conducted would be enforced by both our governments. And that is precisely what already happens in international trade, through treaty undertakings and the like. Nationalism rejects this type of arrangement in favor of territorial homogeneity. Why is this?

Here we need to introduce a distinction additional to those between territorially specific and nonspecific and between essentially territorial and other nationalisms. I refer here to the distinction between those who claim a right to some territory on the grounds of the *fact* of sole occupancy and those who claim it on the grounds of the *desirability* of sole occupancy. Evidently the former justification is available only to those already in sole occupation, while the latter is available both to some who are and to some who are not. The former, though, is the more modest. It does not attempt to *justify* occupancy of a specific territory, or indeed that of any territory at all. It merely observes that occupancy exists; and given that a right to statehood is asserted, it claims that such statehood should be enjoyed within the present area of occupancy.

We may note that a fact-based territorial claim is bound to be specific. Indeed, it may be the claim of an essentially territorial nationalist. For the simplest way to assert a right to a national state in a specific territory is to claim to be a nation in virtue of sole occupancy of that territory and to make this occupation a basis for the right. As it stands, this basis must seem, of course, woefully inadequate. First, the mere fact of occupancy at a particular time cannot be enough to confer a right to statehood. There must be some features associated with the kind of occupancy it is—long term, communal, and so on—which make it desirable that occupancy of this kind[9] should be complemented by statehood. Later in the chapter we shall look at some accounts of what kind of occupancy this might be. Second, the occupancy on which the claim is based must not violate the

rights that others may have to the territory, even if they are not in occupation or not in sole occupation of it. We shall subsequently look at some arguments for such rights claims, too. Third, and perhaps most fundamental, it is not clear why some particular part of the earth's surface should be
picked out as constituting a *single* territory, such that those living upon it
should claim sole occupancy and the right to statehood in it. Some attempts to clarify this point will also be examined in the course of considering arguments for the right of occupation.

Roots

In looking at naturalistic nationalisms, we have already touched upon
one kind of argument for a right to specific territory. The view that people
constitute a nation because they share a common character which is
formed by their particular natural environment generates a reason for
them to occupy that territory—namely, that they are peculiarly well
adapted to it. An area of the earth's surface will be picked out as a single
territory by virtue of being that to which a people with a single national
character are so adapted. Herder, as we saw, opposed "the unnatural enlargement of states, the wild mixing of various races and nationalities under one sceptre."[10] What distinguishes people, he thought, is also what relates them to particular territories: "As every region of the earth has its
peculiar species of animals which cannot live elsewhere, and conse-
quently must have been born in it, why should it not have its own kind of
men? Are not the varieties of natural features, manners and character, and
particularly the great differences in language proof of this?"[11] He illustrated this point by remarking that "the Arab of the desert belongs to it, as
much as his noble horse and his patient indefatigable camel."[12]

Perhaps such stories of adaptation can be recast to eliminate their untenable naturalism. Yet it is hard to see that they could be told in a way
that created a plausible justification for occupancy of a *specific* place,
rather than of a certain *sort* of place. They might succeed in disposing of
the claims of colonists—as Herder intended[13]—but to sustain the claims
of the indigenous inhabitants they would need filling out with some reference to the presumptions of permanency arising from actual occupation
or the like. Before moving on to such considerations we should briefly
note another, more modern form of naturalism which might be invoked
in giving a reason for occupation of a territory. One ethologist wrote: "The
biological nation, as I define it . . . , is a social group containing at least
two mature males which holds as an exclusive possession a continuous
area of space, which isolates itself from others of its kind through out-
ward antagonism, and which through joint defence of its territory
achieves leadership, co-operation and a capacity for concerted action."[14]

"It does not matter," he continued, "whether such a nation be composed of twenty-five individuals or two hundred and fifty million," or whether these individuals are lemurs or Americans. All that is important is the biological drive to defend a certain territory. What if it were so? Rights to territory, we might think, have no place in this picture. But the conclusion drawn is otherwise: that "at the heart of the territorial principle lies the command to defend one's property, but as close to the heart lies recognition of the next animal's rights. . . . [A]nimal treaties will be signed. Rights will be not only recognised but honoured. . . . [T]here is nothing in the territorial principle to deny peace among nations."[15]

It is hard to take this argument seriously. But if we do, we see that the appeal to biology has solved nothing. Though force is needed to defend rights, it is not the case, on this account, that might *is* right, for only rightful occupation, it would seem, will yield a peaceful outcome. The question of what is rightful occupation and what is not remains unanswered. If one holds to a consistently biological interpretation, one will need an account of the ethological principles that determine when recognition is given and when withheld. And a clear account of what principles we do act on here, if it could be found, would go a good way toward clarifying what principles we should act on.

Herder's remark that the Arab belongs to the desert suggests an account of a relation between people and their land which is not naturalistic in a scientific sense but, rather, draws on notions of a *natural* relationship between people and land, in the sense of a relationship which is in harmony with nature. A people's way of life is in tune with their environment in a manner in which that of interlopers is not. This notion, while difficult to get clear, is one that indigenous peoples commonly draw on to distinguish their relation to the land from that of colonists. "How can the spirit of the earth like the White man?" asks a Wintu Indian. "Everywhere the White man has touched it, it is sore." This lack of respect shows itself in an exploitative relation which contrasts with the Indian's: "When we Indians kill meat, we eat it all up. When we dig roots we make little holes . . . we don't ruin things . . . we don't chop down trees. We use only dead wood."[16] There is both a general and a special principle at work here. The general principle may be fairly uncontentious, but one is not certain that it can do the required work. The special principle can perhaps do so, but it is controversial. The general principle is that only those have a right to territory who will not radically abuse it, spoiling the land for others, especially future generations. This principle looms large in the thinking of American Indians and other indigenous peoples.

It also, as I say, seems hard to argue with, since we could not regard a territorial state as desirable if it would inevitably lead to irreparable environmental damage. The difficulty is that what counts as spoiling the land is not always obvious or agreed. In the mid-nineteenth century a Nez Perce Indian wrote:

> You ask me to plough the ground. Shall I take a knife and tear my mother's breast? . . .
> You ask me to dig for stone. Shall I dig under her skin for bones? . . .
> You ask me to cut grass and make hay and sell it and be rich like white men. But how dare I cut off my mother's hair?[17]

The foregoing passage asserts a view of the proper relations between people and the earth quite different from that of Europeans. It is evidently the assertion of some very specific cultural values, which there is an argument for protecting against eradication by European ones. But this would be an argument quite different from that under consideration, which denies territorial rights to those who would spoil land. Indian values involve adherence to the more specialized principle that only those have a right to territory who will not use it beyond necessity and for the mere increase of wealth. Some early European travelers to America were impressed by the resulting way of life of the indigenous people: "Their days are all nothing but pastimes. They are never in a hurry. Quite different from us, who can never do anything without hurry and worry; worry, I say, because our desire tyrannises us and banishes peace from our actions."[18]

This is, however, a very different choice of lifestyle from the European one. If the special principle which underlies it were true, then a good many territorial claims would fall, though the question remains whether it could delimit exactly *what* land was required by a group, much less how different territorial groups should be distinguished. But the special principle is not widely accepted as true, while the general principle, which may be, is much too imprecise and open to different interpretations to be useful in resolving claims.

Instead, we need to ask, not what it is to have respect for one's land, but, however such respect is manifested, does it confer a right to occupancy? In other words, we need to ask whether a people distinguished by a shared attitude of a certain sort to a specific territory thereby have a right to it, and whether those who lack that attitude do not. The relevant attitude can be extended beyond the natural world to what is built upon it, as in Yeats's poem:

> *The enemy has toppled roof and gable;*
> *And torn the panelling from ancient rooms;*
> *What generations of old men had known*
> *Like their own hands, and children wondered at,*
> *Has boiled a trooper's porridge.*[19]

The Norman invaders in this passage evince an exploitative attitude toward Ireland as an environment quite different from that of its original inhabitants, who know and love it. It is the love of country in *this* sense, as contrasted with love of one's fellow countrymen, whose nature and implications we must now investigate.

This love of country is not, as I have just indicated, to be mistaken for "the love of Nature which for so many centuries has inspired and fortified our English poets":[20]

> *O English earth*
> *'Mid the blown seas lying*
> *Green, green,*
> *When the birds come flying*
> *Out of the empty South. . . .*[21]

The "sense of mystic harmony between Man and Nature," here expressed by Laurence Binyon, is rightly thought of as a local rather than a universal phenomenon—in this case, an English one. It is *one* form that the relevant love of country can take in a particular place and time. It is not the love itself.

Consider, nonetheless, the significant fact that the patriotic imagery of the nation is nearly always rural rather than urban: "[R]oots are indeed rural: the imaginary community invoked by the new ethos [i.e., of nationalism] is territorial and has intimate links to the land. By contrast there could be no roots in the city."[22] The nation's need for roots in a peasant past may, as suggested here, be part of the attraction of rural imagery, but this account is too limited, connecting attachment to the countryside too closely with common descent models of nationhood. The phenomenon is in actuality much wider, and more easily explained by the mere fact that nations, unlike the city-states of old, are territorially extensive, taking in many towns and villages. There will inevitably be a preponderance of countryside within their bounds, all of which has to be regarded as somehow apt to fall under the same polity. The territory of the state must itself become the subject of a *single* representation, for which an urban image is inappropriate. A rural one, by contrast, conveys a picture of the land from which all settlements spring, including towns with nothing rural about them. The technique underlying this representation is often that of epitome, particularly effective in verses like Edward Thomas's "Adlestrop." The poet's express train—no doubt plying between cities—makes an unscheduled stop in an idyllic country village of that name:

> *And for that minute a blackbird sang*
> *Close by, and round him, mistier,*

Farther and farther, all the birds
Of Oxfordshire and Gloucestershire.[23]

The birds of these counties serve as a metonym for all the far-flung inhabitants of England connected by their common countryside.

It is worth comparing here two ways in which a people can be associated as one in a common territory. The first is to view them as associated through the similarities between the different places in which they live. Adlestrop, for example, can be taken to epitomize the whole of England (though the risk, as always, is of marginalizing the North). There is then a temptation to suppose, in a Herderian vein, that the inhabitants of such similar places are themselves made similar by virtue of sharing such a land. The inhabitants of England, for example, develop a common "love of Nature." Now this could give rise to an essentially territorial nationalism in which the nation is made one by its territory,[24] and, being one, can claim independent statehood in it. The right to territory is the right to that which fosters and preserves this unity. To have to share it or combine it threatens to change the people themselves, as different objects and images of love of place vie with the old.

The second way in which people could be associated as one nation in a common territory is the reverse of the preceding way. It is that they are a single people independent of their land, through common descent, civil association, or whatever, but they bring a unity to that land through their like-minded actions upon it. The land is shaped in its uniform agricultural organization and vernacular architecture by a common people. On this account we would expect not a "love of Nature"—unadorned, as it were—but love of a manmade countryside.[25] It is not, I think, fanciful to see the latter in nineteenth-century French landscape paintings by contrast with English ones. There is in French landscapes a recurrent emphasis on the fact that the land is shaped and worked—an emphasis which spans, and indeed is presupposed by, the divide between the ethnic conservative representations of official Salon artists and the civic progressive ones of the Impressionists.[26] Rights to a land, on this account, are rights to what people have made their own. We shall have reason to return to them in the next section, but now I should like to resume our investigation of what the love of country comes to, whatever its different forms.

There are, I think, two principal strands in it. One is the idea of a love of what is familiar, *heimatlich.* Only those to whom a land is familiar can appreciate it in the way required for this sort of love. In Binyon's poem, the migratory "birds come flying" . . .

To the old willow,
Ash, thorn, chestnut—
Boughs that they know. . . .

By contrast with the South wind's "wild whisper" of the exotic,

> . . . the things that are dearest
> You have told them never;
> They are deep in our veins
> For ever and ever.

They cannot be told: They can only be felt by those who have repeatedly experienced them, like the beauty of an evening sky: "vast and yet familiar," because it is the same sky that

> . . . I, a child,
> Lifted my face from leaf-edged lanes to see
> Late-coming home, to bread and butter tea.[27]

Even natives of a country may be immune to such things: "One obvious reason for the long neglect of Turner lies in the fact that his genius does not seem to be truly English. Turner's landscape, even when it presents familiar scenes, does not show them in the familiar light. . . . I doubt whether the spirit of English poetry was in him; I doubt whether the essential significance of common things which we call beautiful was revealed to his soul."[28] We have glimpsed this love of country as a special receptivity through quite different forms of expression in American Indian sentiments. It generates a claim based, like theirs, on a highly controversial and conservative view of what is a fitting way of relating to a place.

The second strand in love of country is just that "[t]his is my own, my native land."[29] This sentiment is thought of as a natural affection, attaching to the land that has given us birth, just as it does to our parents. It involves no special aesthetic or spiritual sensitivity. The inhabitants concede, as in the old Russian proverb, that "Mother may be ugly, but she's the only one we've got." The point is precisely the unconditionality of the affection, which only those born or brought up in a place will feel. We shall have to suppose that what makes a land so venerated a single territory is somehow constituted by a coincidence of such feelings among its members: They extend them thus far and no further. But what kind of argument for rights to territory follows from the existence of these feelings? As in so many cases of an appeal to nature, the desirability of the outcome is not addressed. Indeed, in terms of the distinction drawn in the preceding section, this second strand represents a fact-based claim while the first represents a desirability-based one.

Republican critics of what they thought of as *natural* patriotism were quick to pick up this point: "What was the love of their country among the Romans? We have heard much of it; but I cannot hesitate in saying that ... it was, in general, no better than a principle holding together a band of robbers in their attempts to crush all liberty but their own."[30] Indeed, religious writers condemned patriotism as "a disposition to love the creature more than the creator ... undoubtedly a part of a proof of our natural depravity ... this evil principle."[31] There is some justification for their alarm, even if the attachment to one's native land is not regarded as, in any scientific sense, a natural one but, rather, is treated as something that is simply given—a brute fact about people such that "what we can do is to start from the premise that people generally do exhibit such attachments and allegiances, and then try to build a political philosophy which incorporates them."[32] Republicans regard this approach as conceding far too much to unreflective feeling. There is, after all, a good reason for me to love my mother: She *is* the one who bore and nurtured me. But why should a territory of just *this* scope and extent be the recipient of an analogous attachment? The mere fact that people's dispositions coincide in terms of the way they direct their attachment does nothing to answer the question. The nub of the republican criticism of natural patriotism is that there should be a good reason for picking out a certain area of land as the nexus of patriotism. The mere fact of attachment does not provide one. Indeed, far from fostering liberty, it can do the reverse:

> ... the peasant in his little acres is tied
> To a mother's womb by the wind-toughened navel-cord
> Like a goat tethered to the stump of a tree—
> He wanders around and around wondering why it should be.[33]

Republicans like Machiavelli believed, by contrast, that allegiance should be given to lands in which a free life was possible.[34]

In the face of these criticisms, one possible recourse of the naturalist patriot is to claim that the frontiers of nations are themselves natural, a view that readily consorts with the Motherland conception. As early as 1799 an Irish barrister opposed union with Great Britain on the grounds that "the Almighty has, in majestic characters, signed the great charter of our independence. The great Creator of the World has given our beloved country the gigantic outlines of a kingdom."[35] Giuseppe Mazzini believed that "the design of God" was "clearly marked out, as far, at least, as regards Europe, by the courses of the great rivers, by the lines of lofty mountains, and by other geographical conditions,"[36] and Abraham Lincoln thought that this held true of America also. Speaking against secession, Lincoln maintained that "physically speaking we cannot separate. We cannot remove our respective sections from each other."[37] On this point the Nez Perce Indians were more perceptive in their geography than Lincoln, though also more radical in their conclusions: "[T]he earth was created by the assistance of the Sun, and it should be left as it was. . . . [T]he country was made without lines of demarcation and it is no man's business to divide it."[38] At least, if the earth is to be divided, then this outcome must be justified on principles other than those we have considered so far.

Ownership

In the preceding section I discussed claims to the sole occupancy of a territory which depend upon a certain kind of relationship, natural or sentimental, between a land and a people—a relationship which supposedly makes them the *right sort* of occupants for it. In this section, however, I consider claims with a very different kind of basis, one which does not draw upon any such relation: It is one independent of the character of the actual or putative occupants—namely, one based on their alleged *status* as rights holders. But these alleged rights can, as we shall see, be differently grounded themselves.

One sort of claim to a territory is that laid by its indigenous inhabitants. John Locke sometimes conceded this kind of claim:

> [T]he inhabitants of any country, who are descended and derive a title to their estates from those who are subdued, and had a government forced upon them against their free consents, retain a right to the possessions of their ancestors. . . . And who doubts but the Grecian Christians, descendants of the ancient possessors of that country, may justly cast off the Turkish yoke . . . ?[39]

It is, of course, notoriously difficult to establish who *were* the original inhabitants of any country. But at least we know, for example, that the Indians' occupation of America long antedated that of Europeans, and that there are no other claimants; so how should the principle of indigenous occupation be applied in such a case? Locke based his argument on the assumption that people inherit the property rights of their progenitors. But this assumption would scarcely do in the case of Indians for whom the ownership of property is customarily collective rather than individual. Attention to the latter fact does, however, prevent us from falling into the trap of assuming that an argument like Locke's has to presuppose that nations—the groups of people with a relevant territorial right—must be identified by *descent*. This is not necessarily so, if we can find some other way of tracking over time the group that retains the right which it once exercised.

We can regard the fundamental principle in Locke's argument as stating that a group continues to have a right to ownership of land of which it was the first occupant so long as the right is not freely made over to others. Yet immediately we may doubt the acceptability of the principle in determining rights of sole occupancy. Perhaps we who are so implicated in imperialism are too ready to be shocked that "the idea of compensating for historical wrongs, taken to its logical conclusion, implies that all the land which was wrongly taken from indigenous peoples in the Americas or Australia or New Zealand should be returned to them."[40] But also implied are the dispossession and dispersion of people who, because they are born in these countries, have no effective choice as to their occupancy of them. It is by no means clear that they do not also have rights arising from it. As Hume observed, "It often happens, that the title of first possession becomes obscure thro' time; and that 'tis impossible to determine many controversies, which may arise concerning it. In that case long possession or *prescription* naturally takes place, and gives the person a sufficient property in anything he enjoys."[41] Both first and long possession essentially arise from the same factor—an extended period of occupation of a land. If this is what gives a right in the first case, then, the Humean argument implies, it does so in the second, at least so long as the newcomers' possession is not palpably exercised in defiance of the rights of indigenous inhabitants. This may be so less often than we hope and suppose, but it is sometimes so. In these circumstances, a Lockean insistence on the *persistence* of property rights would blind us to the grounding of these rights.

The location of rights of occupation in *property* shows up another deficiency in the Lockean type of account. For suppose that inhabitants of a neighboring country acquire a legal title to land adjacent to it, so that soon they own a large area bordering upon their own home country—as in Jerusalem, for example, or other parts of Palestine. Does this legal title in and of itself strike down the claims that the indigenous inhabitants might make for sole occupancy, in the sense in which such occupancy bears on statehood? Does the title imply that the indigenes have no right to exclude the neighboring inhabitants from permanent occupation? Or that the neighboring inhabitants now have the right to exclude the indigenes, and even to add the area in question to their own state? If we are reluctant to agree, it is because we wish to distinguish the ownership of property from the right of occupation. Tenants, for example, have the second but not the first. States view foreign ownership and foreign immigration very differently and, indeed, do not necessarily regard the former as giving a license for the latter. Note, then, a third notion in addition to property and occupancy which we must utilize here—namely, jurisdiction. It is one thing to own property, quite another to have jurisdiction over it. And there is some question as to whether it should be property rather than occupation that confers a right to jurisdiction, which includes the right to decide what rights do go with property and which do not, and who, in general terms, should be admitted to occupancy and who denied it.

What indigenous inhabitants often claim against newcomers is simply that they have rights of jurisdiction which the newcomers have usurped There may sometimes be a case for saying that such rights can be ancestral rights, but this concession will do nothing to help solve our problem of deciding what *kinds* of group have territorial rights. At most, it would show that groups are, *in certain circumstances,* unjustly deprived of rights they are widely recognized as having. But this point only drives further back the question of what it was by virtue of which their ancestors acquired these rights. National rights to territory may be ancestral rights, but they cannot be founded upon ancestral rights if these are thought of simply as rights of jurisdiction.

In order to see why the Lockean picture links jurisdiction to property, we must return to the model of nationhood as civil association that it suggests. On this model, it will be recalled, a people constitute themselves into a nation by a voluntary contract to become a single society under a common government. Now such a contract may perhaps confer a right to *some* territory, on the grounds that a society of this sort is a highly desirable institution and that it needs some territory to survive and prosper. But how are we to attach a *specific* territory to it? It would, of course, be totally inadequate to say that people have specific territorial rights just because they "wish to constitute themselves as an autonomous political group with territorial rights."[42] Wishing to have rights over a territory cannot confer them. Locke's answer was that the contractors take their property with them into the state they create, and it is the limits of their property which fix the limits of their state. This arrangement is not a mere happenstance, unconnected with the purposes of their entering into a civil association in the first place; for one of the contractors' main aims is "a secure enjoyment of their properties,"[43] which in turn is ensured by creating institutions with "a right of making laws ... for the regulating and preserving of property, and of employing the force of the community, in the execution of such laws."[44] On Locke's account, a right to territorial jurisdiction exists where people already have property and agree to enter a civil association with the power to regulate it.

Certainly statehood can be a very important protection for property rights, and one nationalist motive for claiming it is to protect the property of nations against the encroachments of others. These encroachments can as easily be legal as illegal. Incomers often have financial resources superior to those of natives and are able to buy so much of the natives' land that they are unable to pursue their way of life and retain the communal structures resulting from it. This, to consider but one example, has happened in Hawaii, where American settlers took over traditional Hawaiian lands after their annexation to the United States in 1894. Native Hawaiians now aspire to some form of sovereignty in order to secure legislation which reverses this situation.[45] But this is a completely different thing from instituting statehood to *preserve* rights in property. Rather, such an aspiration looks to the state, or some other state-like sovereign body, to make a division of property which protects the interests of the nation, rather than to uphold a preexisting division of it. The most extreme example of this property claim occurs in what one might call agrarian nationalisms, whereby part of the call for statehood is a call for *ownership* of land, characteristically enjoyed by absentee landlords. Note that the Proclamation at the Easter Rising contains just such a call, in accordance with the theories of James Fintan Lalor,[46] among others. In this case, a right to territorial jurisdiction is sought by a people precisely in order to *dispossess* those who have property.

Locke's account differs in a very important respect from Hobbes's. Unlike Locke, Hobbes held that in the state of nature there is no property but, rather, "a perpetuall warre of every man against his neighbour; And therefore everything is his that getteth it, and keepeth it by force; which is neither *Propriety* [i.e., property], nor Community; but *Uncertainty*."[47] Only when power has been given up to a sovereign can there be "the First Law . . . for the Division of the Land itselfe."[48] So Hobbes could not have based the territorial claims of a nation on their property rights. Since property rights cannot exist except within a particular state, a nation cannot make their possession of them any part of its argument for one. This aspect of statism captures, I suggest, the reaction we may have to the idea that "precisely because a nation's territory is legitimately composed of the real estate of its members, the decision of any of them to resign that membership and, as it were, to take their real estate with them is a decision which must be respected."[49] Such liberal justifications of secession are appealing only if we do think of property rights as attaching to individuals independent of the organized society in which they live, rather than as resulting from social recognition of a certain division of goods.

Locke had an argument for preferring his own view to Hobbes's which is particularly pertinent to the issues before us. Although Locke regarded the Turks as usurping the rights of Greeks, he did not view the colonial settlement of the Americas as similarly usurping the rights of Indians. The reason is that he did not believe the indigenous American had any "fixed property in the ground,"[50] "who knows no enclosure, and is still a tenant in common" of what belongs "to mankind in common."[51] In Locke's view, however, it is not enclosure as such which creates property in land: "As much land as a man tills, plants, improves, cultivates, and can use the product of, so much is his property. He by his labour does, as it were, enclose it from the common."[52]

It becomes his because "he hath mixed his labour with it,"[53] and "his labour"—provided that he is working on his own account—is his alone. People make property for themselves, then, independent of any social institutions. Locke went on to illustrate his claim that "tis labour . . . which puts the greatest part of value upon land" by comparing the value of an acre of land in England with that of an acre of similar land in America, which, because uncultivated, "would be scarcely worth anything."[54] Settlers who enclose it, then, rob no one and benefit everyone at least so long as they leave land over for the subsistence of others—in practice, a condition soon forgotten by those who acted upon Locke's exhortations.

There are several curious features of Locke's account that we may remark upon. Why are Indian lands common "to mankind," rather than to certain groups of Indians? Locke, it appears, was happy to accept the existence in England of "commons, which remain so by compact,"[55] to which only the commoners have rights of grazing, turbary (turf cutting), and so forth. Why not allow that this is the form that all unenclosed property takes in the Americas? For if it can be a form of property in England without tillage, why not in the Americas? I suspect that Locke, an enthusiast for the enclosure of common lands, would have been prepared to admit that, properly speaking, in England it could not be either. Next we may ask why, if Indians have no property, are their lands worth *anything*, however little? Locke would have computed their value from their actual productiveness, which is a function of the labor expended upon them. But it takes *some* labor to gather apples and acorns or to hunt deer. Why is *this* labor not mixed with the land to yield property in it, whereas digging is? Locke's implicit answer was that, unlike digging, it effects no "improvement"—a notion that, as we saw, Locke equated with cultivation and more generally with removing land from being "left wholly to nature."[56] The quite contrary attitude toward nature which Indians take to be appropriate to "the spirit of the earth" is a positive disentitlement on Locke's account to the rights over it that are necessary for a way of life which reflects them.

Rather than considering Locke's account of property on its own terms, I prefer to regard it as an attempt to ground rights to occupancy of territory on principles quite different from, and often at odds with, those of indigenous occupation. As such, it offers an argument which no more requires a reference to individual *property* rights than does the argument from indigenous occupation that it opposes. It is the basis for the territorial claims of many settler groups, but not of settler groups only. It is the argument that people are entitled to a territory which they have by their own efforts *improved*, to use Locke's favored notion. Since those who have not assisted have no rights to the results, so the argument goes, only the group engaged in the great work of *transforming* a country into a national homeland has a right to occupancy and control of it. But, as a former British governor of Jerusalem remarked, "[T]he new and interesting doctrine that the inhabitants of a country can only retain it by proof of 'achievement' seems hardly that of self-determination."[57]

On this doctrine, the right to territory may be claimed either as a reward for what has been done or as a recognition that the land has been made a people's own. Locke's account points in both directions. On the one hand, honest toil should be rewarded. There is a strong suggestion that the Indians are undeserving by comparison with the colonists: They have not earned the right to possession of their land. While people naturally expect to be rewarded with the actual land they have improved, the principle that they should be rewarded for improving it implies only that they should get *some* land. The question of *which* land will be affected by other considerations—in particular, fairness to the subsistence claims of others. Reward is one relevant consideration in a general distribution of land which takes account of all relevant factors. Which land has been improved, however, can become relevant to the question of what is the group to be rewarded. It may be that this group can be independently identified. But it also may be that it is identified simply as the group that has effected improvements extending across just *this* territory. In the latter case the group may exhibit an essentially territorial nationalism, for what makes it a nation is what gives it a right to the national territory.

Such an argument presents several difficulties. The first is that, to be rewarded, one must have done something good. As we noted in the last section, the colonists failed on that count in the eyes of the Indians. And in general there will be differing judgments on this issue. Furthermore, to be entitled to a reward for one's action, *others* must normally benefit from it. If the improvements of settlers benefit only themselves, then there seems no reason why they should expect the further reward of territorial rights. Locke attempted to answer both points by suggesting that the improvement of land benefits everyone, since less is needed for a given level of support. More will be left for others, allowing their standard of living to rise. The underlying principle here can be interpreted as utilitarian: It is a good idea to reward hard-working groups with their own territory, since the well-being of everyone will thereby be increased. Yet it is far from clear that this attempt at an objective measure of benefit will answer the first difficulty. The native peoples of America were, we may suppose, happier in their lot before the colonists' came, despite the fact that "a king of a large and fruitful territory there feeds, lodges, and is clad worse than a day labourer in England."[58] As for the second difficulty associated with the foregoing argument, the proposal will work only if there are mechanisms whereby other peoples benefit from the results of national industry. It is hard to see that they do. The effect of according control of territory to national groups is arguably to make such redistribution of benefits even less likely.

Another way of taking the settlers' claim to territory is as a demand that what they have made their own by their manner of occupation should be recognized as such. The notion that land is made a people's own is likely to be developed in a manner that draws attention to the land being theirs, not just because others are excluded (a fact which provides no argument for statehood) but because it has become their *home*. But if it is in this sense that they have made the land their own, then one would expect the argument for a right to it to turn on considerations of the love of home, as discussed in preceding sections of the chapter. Such love is perhaps particularly well developed among homemakers; but so it is, too, among victims of eviction, and there seems nothing here that would help to decide between their claims.

The National Economy

As noted in Chapter 3, Bertrand Russell wrote that "[a] nation, unlike a class, has a definition which is not economic. It is, we may say, a geographical group possessed of a sentiment of solidarity."[59] But why should a nation *not* be viewed economistically? Is there no way of regarding the nation as a community of sentiment, in which the felt solidarity is one of a shared economic interest that derives from a common geographical situation? For geography can create or sustain what we may view as a single economy, in the sense of a system of economic relationships within definite boundaries distinct from, though not necessarily insulated from, the systems without. Thus what are *thought* of as natural boundaries—seas, mountain ranges, and so on—may not be obstacles to world trade, but they *are* obstacles to the ordinary everyday economic exchanges of going to work, shopping, and the like which take place within the national economy. Rivers and waste places which might readily be crossed within the nation nonetheless set convenient boundaries to it. No doubt the national economy might have been bounded differently; but whatever the case, it has a determinate relation to geography, such that, on the one hand, geographical facts help to explain why there is a single economy where there is and, on the other, the extent of that economy explains the geographical boundaries of the nation.

The kind of economy a nation has within its borders may not be significantly different from that of another, perhaps neighboring, nation. It is not necessary that their members be living a different *kind* of life, only that they be living a *different* life, with exchanges across the border being of a different sort from those within. A nation may often need to find new trading partners; but if trade barriers go up within a country or certain groups make themselves economically independent of the rest, then, on this economic model, a question arises as to whether it really is still a single national community. In this respect, the model seeks to make sense of the connections that some commentators see between the development of nationhood and the growth of internal trade, removal of local tariffs, increased labor mobility, and so forth.[60] It does so by viewing the national community as a system of economic interdependencies in which there is a common interest in its working well to generate wealth for all, as well as a shared attachment to the way of life characterized by these interdependencies. The model is a version of civil society models of the national community, which were briefly mentioned earlier. It differs from Locke's civil association account, however, in two important ways. First, the territorial bounds of the community are fixed by facts about the relationships between members, not by facts about them as individuals—namely, their property holdings. Second, it presupposes an ongoing economy in which for the most part people find themselves involved, rather than one which they deliberately accept as in their interests. There *is* a common interest, but it need not be transparent to members of the group. Yet so long as they are motivated in their relationships by some intention to promote the general interest, however vague they are about what it comes to, then there exists an overall community "possessed of a sentiment of solidarity."

Economic nationalism identifies a nation as a territorial group working toward economic well-being in such a way that statehood is necessary for the achievement of its ends. This notion can be viewed as having both an ethical and a metaphysical aspect. The ethical is that a nation *should* aspire to achieve the economic well-being of the group. There are different ways in which this point can be interpreted. First, well-being can be construed as prosperity: the increase of national wealth. This is a source of national pride or a measure of achievement because what counts as wealth just *is* what is valued in a group's material culture, and that will differ between cultures. On this interpretation, economic nationalism is, in a sense, essentially progressive in comparison with the bare maintenance of well-being. What is more, it provides an argument for statehood—unitary as well as independent—from the need to control the outflow of wealth from the nation that produces it. Second, however, what counts as wealth, or even well-being, can be variously construed in terms of its ownership. Collective wealth, expressed in terms of great public buildings and the like, is a very different thing from widespread individual wealth, and divisive disparities in the latter produce a very different society from the "one nation" aspired to, for example, by conservative followers of Disraeli—a society which is different again from a socialist one.

The metaphysical aspect of economic nationalism, in turn, flows from the ethical. It is that for a group to be a nation it must, as we have seen, be economically viable. This outcome does not require autarky, but it does rule out more or less permanent dependence of a sort to which nineteenth-century imperialists believed their colonies were doomed. In short, viability is viewed as a necessary condition of forming a separate community, for without it the group's ethical objective will be impossible.

In order to mount an argument for independent statehood for an economically conceived nation, one must overcome the objection noted earlier that it is not necessarily morally desirable to recognize groups defined by communal *self*-interest. But what does the objection amount to? It is not, I shall assume, a general objection to the system of states[61] in favor of world government but, rather, an objection to this proposed way of allocating rights to statehood. It is a powerful objection metaphysically as well as morally, because claims from self-interest provide no principled way of deciding between rival claims. An economically powerful group, such as northern Italy, may claim a right to independent statehood which a larger one containing poorer sections, such as Italy as a whole, will deny. The metaphysical objection, then, is that if an economic unit is discerned through its members' common interest, we will not be able to tell *which* is the unit to be accorded the right when there is this kind of conflict of interests. Nor will it do simply to allow secession to, say, any group with a separate economic interest, for it is not morally desirable to permit groups of this kind to break away and leave others worse off. Precisely similar considerations hold for groups that currently have separate states, when it is in the economic interests of a poorer state to merge with the richer ones. Thus a separate economic interest cannot ground a right to statehood.

There are several possible rejoinders to this objection. The first is to deny that the group is defined by its attempt to maximize its own self-interest in a way that might contrast with maximizing a wider one. The group is defined by an ongoing economic system which is what generates the common interest that sustains it. The group is then simply intending to develop to best advantage the resources it has been given through the geographical and other factors which constitute it into a single economy. This objective requires independent statehood for its fulfillment. Any attempt to draw others in—the inevitable consequence of a wider state—can only do damage to all the communities involved. Given the facts of geography and past economic performance, it will be argued, there will inevitably be rich and poor groups side by side. But the interests of both are served if the communities are recognized as requiring separate statehood, rather than as needing to be merged into an entity whose interest does not correspond to anything that people currently aim at in their everyday relationships.

There are different ways of developing this argument from economic nationalism. One is to emphasize the way that the relationships of mutual interdependence which constitute a national community are shaped by its specific economy, dependent in turn upon its geographical location. These relationships are not widened but irretrievably lost if any attempt is made to realize the Enlightenment aspiration

> *[t]hat every distant land the wealth might share,*
> *Exchange their fruits, and fill their treasure there;*
> *Their speech assimilate, their empires blend,*
> *And mutual interest fix the mutual friend.*[62]

For what is lost is a distinctive way of life. In Christina Rossetti's strange poem "Goblin Market,"[63] the sisters Laura and Lizzie live in a clearly northern land and engage in its strenuous economic activities.

> *Early in the morning*
> *When the first cock crowed his warning,*
> *Neat like bees, as sweet and busy,*
> *Laura rose with Lizzie:*
> *Fetched in honey, milked the cows. . . .*

And so forth. But Laura is distracted by the "fruit-call" of goblin merchants from the South:

> *"Come buy our orchard fruits, . . .*
> *Melons and raspberries,*
> *Bloom-down-cheeked peaches,*
> *Swart-headed mulberries . . .*
> *All ripe together*
> *In summer weather. . . . "*

Bewitched by this sensuous, somnolent litany, Laura succumbs to what Lizzie recognizes as dangerous to their way of life and, after eating the fruit,

> *[s]he no more swept the house*
> *Tended the fowls or cows, . . .*
> *But sat down listless in the chimney nook*
> *And would not eat.*

It is the familiar tale of a person's loss of economic identity and vigor when exposed to new products and relationships. Rossetti's implied remedy is a radical autarky which repudiates even trading contacts. A particular way of life is founded upon the modes of production and consumption made possible by a place. There is no viable alternative to it.

The difficulty with this approach is twofold. First, it almost inevitably tends toward xenophobia, given that aliens of any sort are viewed as threatening a way of life. The goblin merchants in Rossetti's poem are depicted as only semi human: "Ratel and wombat like . . . Parrot voiced and whistler." As such, they endanger a way of life that is seen as more fully human than one in which the ready availability of food and, by implication, unregulated sex is dehumanizing, animal. All this is odd in view of the fact that Rossetti was herself three-quarters Italian, and southern Italian at that. But the price that assimilation into English society exacts from her is this uncompromising affirmation of what is clearly valorized as an English way of life. The potential advantage of economic nationalism is that it is inclusive, allowing membership to all, whatever their ethnicity, so long as they make an appropriate economic contribution. Emphasis on a particular way of life as what realizes economic relationships undercuts this inclusiveness.

The second related problem with this approach is its conservatism. The household-based economy that Rossetti describes was disappearing even as she wrote, destroyed not only by imports but by changes internal to the economy, such as expanded mass production and division of labor. A way of life is bound to be identified through its cultural manifestations. But emphasizing the preservation of these can obscure the underlying economic relationships. What continues to look, for example, like a farm run on the same lines for generations, with service on it running in families, can turn out to have changed from a feudal to a capitalist institution, though only some crisis might reveal it. So it is, too, with larger economic units like nations, as conceived on the economic model. Either they might cease to be discernible as separately identifiable economic systems, despite their continuing cultural distinctiveness, or they might no longer be systems in which a common interest across all sectors of the population can be attributed, since relationships apparently motivated by reciprocal concern have become exploitative.

This brings us to a second possible response to the objection that economic nationalism is simply collective self-interest. It is that the relations within the economic system are themselves worth cultivating, since they are based on the recognition that the interest of the community as a whole should be pursued. Admittedly, the reason is that what benefits the community is thought to benefit the members in the long term. But this is not to treat one stratum of society as helots, or one area of the country as a colony. In other words, it is not to regard some people as existing to serve the interests of others rather than to participate in pursuing a common interest. This state of affairs, so the argument goes, is a morally desirable one which independent statehood should foster and reinforce.

There is a well-known Marxist riposte to the foregoing line of argument. It is that, at least in capitalist societies, there is no community of interest between the different classes involved in an economic system. The interests of the working class are in conflict with those of the capitalists. Thus, as Rosa Luxemburg observed,"[i]n a society based on classes, the nation as a uniform social and political whole simply does not exist. There literally is no social arena from the strongest material relationship to the most subtle moral one, in which the possessing classes and the self-conscious proletariat could take one and the same position as one undifferentiated national whole."[64] Here Luxemburg assumed an at least partly economic account of what a nation would be and, because under capitalism she discerned no economic system which brings its participants together with a common interest, denied that nations exist there. Nationalism in its political manifestations is, on this account, an ideology which obscures real socioeconomic relations in the interests of the dominant capitalist class.

The classic Marxist position was criticized by Antonio Gramsci, who, like Christina Rossetti's father, was a native of southern Italy and a defender of an Italian national unity under threat. Despite his socialist internationalism, Gramsci argued that "today the national class is the proletariat. The multitude of workers and peasants ... cannot allow the dismemberment of the nation because the unity of the state is the form of the apparatus of production and exchange built by Italian labour, the heritage of social wealth."[65] Gramsci believed that national unity was in the interest of the people generally, both urban and rural, because it sustained an economic system in which people *could* have a common interest, even if in practice their class relations brought them into conflict. The recognition that the pursuit of a common interest was possible constituted the formation of a "collective will," achieved despite "the efforts of the traditional classes to prevent the formation of a collective will of this kind, and to maintain 'economic corporate' power."[66] Gramsci believed that the formation of a collective will in Italy was impeded by a view of southern Italians as responsible for their own exploited situation: "If the South is backward, the fault is not to be found in the capitalist system or in any other historical cause, but is the fault of nature which made the southerner lazy, incapable, criminal, barbarous."[67] Here is a criticism of precisely those xenophobic tendencies which, paradoxically, we noticed in Christina Rossetti's version of economic nationalism. Gramsci's position is that the relations of economic interdependence need to be seen for what they are. And once they *are* seen, there is a morally desirable way of giving expression to them in social relationships. It is these that statehood can assist in developing. But doing so is a very different thing from preserving a way of life which might itself no longer reflect economic realities.

These two ways of defending economic nationalism point, however, to a tension in it that may be hard to resolve. The economic unit which is the nation is identified by a system of relationships in which people engage in the pursuit of a common interest. But the relationships are one thing, the sense of a common interest is another. Gramsci stressed the real relationships of mutual interdependence between North and South which make them one nation. Rossetti, by contrast, stressed the sense of a common interest among the northern agriculturalists which they do not share with the southern fruit growers. Yet both positions can lead to problems. Gramsci's risks overemphasizing economic facts and neglecting psychological ones. But there is no worthwhile national community unless the relationships are motivated in part by a sense of common interest. Rossetti's is in danger of confusing people's *thoughts* about where their common interest lies with *facts* about it. But the economic model is not a subjectivist one. So long as the members' behavior is motivated by a sense of common interest, it does not matter if they cannot articulate that sense and say what their common interest is. Indeed, if they do, they may well fall into error about it, perhaps through failing to grasp what real economic relationships underlie their way of life.

The possibility of error that this account allows is a strong point in its favor. It is appropriate participants in its socioeconomic life who are members of the nation, but some may go wrong in thinking that participation requires a certain ethnicity or whatever, even though they in fact have the right relationships with those who lack it. Yet the error that the model permits may be more far-reaching. There may have been such economic nations from time to time, separated from others by a geographically determinate system of economic relationships which are motivated in part by concern for the common interest. But Rosa Luxemburg was surely right in thinking that exploitation by a dominant class will sometimes disqualify the group that is taken to be a nation as lacking the appropriate motivation. Furthermore, widening circles of economic interdependence, lowering of trade barriers, and so forth make it hard to discern separate geographically determinate systems. If economic nationalism is correct, perhaps there are now far fewer nations than people think. Perhaps there are none.

Summary

This chapter has aimed to identify nationalisms in terms of their arguments for territorial rights. I distinguish those that argue for some territory from those that argue for a specific one, and those that are essentially territorial in grounding their right to statehood in a territorial claim from those that are not. These distinctions structure the more substantive nationalisms that I go on to identify. There is first a family of doctrines which bases territorial rights on a natural or sentimental relationship to a land; but it provides no clear account of why territory of the scope selected should correspond to a nation. A second set of nationalisms identifies the territory claimed in terms of ownership; but it cannot give a convincing explanation of why ownership yields rights of political jurisdiction. Finally, a third type of nationalism views the national territory as that within which a distinct economy operates. This last category, I suggest, is the most plausible one; however, it not only fails to show why a separate state is ethically desirable to promote collective self-interest, but also unrealistically presupposes that we can identify suitably distinct economies in the contemporary world.

Chapter Seven

Language and Culture

Effective Communication

The economic model of the nation regards it as a certain sort of society: "[A] society in this sense is a group of individuals connected by an intense division of labour, and separated from other societies by a marked drop in this level of intensity."[1] But a society so understood may be *contrasted* with a community which "consists of people who have learned to communicate with each other and to understand each other well beyond the mere interchange of goods and services,"[2] such that membership of a national community may be regarded as consisting in "the ability to communicate more effectively and over a wider range of subjects, with members of one large group than with outsiders."[3] We can call this the *communication model* of the nation. It is one species of the view that a nation is constituted by a common culture, and it provides one kind of explanation of the phenomenon whereby national identity is very often attributed on the basis of a common language. However, a common language is not necessary in all versions of the theory; for example, "the Swiss may speak four different languages and still act as one people," for each can "communicate more effectively with other Swiss than with the speakers of his own language who belong to other peoples."[4] The culture they share, though not involving a common language, is analogous to a language in being a symbolic system for social exchanges. I shall refer to it as a *language culture*. The communication model of the nation identifies it, then, as a group with a shared language culture.

Some have made the stronger demand that a common language itself is necessary, or even sufficient, for nationhood. "Wherever a separate language is found," wrote Johann Gottlieb Fichte, "there a separate nationality exists which has the right to take charge of its affairs and to govern itself."[5] Which version is preferred depends upon how we answer the theoretical question as to how a language culture functions and the apparently empirical one as to what degree of intertranslatability is possible between separate languages. The latter is a question I disregard in this book, so I shall say no more here about the stronger demand.

How might a language culture constitute a group as a nation—that is, as a group of a kind with a right to statehood? There are numerous possible answers, all pulling in different directions. Indeed, they stem from different views about what it is for members of the same national group to communicate. Consider, for instance, the following remarks of Thomas Macaulay on the requirements of British rule in India:

> We must . . . do our best to form a class who may be interpreters between us and the millions we govern—a class of persons Indian in blood and colour, but English in tastes, in opinions, in morals and in intellect. To that class we may leave it to refine the vernacular dialects of the country . . . and to render them by degrees fit vehicles for conveying knowledge to the great mass of the population.[6]

That Macaulay was writing about a colonial state here is immaterial, as his point applies to any state as regards the requirements of communication which it presupposes. Paramount among these is the need to be able to convey "knowledge" to the governed. This requirement may necessitate changes to their languages—Macaulay mentioned the addition of scientific vocabulary—which will make them more uniform in their capacity to transmit information. If people are to enjoy common statehood, they must be able to communicate on relevant matters with the government of their state; and hence they must have a shared language culture, one capable of handling a shared body of information relevant to their membership of the state, whatever other cultural capacities they differ in.

Such a shared language culture need go beyond what is required for "the mere interchange of goods and services" only in that it also adapts people to a shared state. They will have to have a common understanding of the features of their way of life which are subject to regulation by the state. They will have to share, in one sense of the phrase, a public culture. Now those who already share it—through, for example, sharing a language that unambiguously articulates the relevant concepts—may seem to have a right to statehood from considerations of their aptness to form a successful state. Yet such an argument would be strong only to the degree to which it would be difficult to bring people to a common political understanding if they did not already share it. That it would be difficult is not clear, however. Macaulay was in little doubt that such an understanding would be possible in India, and most states, including multilingual ones, have indeed been able to create a basic public culture. The capacity to communicate the information required for a particular economic and political system to function successfully is apparently not specific to one *kind* of group. It seems that others, too, can readily acquire it: "Modernization" is all that is normally required. But what makes a group a persistent kind of group—a potential nation—must be something more deepseated and resistant to change than this.

Macaulay's remarks on India introduce, however, a very different notion of language culture from this relatively superficial and instrumental one. It is a conception which links having a common language culture to being a certain kind of person. While the masses of India need only to be able to transmit the bits of information required for their exchanges as citizens, the governing class needs to be "English in tastes, in opinions, in morals and in intellect," even if it is "Indian in blood and colour." What is it to have this kind of culture? What does the possession of this kind of culture allow people to communicate? Consider the celebrated opening of E. M. Forster's *A Passage to India*, published in 1924—the year when the Indianization of the All-India Services got under way.[7]

> Except for the Marabar Caves—and they are twenty miles off—the city of Chandrapore presents nothing extraordinary. Edged rather than washed by the River Ganges, it trails for a couple of miles along the bank, scarcely distinguishable from the rubbish it deposits so freely. There are no bathing-steps on the river front, as the Ganges happens not to be holy here; indeed there is no river front, and bazaars shut out the wide and shifting panorama of the stream. The streets are mean, the temples ineffective, and though a few fine houses exist they are hidden away in gardens or down alleys whose filth deters all but the invited guest. ... The very wood seems made of mud, the inhabitants of mud moving. So abased, so monotonous is everything that meets the eye, that when the Ganges comes down it might be expected to wash the excrescence back into the soil. Houses do fall, people are drowned and left rotting, but the general outline of the town persists, swelling here, shrinking there, like some low but indestructible form of life.[8]

How might the Indian civil servants whom Macaulay anticipated react to this passage? What would it say to them?

We are not forgetting, of course, that Macaulay was writing in a context of empire. He thought of English culture as creating an imperial rather than national governing class. Nor did he think of independent nationhood as constituted by a separate culture: He anticipated that as a result of English acculturation "the public mind of India may expand under our system until it has outgrown that system. ... [T]he sceptre may pass away from us."[9] But we can, perhaps, see more clearly what a certain sort of cultural conception of nationhood comes to if we appreciate what it is that is communicated within the culture it invokes and not beyond it; and Forster's description of Chandrapore is surely typical of an exclusively English culture or, rather, "typical of a particular English social group at a particular time."[10] It is precisely by virtue of possessing this kind of culture that, as another critic writes, "the English colonial power, for which Chandrapore is represented as the proper field, is no less imperialising for working aesthetically."[11] Whatever its intentions, imperialism excludes those it colonizes, and English culture of the kind epitomized by Forster excludes others in the act of representing them. Thus Forster's description "is an assured passage, sure of its own stance before its material, sure of the responses it will draw from its audience. It's undramatic; the movement of its feelings, the way it approaches the experiences with which it is dealing, its obliqueness and quietness, all this is like subtle piano playing rather than large orchestration. It is an admirable passage."[12] But its stance is an outsider's. The responses it elicits could not be expected from "the inhabitants" seemingly made of "mud moving" who "are drowned and left rotting." They could scarcely be expected to see themselves as contributing only to Chandrapore's lack of aesthetic distinction. Nor could they, as Hindus, appreciate Forster's ironic report that "the Ganges happens not to be holy here" or that "the temples are ineffective." For that matter, much of the point of the passage would be lost if they could. For its point is precisely to locate its audience as a group with shared expectations and reactions, but ones quite different from those of Chandrapore's Indian inhabitants. Indeed, *their* outlook—and this is part of the book's theme[13]—is unfathomable: "How could the mind take hold of such a country? Generations of invaders have tried, but they remain in exile. . . . India knows of their trouble. She knows of the whole world's trouble to its uttermost depth. She calls 'Come' through her hundred mouths, through objects ridiculous and august. But come to what? She has never defined."[14] Communication with the English is disallowed.

What Forster can communicate to his English readers, but Indians cannot, are, we might say, *attitudes*. But this point may be misleading since it might give the impression that attitudes could exist without the specific kind of cultural vehicle which communicates them. Yet the urbanity of attitude, the reserve: These are not separable from particular utterances (and avoidance of utterances) that receive their canonical expression in certain types of literary English prose—prose to which "several centuries of civilised intercourse have given a texture, a variety of weight, an obliquity, an irony."[15] To talk like this is to manifest these attitudes and to place oneself, perforce, within a persisting cultural milieu. In what way might membership of such a milieu constitute membership of a nation? For viewing such membership in this way is certainly one important conception of the nation. It is manifested, for example, in an influential government report on the teaching of English in schools, published shortly after *A Passage to India*. By means of an education in English literature, "the common possession of the tastes and associations connected with it, would form a new element of national unity, linking together the mental life of all classes by experiences which have hitherto been the privilege of a limited section."[16] How might this national unity be achieved?

There are a number of possibilities. One is that a language culture of the sort I have just sketched (which may correspond to speakers of a single language, to a section of its speakers, or to speakers spanning several languages) serves simply to mark and to maintain a boundary between them and others.[17] Features of the language culture are symbolic of national identity, so that what counts as familiar or as foreign depends upon their presence or absence. These boundary markers are internalized: We feel at home in our own language culture, and vulnerable outside it,[18] as are the English in Forster's India. In that sense the language culture makes us a particular kind of people, but there is no more to it than that. Our group similarity, our difference from others, consists in nothing more than our attachment to certain cultural markers and our alienation from others.

This account of national culture is, however, gravely inadequate. For what distinguishes *national* cultural groups from others—from, say, class-based ones such as we may detect in Forster's intended audience? There are many sorts of boundaries and many ways of being an insider and an outsider. What would have to mark people off culturally as a nation is an appropriate relation to statehood, and for that the boundaries marked must be territorial ones. But first, it is not easy to see, on this account, why it should be anything other than a brute fact that boundaries are sometimes drawn in just this way, transcending class divisions and so on. Second, when they are so drawn, it is hard to see how they are anything other than quite arbitrary. What kind of case for independent statehood can be envisaged for a group conceived as a cultural unit in such an austere way? The mere fact that people separate themselves from each other by reference to certain cultural markers has so far no implications for their political organization. What might have such implications would be its presumed consequence that those who occupy distinct cultural groups in the sense under discussion do not extend sympathy and loyalty across their cultural boundaries. But why should this consequence follow? There is a danger that its following is itself taken as criterial of the appropriate boundary being marked, and then it explains and justifies nothing. In the closing paragraphs of *A Passage to India*, Fielding and Aziz, the Indian, ride together, talking of Indian independence. "Why can't we be friends now?" asks Fielding:

"It's what I want. It's what you want."
    But the horses didn't want it—they swerved apart; the earth didn't want it, sending up rocks through which riders must pass single file; the temples, the tank, the jail, the palace, the birds, the carrion, the Guest House, that

came into view as they issued from the gap and saw Mau beneath: they
didn't want it, they said in their hundred voices, "No, not yet," and the sky
said, "No, not there."[19]

The impossibility of amity is inexplicable, brute, an aspect of inescapable
barriers to mutual comprehension. The simpler but less exciting explanation of a radical divergence of *interests* between the imperializing English
and the colonized Indians is disregarded. Yet until such explanations are
ruled out, Forster's mistier metaphysical picture should not entice us.

Membership of a language culture which communicates attitudes as
well as information might constitute membership of a nation in a different way. For participation in such a culture might be taken to be engage-
ment in a certain kind of life. We must be careful, however, to distinguish
between two sorts of account. In one, the way of life is identified in, for
example, social and economic terms. Its culture is characterized independently—for example, in terms of the speaking of a certain language
through which the way of life is transacted. Life and culture are characterized independent of each other, and it is the shared life, not the culture required for it, that constitutes the nation in the sort of way we considered
in the last chapter. By contrast, the way of life may be construed as identifiable only through a culture that constitutes its relationships as those of a
shared life. It is this idea that theorists have in mind who understand culture in terms of "the particular way of life"[20] of a social group. Then
membership of that culture is criterial for membership of the nation
which the social group makes up. Note that the account can be quite
nonsocietal, in the sense that it refers to characteristics of members, not of
their social relationships. For though the life itself must involve such relationships, participation is made possible by characteristics of individuals—their possession of a certain language or an analogous capacity to
manipulate certain symbolic codes. People isolated from others of their
culture are members of the same nation on this understanding, and there
can be last members of them after their communities have gone—as
American Indian tribes die out, for example.

This conception of culture is more powerful than the austere boundary-
marking one we looked at previously. It explains why a mode of communication which serves "well beyond the mere interchange of goods and
services" should form people into a national group. It does so because it
gives them a common way of life within which a wide variety of relationships is possible, but beyond which only a relatively narrow one is. Now
a separate state, it may be argued, is both needed for the preservation of
such a life and made effective by it: The state's boundaries should be
those of the culture which identifies this life as a separate one. The present argument, which goes beyond the claim that *independent* statehood is

required for cultural protection, has been attractive to many, but it over-looks a crucial distinction noted earlier—namely, that between a kind of life and a particular life, which phrases like "a particular way of life" conspire to blur. As we observed in considering the economic model, more than one society can involve the same kind of life, characterized by the same culture, but these societies may be living different lives, with no significant exchanges between them. There will be many arguments as to why these separate communities are not apt for shared statehood; and, indeed, shared statehood will seldom be claimed for them. Calls for a union of France and Quebec, for example, have not loomed large in Québécois secessionism. Where such calls have been significant in German irredentist claims, say—it is because the formation of a single community of members of a common culture has been thought feasible. A common kind of life has been thought to facilitate a common life.

It may seem, however, that a common life requires a common *kind* of life in the cultural sense under discussion. Yet what constitutes the kind of life constitutive of this sort of cultural nation is open to question. There is a tendency to suppose that a national culture must provide a system of representations for the whole of life, disqualifying as members of the same nation those whose cultural representations of parts of life are radically different. But why should a life so comprehensively the same be needed for shared statehood? If political exchanges or economic exchanges or both are not enough, then perhaps further exchanges short of the kind that rule out important differences of attitude and outlook are. Membership of a national society demands a grasp of what the relevant exchanges consist in and require. This understanding implies common, or rather intertranslatable, representations of the way of life that is shared. Whether it demands any more than this is not obvious, for many features of, for example, personal life may not be shared. A life may be shareable to the degree required for statehood and thereby be a national life without a comprehensive national culture.[21]

"I Owe My Soul to Shakespeare"

Membership of a supposedly national culture is commonly taken to be constitutive or partly constitutive of national membership, but different accounts can be given of what membership consists in and the kind of cultural nationalism advocated varies accordingly. Macaulay's suggestion that the Indian elite become "English in tastes, in opinions, in morals and in intellect" is, as we saw, a species of cultural imperialism. But the principle involved can readily be adapted to cultural nationalism. Perhaps the practical difference[22] lies in the fact that cultural imperialism seeks to extend a culture beyond its usual bounds; and cultural nationalism, to maintain it within them. In both cases the mechanism may be thought of as the same: People voluntarily take on a given culture. They may do so with enthusiasm, as in the case of immigrants entering a country whose culture attracts them, or they may have little alternative, whether as immigrants or as colonized peoples. And what goes for immigrants holds for those already living within a certain culture: Their relation to it is conceptualized as essentially one of voluntary acceptance of it as their national culture. The kind of cultural nationalism involved here is, then, a species of voluntarism, which we may call *cultural voluntarism*.

As we saw in the context of voluntarist accounts of the nation generally, there are different ways in which a nation can be thought of as constituted by its members' coincidence of wills. What is common to cultural voluntarisms is that they view a culture, rather than a polity or civil society, as the nexus of voluntary association. We can thus exclude contractual association as relevant to cultural voluntarism. At least as far as language culture is concerned, it would be quite implausible to postulate a contract between members to communicate through the same cultural codes. There is no way in which a cultural association could be produced by the will of its members that would outlast their desire for it. If their cultural commitments wane, then, according to cultural voluntarism, their cultural association withers—much as some French politicians fear, for example, that Americanization threatens the cultural association that is France. There could be cultural associations without an *explicit* commitment to a culture, perhaps because their members lack any determinate concept of it. This, however, is not the position most characteristic of the kind of cultural nationalism under discussion. Rather, "nationalism reifies culture in the sense that it enables people to talk about their culture as though it were a constant."[23] A nation is taken to be a group with a common commitment to employ the resources of a culture which people can identify as what thereby unites them together and separates them from others. It is this *subjectivist* version of cultural voluntarism that we shall consider.[24]

On this account, national obligations to sustain the culture proceed from its members' sense of cultural membership just because their sense of membership implies the assumption of a voluntary commitment.[25] As in other versions, this voluntarist account of national obligations applies whether their membership derives from birth or from entry. Similarly, the right to independent statehood ultimately derives from the liberal right to freedom of association. This right is exercised here through cultural association. What makes cultural voluntarism a form of nationalism is that it holds that such an association may require the protection of separate statehood.[26] In order to be effective in their desire to associate together through the mediation of a certain culture, members may need to have a state which can exclude nonmembers or regulate the affairs of the cultural association without having to take account of nonmembers' concerns. They therefore claim a *right* to statehood even if alternative forms of government may avert their need to exercise the right to a state through protecting their cultural association adequately without it.

Attending this picture are the usual difficulties of voluntarism already considered. There are additional ones. Some, such as are posed by the presumed right to cultural homogeneity, I shall defer until the next chapter. Others derive from the specific problems of choosing a culture. Cultural voluntarism may adopt a quite distinctive view of culture, which not only appealed to imperialists but continues to appeal in, for example, the "melting pot" vision of America. "In America," wrote Charles Wentworth Dilke, advocating a union of Great Britain and the United States, "the peoples of the world are being fused together, but they run into an English mould: Alfred's laws and Chaucer's tongue are theirs whether they would or not."[27] This model of language culture as a form or "mould" emphasizes the possible acquisition of national identity by acculturation. Dilke decouples acculturation from voluntary commitment, but it is evident that cultural voluntarism requires something like his model if a cultural association is in principle joinable by outsiders, by those who do not already have the culture in question. Whether they have it or not, it is a culture that people choose as their own. The model of culture as a "mould" that forms people is conducive to this conception of someone's culture as what they have chosen.[28]

Nonetheless, the idea that I *choose* my culture is deeply problematic. I have cultural affinities with others whether I wish it or not. Thus, for example, Yeats found himself unable to disown English culture, despite his Irish cultural nationalism: "No people hate as we do in whom the past is always alive. . . . [T]hen I remind myself that . . . all my family names are English; that I owe my soul to Shakespeare, to Blake, perhaps to William Morris, and to the English language in which I think, speak and write; that everything I love has come to me through English. My hate tortures me with love, my love with hate."[29] Yeats, like others of the Anglo-Irish, could not choose *not* to be English by choosing to be Irish. He could and did take on obligations which focused on Irish culture, but those obligations did not follow from a choice of culture. Rather, they followed from a choice of whom to associate with culturally from among the possibilities open to him. He could have chosen to associate with the English, but he chose the Irish.

This example suggests a model of culture different from that of a form available for impressing a cultural identity upon people. It is a model congenial to those who do not think that a nation can necessarily be joinable at will but nonetheless locate its identity in a voluntary association.

There is no contradiction here. A culture can be thought of as a system of cultural characteristics which members of a certain group share. Yet since one is a member of many different groups with their own distinctive cultural characteristics, a commitment is required in order to identify a specific culture as the *national* one. People already share a culture, but they become a nation only through choosing this culture as that through which they will associate in a way appropriate to statehood.[30] The model of a particular culture at work here is, as it were, that of a cross-section taken through people's cultural bodies, which differ in their overall configuration but which can have, in various planes, cross-sections in common with others. On this model, I cannot choose my culture in the sense of choosing its overall form. That overall form is the product of factors over which I have only limited control. But I can choose to orientate myself, so to speak—to display the same cross-section as a selected group of others. This is what is involved in the choice of a cultural association.

The version of cultural voluntarism under discussion, attractive though it is, seems fundamentally unstable. If it is because people *choose* a certain cultural association which yields them a right to statehood, then whether there really *is* a cultural similarity between them which differentiates them from others seems irrelevant. It might as well be an illusion—and in the case of many language cultures, it is. It is well known, for example, that languages which merge imperceptibly into each other are often individuated quite arbitrarily for political reasons. Consider the question of whether English and Scots are separate languages or whether Scots is just a dialect of English.[31] What counts as similarity and difference here is itself a matter of choice, and political choice at that. Cultural facts fall away as irrelevant. If, on the other hand, cultural facts are relevant to claims for statehood, a shared will is not sufficient. How, then, do cultural facts contribute to generating a right to statehood? The model has no obvious answer. We shall return to the question of whether this instability can be overcome at the end of the chapter.

I turn now, however, to a different kind of cultural nationalism, which I term, for reasons that will become apparent, *cultural contextualism*. On this account, culture is not something we *can* choose, and that is because it forms our "context of choice." That is, it provides "the media through which we come to an awareness of the options available to us," which are "a precondition of making intelligent judgements about how to lead our lives."[32] A culture viewed in this way will include language, or whatever translinguistic or intralinguistic systems of representation provide people with the same context for making choices. A nation is individuated by a culture as so understood.[33] There is no room here for the idea that a nation is a voluntary cultural association. People are brought together through the sharing of a culture into a group whose members share the same context of choice. They are thus able to pursue a common life since they decide how to live together within a shared understanding of what is possible for them. What indicates the existence of a national culture is therefore the successful functioning of a national community, a group in which people find that they can live together rather than an association in which they deliberately set out to do so. Cultural contextualism can dispense, then, with the subjectivism of cultural voluntarism. A national culture does not need, on this account, to be explicitly grasped by its members for what it is. They can get by with only the vaguest idea of its nature and extent so long as it plays the appropriate part in their common life.

Cultural contextualism locates a nation's right to statehood in the need to protect a culture. But it can give a better account than cultural voluntarism of why this is worthwhile. For the loss of a culture is the loss of the background necessary for meaningful choice, and it plunges people into an aimless and anomic existence in which a good life is impossible. The value of the culture is not that it is instrumental in enabling people to achieve their chosen goals—to speak a certain language and so on. On the contrary, as their goals are shaped by it, its value lies in its creating their moral identities.[34] Their obligation to preserve their culture is simply an extension of their obligation to conduct their lives in a responsible and rational way—in this case, by safeguarding the preconditions of such a life. The right to the political means for fulfilling these obligations flows from their overriding importance in people's lives. For others have a duty to give them the opportunity for realizing the good of cultural membership, just as for such other goods as liberty.[35]

Cultural contextualism provides, furthermore, a good explanation of why people value their own culture and feel an obligation to protect it. They find a value in it that may be inaccessible to others, precisely because it provides their *own* context of choice, which is not necessarily translatable into that provided by another culture. This finding of value in a culture has nothing to do with making a judgment of *comparative* value. One cherishes one's language, say, as one cherishes a loved one, without any comparison with others. "Despise the language and you despise your nationality; honour your language and you honour your nationality,"[36] as Jan Hofmeyr, leader of the Afrikander Bond, said in defense of Afrikaans against the supposed superiority of English. To cherish a language culture is to feel an obligation to preserve it against loss or damage, not only for oneself but for others. Cultural contextualism can handle the desire that one's own culture survive and the political demands which have this as their objective.[37]

There are, however, aspects of cultural contextualism which are less satisfactory. How, in particular, can it explain our obligations to compatriots? For surely it is loyalty to *people*, rather than to a language, say, which should lie at the bottom of national obligation. If nationalism, as on this account, "conceives the natural object of human loyalty to be a fairly large anonymous unit defined by shared language and culture,"[38] then why should sharing a language and culture generate loyalty to fellow members of the unit? On the assumption that the cultural community is constituted by mutual obligation, one may put the same point in another way: Why should people who share a language constitute community? There is a tendency among cultural nationalists simply to *assume* that it does, so that it is not always clear whether they are offering a societal or nonsocietal account of nationhood. Yet, as noted earlier, there can be isolated members of a culture who form no part of any community associated with it. Do they have a reason for loyalty to others who speak the same language?

If they do, it is surely only because they *could* have certain sorts of relationship with them which they could not have with others. It is these relationships which are valued, as indeed it must be social relationships which are valued if I am to recognize obligations to my fellow participants in them. Yet to admit this is a dangerous move for cultural nationalists. For if they ground obligations to fellow members not in culture itself but in the value of the social relationships it makes possible, then questions can arise about whether these relationships really *are* valuable. These are not questions of a sort that could arise about the culture, conceived solely as a means of social communication. For a culture so conceived is neither good nor bad in itself, though it can make possible either good or bad relationships; and it may turn out that the relationships which constitute a national community are bad ones—ones based, for example, on uncritical loyalty or collective uniformity. It is far from clear that a supposedly national community of this sort should be accorded a right to statehood.

"Land of Heart's Desire"

What is it that makes a culture a *national* culture? We must try to answer this question regardless of whether we are tempted by cultural nationalism to hold that what makes people a nation is that they share a culture. But in trying to answer it we need to distinguish between two other questions which are not, unfortunately, totally unrelated. One is the question which produces the sort of answers I have already mentioned. It is a question about what conception of culture is needed for a certain sort of nationalism, of which the mould and cross-section models are examples. These conceptions are, as I said, related to the issue of whether nations are joinable by outsiders and, if so, how. A conception which makes nations radically nonjoinable is what we may call the *closed-container model*.

The picture usually associated with the notion that speakers of German thereby constitute a single nation exemplifies this model.

Fichte, the most influential proponent of the view, aimed to explain "what is the characteristic of the German as such . . . ever since he began to exist." He located it as follows:

> The cause of a complete contrast between the Germans and the other peoples of Teutonic descent is . . . the change of language. Here, as I wish to point out distinctly at the very beginning, it is not a question of the special quality of the language retained by the one branch or adopted by the other; on the contrary the importance lies solely in the fact that in the one case something native is retained, while in the other case something foreign is adopted. . . . [T]he importance lies solely in the fact that this language continues to be spoken, and men are formed by language far more than language is formed by men.[39]

German speakers form a nation because they speak their *native* language. Indeed, this criterion operates in many cases where a linguistic group claims to be a nation. It is not the speaking of a different language from others that is crucial, but the speaking of the same language as their predecessors. Outsiders cannot join, or cannot fully join, for they cannot acquire an identity as deep-seated as that possessed by those who grow up in the language culture. Since it cannot be their native language, it cannot form their fundamental identity; but national identity is fundamental and not acquired.

It may seem that the cultural contextualism we looked at in the last section is committed to this closed-container model. But it is not.[40] It is able to accept that a culture can be acquired;[41] and this is because it is not committed to a view of cultural identities as homogeneous and unchanging, as Fichte was—a view in which diversification and change threaten the existence of identity itself.[42] Why did Fichte hold this sort of view?

It is, I suggest, because he gave a particular answer to a second question that I wish to distinguish from the first concerning nationalist conceptions of culture. This second question is one about the metaphysical status of national culture: Is its existence a discoverable fact, the outcome of factors beyond the control of its members? Or is it the product of their social choices, and modifiable by their voluntary acts? Fichte took up the former, *essentialist* position. He located national culture in a language which is not to any extent "formed by men" but, rather, has "issued from the force of nature."[43] He thought of national character as distinctive in consequence of the distinctiveness of national culture; though the opposite position is equally an essentialist one if character is thought of naturalistically. Cultural contextualism, on the other hand, is not committed to an essentialist account of culture. People cannot choose their cultures, nor are the cultural communities they form voluntary associations; but this does not imply that their culture is not the product of collective choices or that it cannot be changed by them. Thus, for example, a language can change over time by the deliberate importation of foreign words with a resultant change in the context of choice. But such changes need not lead to the "perversion" and "degradation" that Fichte regarded as inevitable,[44] and inevitable because the clearly discernible outlines of a national culture are thereby obscured and perhaps eventually lost.

The alternative position to essentialism is the *social constructionism* we encountered earlier, on which a national culture is, so to say, invented rather than discovered, because it is shaped as such by social agents (albeit from inherited cultural materials). This distinction has considerable implications for cultural nationalism. For the essentialist view allows that the possession of an appropriate shared culture is the kind of thing that should persuade people that they have a common national identity and therefore, perhaps, that they ought to associate together politically. If, on the other hand, a national culture is constructed, then a consequence apparently less favorable to cultural nationalism follows. The fact that I share in the national culture is a product of the choices that have been made to determine what is to count as that culture. Hence I cannot take at face value the claim that I have a similarity to others which justifies me in seeking statehood with them. The supposed similarity is subject to manipulation which determines who it extends to and who not, and which might have been contrived differently. While I cannot opt out of the culture, I can question its construction and wonder whether it really does provide a good reason for political association. It is not the possession of a culture *per se* but, rather, the possession of one constructed in a way that does provide a reason for political association which might convince me of my national identity. Skepticism of this sort undermines the easy appeal of cultural nationalism and forces it to address the question of what sort of cultural construction might lay a claim to the protection of statehood. To avoid confronting this question, cultural nationalists tend to assume the truth of essentialism; but are they right to do so?

In order to simplify the question, let us look at a relevant aspect of a national culture: national literature.[45] And in order to tackle the question of whether the nationality of a literary work is an essential or a constructed feature of it, let us ask how we might go about determining whether the work of a given author qualifies for it or does not. Indeed, we need to know how to answer questions of this sort if we are to grasp how cultural nationalism can work as a criterion of national membership. Consider the case of Irish literature, construed as including works written in English: "Why Goldsmith, Sterne and Sheridan do not belong to Irish literature, while Yeats and Joyce do, needs an answer."[46] I shall investigate the question of whether the work of Elizabeth Bowen falls into this category. Elizabeth

Bowen was born in 1899 into an old Protestant Anglo-Irish family and re-tained the family seat as her Irish residence for most of her life. This, how-ever, was largely spent in England, leading one critic to write that she was "mainly an 'outsider' closer to Oxford and the Bloomsbury group than to Ireland"[47] and another to suggest that "the 'Irishness' of Elizabeth Bowen may seem especially suspect."[48] She herself thought otherwise: "I regard myself," she said, "as an Irish novelist. As long as I can remember I've been extremely conscious of being Irish—even when I was writing about very un-Irish things."[49] And Sean O'Faolain agreed, exclaiming of her novel *The Last September*, set during the Irish War of Independence, that "[i]t's so en-tirely Irish, if that matters a damn."[50] For our purposes it does matter. What did O'Faolain detect in Bowen's work? Was it some essential Irishness which any discerning reader must acknowledge? Or was it just that it moved him and other Irish readers to acclaim it as Irish, to admit it to a cul-tural canon over which they had control?

I have time here to look at only one aspect of one novel, *The Last Septem-ber*[51]—namely, the language. For the language must surely be what princi-pally bespeaks a literary work's national identity. It is not just that the lan-guage of a nation is distinctive, even when it is shared with others. It is, as I suggested earlier in speaking of cultural contextualism, that the language is cherished, is heard as beautiful, even when it is the language of the colonists adopted by the colonized. "The Saxon took our lands from us and left them desolate," wrote Oscar Wilde. "[W]e took their language and added new beauties to it,"[52] and those beauties have a characteristically Irish rhythm and tone. Epigrams like Wilde's definition of a cynic as "a man who knows the price of everything and the value of nothing"[53] or wisecracks like "I have nothing to declare except my genius"[54] have almost an Irish accent about them. Elizabeth Bowen displayed little of that *élan*. Her diction had all the restraint of the Anglo-Irish gentry. Yet there is a bleak irony which Bowen detected in Irish talk and replicated in her prose. In one scene in *The Last September*, a Sinn Fein gunman confronts two An-glo-Irish women out walking. "The man's eyes went from one to the other, and remained ironically between them. His face was metal-blue in the dusk and seemed numbed into immobility. 'It is time,' he said, 'that yourselves gave up walking. If you have nothing better to do you had better keep in the house while y'have it.'"[55] The same irony at the expense of those deemed un-Irish is deployed in characterizing an English officer who is hunting the gunmen: "Gerald would have wished to explain that no-one could have a sounder respect than himself and his country, for the whole principle of nationality, and that it was with some awareness of misdirec-tion, even of paradox, that he was out here to hunt and shoot the Irish."[56]

Bowen's diction, I suggest, has features which might identify it as Irish. Her ear for the speech of "the Irish properly so-called"[57] is unfailing, and unfailingly sympathetic, as demonstrated in the penultimate passage quoted earlier. It is without the condescension toward or conscious distancing from Irish speech that is typical of much Anglo-Irish writing—for example, that of Edith Somerville and Martin Ross (Violet Martin):

> "The blood was dhruv out through his nose and ears," continued Slipper, with a voice that indicated the cream of the narration, "and you'd hear his bones crackin' on the ground. You'd have pitied the poor boy." . . .
> "Was he hurt, Slipper?" asked Flurry casually.
> "Hurt is it?" echoed Slipper in high scorn: "killed on the spot!" He paused to relish the effect of the dénouement.[58]

Such language may be "closely observed . . . with love and glee,"[59] but it is love of something which cannot be taken seriously—at least so far as this kind of treatment of it is concerned. Bowen took it seriously, but it was not *her* language: How, then, might she qualify as an Irish writer? Condescension and superiority would, I have implied, disqualify her. But why is this? What could an answer have to do with her diction possessing or not possessing some essential Irishness? There is no compelling fact about it which forces her to be admitted to Irish literature or banished from it. And similarities to canonical examples can be emphasized or discounted by comparison with her Bloomsbury aesthetic. What is being done here fits the constructionist rather than the essentialist model, and this is surely clinched by the fact that condescension toward Irish speech would disqualify Bowen just because it would discourage Irish readers from admitting her to their canon. They would be unable to treat her work as part of their language culture precisely because it distances itself from it. But Bowen does not place herself outside the culture, and the option of admitting her remains open. Whether it is taken, whether her diction *is* a part of that culture, calls for a decision and not discovery, just as in the other constructions of Irish identity we looked at earlier.

This is a very summary treatment of a difficult issue, and with a conclusion too baldly stated. It should not be thought, however, that social constructionism rules out cultural nationalism. Rather, it changes its nature, for it transforms the character of the cultural considerations on which it relies. Instead of being inescapable facts which classify people into national groups, cultural characteristics become malleable templates which people fashion to classify themselves and others. It follows that people can resist the classifications that are applied to them and seek to change them. One reason for doing this might be the conviction that the way one is classified culturally is the work of *others*, not of those one is classified with. Thus, for example, the Yeatsian Irish Literary Revival through which a particular kind of Irishness is constructed was accused of being engineered by *British* interests: "The Irish Literary Revival was an offshoot of British needs. Materialistic, monied, torpid late Victorian society wanted an anti-materialistic Land of Heart's Desire. . . . Yeats and his friends elected to supply such a Never-Never Land."[60] If people acknowledge this, then they can reject the Literary Revivalist construction of their identity. But Yeats, of course, could have claimed to be Irish, so that the construction in which he was involved looks more like a sectional than an alien one. As we saw earlier, it figured in a contest as to what Irishness should consist in.

Success in this contest goes to those who manage to define a literature—or, more broadly, a culture—which a people can accept as their own. What makes them a people may just be this shared cultural attachment. There may be no way of identifying them as an entity independent of this criterion. In that case, and that case only, we can plausibly attribute national identity on the basis of a common culture, but we would do so without presupposing the essentialist view of culture which underlies cultural nationalism as ordinarily understood. Now it will be immediately apparent that this basis for the attribution of national identity makes cultural nationalism a form of voluntarism, since it makes nationhood depend upon the will of its members. But it is, in the first place, a different form of voluntarism from those I introduced earlier in the chapter, for it obliterates the distinction between the possession of a culture and the choice of a cultural association.[61] It is this distinction which produces the instability previously noted in the associative version of cultural nationalism. The instability disappears if the cultural considerations relevant to claims to statehood are themselves the product of what people will. For then what they will and what cultural classification applies to them are no longer *competing* criteria for their national identity.

In the second place, however, obliterating the distinction between possession of a culture and choice of cultural association closes the gap between cultural voluntarism and cultural contextualism. For there is no need for people to choose to associate on the basis of a culture if they are already brought together through sharing one. But their sharing a culture, under social constructionism, just *is* their making the same choices as to what is to count as their culture and what is not. These choices, however, are made from within an existing culture, as under cultural contextualism; they are not, as in the first version of voluntarism we considered, somehow made outside of it and so themselves culturally inexplicable.

Cultural nationalism thus reconstructed still encounters the difficulties of any voluntarism which cannot deliver complete consensus. What are we to recognize as a nation in a society divided in its will? The difficulty emerges clearly if we consider the argument that a self-constructed cultural group might have for statehood, unitary as well as independent— namely, that it would ensure its continued control of its own culture and hence of the cultural identity of its members. This argument from the need for autonomy is convincing only to the degree to which the people who would fall under the state are culturally homogeneous. If they are not, then independent statehood will further the autonomy of a culturally dominant group at the expense of that of others. This explains the drive toward such homogeneity in the nation-building endeavors of groups attempting to construct themselves as cultural nations. Even homogeneity, however, does not imply collective control, whereas only such control could plausibly constitute people as a nation—first, because all members must somehow be involved in the construction for it to count, on this model, as *their* culture, but second, because only collective control could generate a convincing argument for statehood. Yet the reason the latter holds true is surely that such collectivity expresses a regard for certain *values*. This is a consideration that goes beyond those that can be adduced on behalf of nations conceived solely in terms of language culture. As I suggested earlier, it is not the value of a culture produced in a certain way but the value of the communal relations which go into producing it which here seems to be doing the work of justifying statehood. It is to the subject of culture as articulating values that we now turn.

Summary

In this chapter I have looked at a class of so-called cultural nationalisms— namely, those in which a common culture is thought of in terms of a common language or other system for social exchanges. This investigation has generated what I call the communication model of the nation, which admits of various versions. One version treats a national language culture as merely an instrument for political dialogue; but this approach is too shallow to provide a plausible basis for separate states. Another regards it as communicating intellectual attitudes and thereby shaping a common character. Yet it is not clear that the common life that would be required for nationhood depends upon such deep-going cultural commonality.

In any event, there is the further question of what membership of a language culture consists in. Cultural voluntarism views it in terms of choosing to participate in a cultural association; and cultural contextualism, in terms of employing a language willy-nilly as a shared context for life choices. Both are open to criticism. But a major problem for all cultural nationalisms is how to demarcate a specifically *national* culture. The solution may be to reject essentialist answers in favor of a form of social constructionism, which in turn promises to reconcile cultural voluntarism and contextualism: People share a national culture through making the same choices as to what is to count as that culture. But this outcome demands a degree of cultural homogeneity which may be both unrealistic and undesirable.

Chapter Eight

"An Outlook on Life"

Language and Values

A common language is a means of communication and is appealed to in nationalist arguments, as we have seen, because communication is necessary for a common life. But language is more than this, as our discussion of national literatures implies. Its expressive potential is held to reflect national character, whether because it shapes or is shaped by it. And, in particular, it is held to reflect national character as embodying distinctive *values*, an aspect of culture which we have unrealistically split off from others and so far ignored. The supposed connection between language and values was voiced by Eamon de Valera. Speaking of Gaelic, he said:

> It is for us what no other language can be. It is more than a symbol; it is an essential part of our nationhood. As a vehicle for three thousand years of our history, the language is for us precious beyond measure. As the bearer to us of a philosophy, of an outlook on life deeply Christian and rich in practical wisdom, the language is worth far too much to dream of letting it go.[1]

What this outlook on life comes to we learn from the same speech: "The Ireland which we dreamed of would be the home of a people who value material wealth only as a basis of right living, of a people who were satisfied with frugal comfort and who devoted their leisure to things of the spirit." Among the "things of the spirit" de Valera cited first the speaking of Gaelic. Talk is itself to be valued, and the value of talk is implicit in the language itself, with its long oral traditions.[2]

The idea that a particular language might convey a certain system of values is a difficult and puzzling one. It has, I think, at least three distinct implications. First is the notion that some ethical concepts might be expressible in some languages but not in others. Consider, for example, the Maori concept of *mauri*.[3] Sometimes translated as "life-force," *mauri* is what people seek to extend in themselves but also to respect in the natural materials they work with—in weaving, for instance. But weaving has its own *mauri*—the weaver being a vehicle for the activity of the gods—and so does the acquisition of knowledge. It is evident that no straightforward translation will work here, and that what the concept comes to can be grasped only from its place within a network of linguistic concepts and against the background of a way of life in which they are applied. Yet what follows from this? It does not appear to follow that those who do not speak the Maori tongue could not acquire a sense of what *mauri* and related value concepts mean. Indeed, it is sometimes suggested that Pakeha—white New Zealanders—should acquire such a sense as part of the development of a distinctive New Zealand national culture.[4] They would thereby be acquiring new attitudes of respect for work, say, but not, it seems, attitudes inconsistent with their wider Western values.

A second way of taking the idea that language conveys values is suggested by a criticism that might be made of the importation of concepts like *mauri* into Pakeha discourse—namely, that they could not make the connections with other concepts in the English language which they do in Maori. Only in a particular language, it may be suggested, are certain values firmly rooted in a coherent way of thinking about things. Outside of it they can command no genuine comprehension and attachment. Johann Gottlieb Fichte made this point as part of an attack on Enlightenment values: "If instead of the word Humanity [Humanität], we had said to a German the word *menschlichkeit*, which is its literal translation, he would have understood us without further historical explanation; but he would have said: 'Well to be a man [Mensch] and not a wild beast is not very much after all.'"[5] Fichte denounced the "degradations of their former ethical standard because of inappropriate foreign symbols"[6] by some of the Teutonic peoples. Yet Fichte's concern here with intelligible etymologies, later taken up by Heidegger, surely lays the emphasis in the wrong place. If the Germans were unable to grasp the ethical concept of Humanity, it was not because the word has Latin roots.

A third way in which language may be said to convey values seeks to explain what *is* required for value concepts to be applied with clarity and conviction. It is that only specific languages or uses of language can be vehicles for the social relationships which embody them. In particular, so the claim goes, it is only when a language is vigorous and demotic that humane relationships are possible. Thus, for example, F. R. Leavis describes Bunyan's *The Pilgrims' Progress* as "a humane masterpiece."[7] "What is involved," he explains,

> is not merely an idiomatic raciness of speech, expressing a strong vitality, but an art of social living, with its mature habits of valuation. We must beware of idealising, but the fact is plain. There would have been no Shakespeare and

no Bunyan if in their time, with all its disadvantages by present standards, there had not been, living in the daily life of the people, a positive culture which has disappeared and for which modern revolutionaries, social reformers and Utopists do not commonly project any serious equivalent.[8]

The English language of the seventeenth century conveys the humane values of pre-industrial social relationships, or does so at least insofar as it resists the Miltonic Latinizations which cannot provide a vehicle for such relationships.[9] Leavis has been charged with a particular species of English cultural nationalism:

> This Leavisite nationalism is evident, for example, in the peculiar centrality attached to the notion of a national literary canon. It is evident too in Leavis's own peculiar theory of language, with its improbable affirmation of the non-arbitrary nature of the (English) sign. . . . The result is a nationalistic preoccupation with the superior virtues, if not of the contemporary English, then of their peasant ancestors and of the language bequeathed them by those ancestors.[10]

Yet this seems wide of the mark. For Leavis does not appear to specify values distinctive of the English which their language conveys. Rather, he seems to be thinking of certain universal human values sometimes being realized and sometimes not; but that when they are realized in certain sorts of social relationships, then their realization is mediated through distinctive uses of language which instantiate corresponding aesthetic values. This conviction can support an insistence on preserving the language which may look nationalistic, but it is not a nationalism based on an identification of the nation as pursuing values specific to it.

It is this last mentioned kind of nationalism which we need to concentrate on now, a kind of cultural nationalism in which a culture is taken to be distinguished principally by the values of the way of life it characterizes. I shall refer to this as a *value culture*. It is, I believe, quite artificial to regard culture as of the one sort or the other, though cultural contextualism does seek to eliminate value from culture since values are thought of as subject to choice rather than as part of its context.[11] Yet it is permissible to differentiate language culture from value culture because some kinds of cultural nationalism emphasize the former and some the latter, as de Valera seemed to be doing in the passage with which we began, despite his ostensible concern with language.

By "values" in this context I intend to include a wide range of notions, not only moral values but aesthetic ones, and also rules of taste and manners. There are important differences here which we shall touch on. But some elementary general principles must inform those nationalisms which individuate nations by their value culture, whichever sorts of value they lay stress on. One of these is that the attachment to certain values shall clearly differentiate nations from one another. De Valera no doubt had a contrast with England in mind when he maintained that the Irish were satisfied with "frugal comfort" and valued wealth only "as a basis of right living." The image of the English as mercenary had long been common, and not only among foreign observers like Heinrich von Treitschke:

> The English possess a commercial spirit, a love of money which has killed every sentiment of honour and every distinction of right and wrong. English cowardice and sensuality are hidden behind unctuous theological talk. . . . In England all notions of honour and class prejudices vanish before the power of money, whereas the German nobility has remained poor but chivalrous. That last indispensable bulwark against the brutalisation of society—the duel—has gone out of fashion in England.[12]

This image was also shared by some Englishmen themselves, such as Matthew Arnold who wrote of

> *. . . England, bent but to make pour*
> *The flood of the world's commerce on her shore.*[13]

But evidently such English people could not view English culture so conceived as a proper basis for national identity. The second principle guiding value culture nationalisms, then, is that the values attributed to the nation must be capable of being presented as *worth* valuing.

This principle need not involve a different view of what sort of pursuit is characteristic of a nation from that suggested by its critics, only a different valuation of its objects. The nineteenth-century English pursuit of money can be presented as a creditable exercise of individual freedom. Consider this example of the sort of pronouncements that have contributed to the most recent species of English nationalism:

> [S]ocialism has brought economic paralysis and/or collapse to every country that tried it. . . . England, once the freest and proudest nation of Europe, has been reduced to the status of a second-rate power. . . .
> Racial and/or religious persecutions of minorities stood in inverse ratio to the degree of a country's freedom. Racism was strongest in the more controlled economies, such as Russia and Germany—and weakest in England, the then freest country of Europe.
> It is capitalism that gave mankind its first steps towards freedom and a rational way of life.[14]

Freedom is, of course, something that everyone should want, so it may seem paradoxical to represent it as the special goal of the English. Where values are universal in this way the cultural nationalist must claim that his nation has a special relationship to them, of origination, guardianship, or interpretation. That is the third principle of value culture nationalism.

Not all values, however, are universal in this way. F. M. Forster, comparing English with German culture during World War II, wrote that "[t]he English love of freedom, the English countryside, English prudishness and hypocrisy, English freakishness, and our mild idealism and good-humoured reasonableness have all combined to make something which is certainly not perfect, but which may claim to be unusual."[15] Most of these valuations have to do with matters of taste and manners rather than with morals: There is no suggestion here that others should be what Forster ironically described as prudish, hypocritical, or freakish, for example. Merely to display such a mixture of nonuniversal valuations may be enough to identify someone's cultural nationality—which is a fourth principle. But for a fifth and last, we have to distinguish what valuations are essential to national identity from those which are merely accidental. Forster said that the English culture he described "springs naturally out of our way of looking at things, and out of the way we have looked at things in the past. It has developed slowly, easily, lazily,"[16] he continued, contrasting it with the governmentally imposed culture of Nazi Germany. At least two notions are at work here to distinguish what is essential from what is not. First is the idea of what is relatively persistent over time as against what is a response to changing circumstances. National values must be rooted in national history, as nineteenth-century English capitalism, perhaps, is not. Second is the idea of what is spontaneous, in not being imposed but also in not being deliberately selected for valuation. These criteria, I take it, are implied by Forster's remarks. I do not suggest that they apply to *all* value culture nationalisms. Different nations may employ different criteria, but *some* criteria are required to identify what is essential to what they value and what is not.

The account of value culture nationalism which I have offered will usually make religious nationalism a species of it. It is significant that de Valera included in his culturalist characterization of Ireland "an outlook on life deeply Christian," which he understood to be a Roman Catholic one. Yet the Catholic religion is not, of course, unique to the Irish. It must be annexed to other elements if it is to individuate them as a nation, and this is in general true of religions. What is more, it may not be moral values specific to their religion which mark people off from their neighbors of a different faith. Notoriously, the versions of conservative morality which stem from the religions of Irish Catholics and Ulster Protestants are very similar. But religion is held to mark a moral difference despite that: "The Ulster Protestant is a strong, robust character, with a fierce loyalty to his friends. . . . [T]he Ulster Protestant has no time for double dealing, shady dealing, hypocrisy and weakness. He despises traitors, political puppets, ecumenical jellyfish, opportunists, liars, crooks, apologists and snivellers."[17] Many of the supposed characteristics of Irish Catholics are reviled here, but they are not (with the exception of ecumenism) religious characteristics as such. Yet, like many religious nationalisms, Ulster Protestantism is characterized by a firm conviction of its possession of the truth. It is others' lack of it which makes them suspect, even when they are apparently acting rightly. They do not value the truth, as true believers do, because they persist in error. It is, perhaps, notions like this that enable religious groups to distinguish themselves most sharply from others and thus, given the appropriate factors, to represent themselves as different nations.

The very fact that most religions claim a monopoly on the truth has seemed to some to make their profession incompatible with nationalism. If everyone is potentially a convert, then the distinctions between peoples which nations represent cannot be of lasting significance when based upon religious differences. In the case of some religions, such as Islam, which seek a major role in the structures and procedures of the state, it is supposed that religious and national claims to statehood are incompatible, the former presupposing a changing and theoretically unlimited entity, the latter a stable and bounded one.[18] In the light of the constitutive principle of nationalism, however, we would do better to regard this as a conflict of nationalisms rather than as a conflict between nationalism and religion. Describing the challenge from Egypt and Syria to the Baghdad Caliphate in early Islam as constituting a conflict which has never been resolved, one commentator writes that "under the traditions and unwritten rules of Islam there can be no such thing as an individual and sovereign Islamic nation set apart from the rest of Islam: all Islam is a single nation."[19] This strikes me as the right way to express the matter.

"Worthwhile Ways of Life"

A wide range of arguments for a right to statehood employ the fact of common culture as a major premise. Many of these arguments apply equally to value and to language culture; others, which do not rest on the communicative or contextualizing function of a culture, only to the former. But often the arguments confuse two questions which I wish to keep separate here: the question of whether a group has a right to statehood and the question of whether only statehood, as opposed to some other arrangement, could safeguard a culture. I am concerned here solely with the first of these. I take it that a cultural group can assert a right to statehood just because circumstances *may* arise in which statehood is the only means to safeguard its culture. In other circumstances, alternative arrangements would be effective and the group might be wrong to resist them and insist upon its right. If it is objected that the group possesses a right to statehood *only* when statehood is the sole option for safeguarding its culture, I reply that the right is not then a *national* right and the group is not being regarded as a nation. Rather, it is being treated as a group which finds itself in circumstances where it risks a certain sort of oppression, and which then has a general right to protect itself by seeking statehood. This, as I have insisted earlier, is quite different from its claiming a national right by virtue of the kind of group it forms.

There are several different sorts of argument for value culture groups to enjoy a right to statehood. I shall arrange them into four categories. The first two categories contain arguments which seek statehood for the protection of cultures, strictly speaking. The first seeks it to preserve the values enshrined *in* a culture; the second, to preserve the value *of* a culture. The third category of argument asserts a right to statehood for the protection of certain other rights, which we can refer to as cultural rights. All three categories provide what I have called entitlement considerations for statehood. The fourth category contains arguments from the aptness for shared statehood of groups with a common culture. While it is not always easy to classify a particular argument, this framework will, I hope, serve to identify the possible elements in a cultural argument for statehood. It goes without saying that a given argument may draw on several different elements. Yet, as always, the strength of the whole cannot be greater than the strength of its parts.

We start with arguments from the values promoted within cultures. First, it could be claimed that statehood protects values that are essential to any good life and which are therefore recognized in all cultures. Are there such values? Perhaps liberty is one. But insofar as such values are universal, it seems hard to make a case for correlating statehood with a particular culture, since statehood is justified by features which all share. Perhaps, though, the membership of some particular culture is itself a universal value. It would be if the pursuit of values was possible only within a particular culture, as cultural contextualism maintains. I shall treat this observation, however, as providing an argument for the value *of* a culture rather than as discerning a value promoted within cultures.

Second, and more promising, it might be argued that statehood is needed to protect the distinctiveness of cultures. The implication is that the values promoted by a culture by virtue of which it has a claim to separate statehood are precisely not those it has in common with other cultures but those by which it differs—whether because these are distinctive values, as the Maori notion of *mauri* mentioned earlier may be, or whether because more familiar values are presented in a distinctive constellation, as may be suggested by de Valera's "dream" speech. Undoubtedly there are many threats to distinctive cultures, not just because of the specific circumstances of the present—for these would not support a *national* argument—but because of the inherent fragility of cultural distinctiveness in an environment of cultural diversity. Should a right to statehood be admitted in order to avert these threats?

An objection which may arise is that the culture to be protected may be distinctive but not, on that account alone, worth preserving. The processes whereby a society loses such a culture may be welcomed as leading to a better one, just as J. S. Mill welcomed the decline of a distinctively Breton or Basque culture in favor of a supposedly superior, more open and liberal one. Indeed, the distinctive values of many cultures can be so rebarbative in terms of, for example, their attitudes toward war or women that it is hard not to concede the objection. There may, however, be a value in distinctiveness both to those within a culture and to those without. For the participants it may ensure a clear and coherent system of values to pursue, which is otherwise not possible, with the result that the pursuit of any value at all becomes problematic. And for outsiders it may conduce to respect and toleration, and to critical reflection upon one's own culture. But these are liberal virtues, and it might be claimed that in their absence the greater the degree of distinctiveness the more alien and unsympathetic the culture will appear, while in guarding its purity its practitioners will themselves run to fanaticism. Against this uncertain balance the claims of some unappealing cultures to the protection of statehood would scarcely seem compelling.[20]

A third argument seeks to avert this conclusion by insisting that the values within particular cultures require the protection of statehood precisely so that they will not be judged by standards external to themselves. Each culture, it is claimed, has its own distinctive values or scale of values which are not commensurable with those of another culture. It is, in consequence, quite impossible for more than one such cultural group to be governed within a single state which will apply evaluative judgments alien to at least one of them. But then the state will be regarded as oppressive by members of that group and cannot command their loyalties, although they are entitled to a state which can, whatever others may think about their values.

This argument makes at least two highly questionable assumptions: first, that values are incommensurable, a relativist doctrine which we have touched on earlier; and second, that a state would have to espouse the substantive values of one cultural group or another. The latter could be denied on the liberal ground that the state need appeal only to neutrally justifiable principles of justice within which a variety of conceptions of the good can be followed up. It is highly doubtful whether this view of the state as neutral can be sustained.[21] But even if it can, it must be conceded that only a well-functioning liberal state would be neutral, whereas a cultural group could claim that it needed a degree of protection greater than that provided by such a state. The counterargument must be that a cultural group with this agenda has no motive for instituting a liberal state and, therefore, that the right to statehood which it claims is too extensive in its ambitions to be entertained, since the state it is likely to institute will leave no room for the alternative values which individual citizens may choose to follow. This is, of course, a liberal argument to which exception might be taken. Yet there is no alternative to standing upon *some* moral ground if the right to statehood is claimed to be a moral one. Those nationalisms which, like fascism, simply *assert* the right, and do not seek to justify it to liberals, have at least understood this point, even if their response to it is an odious one.

Cultural arguments in the aforementioned second category highlight the value of a culture itself as the reason it deserves the protection of statehood. We can distinguish between two types of such arguments, one asserting the intrinsic value of a culture, the other its instrumental value. Within the first type we can differentiate those arguments which find an intrinsic value in a certain sort of culture from those which find it in cultural diversity. The former starts from the position that certain cultures are of value in themselves, without endorsing the values they promote or even conceding that such an endorsement or repudiation is possible. The model at work here treats these values as aesthetic or as analogous to aesthetic values. They encapsulate shared tastes, as with a national cuisine[22] or a national folk music and dance. Outsiders may find it hard or even impossible to acquire these tastes or the more deep-going values modeled on them. Yet they can appreciate the value of a culture which brings them together into an integrated system. This value may itself be thought of as akin to an aesthetic one, with the aesthetic virtues of richness, harmony, ease, and so forth. But these are the virtues of a vehicle for living a life, and it is as such a vehicle that the culture has its value. Harmony, for example, need not be *promoted* by the culture but can nonetheless be achieved in the life lived through it. Cultures which possess this sort of value are, according to this argument, entitled to the protection of statehood. Without it, a culture can succumb to the alien influences of those who lack a feeling for its tastes and customs, and no longer show the virtues that made it worthwhile.

Though in many ways an attractive picture, this is potentially a deeply conservative one. Its image of cultures as possessing the unity of works of art makes changes to them as sacrilegious as drawing a mustache on the Mona Lisa. But the image is misleading as to the actual nature of cultures, for even those so-called primitive cultures once thought to be immune to revision are in fact open to evolution and influence, with results that are as often exciting as dispiriting. A style would be a better model than an individual artwork, for a style is subject to such changes and, so long as it is under the control of its practitioners rather than of others, these changes may reflect growth rather than loss of vitality. The difficulty is that a style is not so readily individuated as an artwork, and nor is a culture, when it is construed as something of value to be preserved. As we discovered in the earlier discussion about a national literary culture, it is not easy to see how to identify a culture except as the focus of its participants' commitment. But that suggests a very different conception of a culture's value from the one presented in the argument considered here, and it is a conception to which we shall shortly return. It is, what is worse, a conception which accepts, as this argument cannot, that some cultures are *not* valuable in themselves: Perhaps, like bad artworks, they are even vicious.

These difficulties also affect an argument from the value of cultural diversity. One defense of nationalism, against the claims of an ethical universalism which sees no reason why states should correspond to particular cultures so long as they are just, is the view that "there is, in historical reality, an irreducible diversity of worthwhile ways of life, each with its own virtues and excellencies, and to any of which a reasonable and specific allegiance may be owed."[23] This may be asserted simply as a brute fact which political arrangements have to respect, in which case the *protection* of a culture is not the point and an aptness rather than an entitlement argument is being advanced. But it may also be seen as a fact to welcome and embrace. If so, the reason may be, in a liberal vein, that cultural diversity displays the range of possibilities available to an individual in choosing a way of life. Choice itself would be restricted if that range were diminished, and cultures need separate statehood to protect it. Diversity is intrinsically worthwhile and deserving protection just because choice is. This argument unrealistically assumes the openness of cultures and their amenability to choice, which we have already had reason to question. Yet it is not the only, or even the best, argument from diversity. Indeed, one might query whether it treats that diversity as genuinely valuable in itself rather than instrumentally valuable. A different tack is to regard cultural diversity as worthwhile simply because the exhibition of diversely conceived ways of living is valuable. It has the same sort of value as the diversity of plant and animal life. We are diminished by its reduction in a way not susceptible to further explication.[24] Yet we do destroy some species where they threaten us; and so, it might be argued, diversity, valuable as it is, must take second place to other values in the world—peace, security, and so forth. No national right to statehood can be conceded irrespective of the character of the culture that statehood would foster.

One is hard-pressed to see how the third argument in the present category can escape this criticism either. It is the instrumental argument that
cultures are valuable because of the benefits they bring to their members.
Whereas the preceding two arguments should be regarded as societal,
since they take the nation to be constituted by culturally mediated relationships, this instrumental argument is not; however, as indicated earlier, the distinction between a culture as providing benefits and a community as doing so is not religiously maintained.[25] The instrumental case can
be quite straightforward: "[I]n the last analysis, a sane nationalism is to be
justified by a utilitarian argument—that most men and women are happy
only when their way of life prolongs customs and habits which are familiar to them."[26] Here the "customs and habits" of a culture are regarded as
worth protecting because they contribute to human happiness. As in the
more restricted argument from language culture considered earlier, people feel at home in them and are uneasy when they change. Yet this is true
at many levels—local, professional, domestic, and so forth: Why should
supposedly *national* cultures be privileged by special protection?

One response is to argue that we identify with our national culture
more than with others.[27] In part, the reason is that our membership of the
culture is "a matter of belonging and not of accomplishment." Such invol-
untary membership is a more secure anchorage for self-identification, and
"secure identification at that level is particularly important to one's well-
being."[28] This version of the argument implies an identity-constituting
version of nationalism. To lack a nation-state is for one's identity itself to
be imperiled by lack of protection for the culture which helps to constitute it. Yet even if this is so, it is not clear that to have the identity constituted by some cultures is better than to lack a secure identity at all: Root-
lessness, which is after all the fate of many, may be better than roots
anchored in a toxic soil. Nor is it easy to see how to construct a utilitarian
argument to the effect that, despite such cases, it is to the general good
that certain cultural identities should be given the protection of statehood, unless it is an aptness argument of the kind we shall be coming to.

Cultural Rights

It has been a constant refrain in the preceding section that not all cultures
merit the protection of statehood and, therefore, that culture cannot sustain a national right to it. An obvious and impatient response is to assert
that people have *rights* from which their right to statehood flows, and
whose exercise is not to be hindered by moralists and cultural imperialists treading in the footsteps of Mill. Arguments for statehood based on
the need to protect cultural rights exploit this reaction. I shall look at three
of them. The first is that people have a right to the conditions for a good

life, of which their cultural membership is one: "[W]e should treat access to one's culture as something which people can be expected to want" and, therefore, as "something to which one is reasonably entitled."[29] This point can be argued on a contextualist view of culture, but it is defensible independent of it—if, for example, we doubt whether the sharp divide between language and value culture which contextualism requires can be sustained.[30] We can regard people's attachment to their own culture as a brute fact and, thereby, as something which generates a right, just as the rights to family life, for example, might be thought to be generated. A right to statehood may now be derived as a right to the political arrangements needed to protect the cultural membership one has a right to enjoy.

With this argument we encounter again the problem of how to identify *which* culture it is that must be protected by statehood. But even after setting it aside, we still have the problem of justifying the claim that there should be a right to political structures which reflect and safeguard cultural membership. One suggestion is that such structures are needed because culture requires public expression—in, for example, "the architecture of public buildings; the pattern of a landscape; the content of education; the character of television and film."[31] These things are under political control, and could be used for the suppression of a culture rather than for its expression, unless under the control of the culture's own state. Yet exactly analogous points could be made about a specifically religious culture. It would be far less appealing to cite them as reasons for a theocratic state. The reason is evident: We should fear the imposition of a religious culture from which some individuals might wish to dissociate themselves. The case is the same for cultural membership more generally: If the right to membership of a given culture is an individual right, and indeed it is, then the right to nonmembership—and similar rights to public expression of one's position—must be conceded also. But this condition would place limits on the extent to which a state can reflect a given culture, thereby undercutting its adherent's argument for separate statehood rather than for, say, a role within a multicultural state.

A second argument[32] starts with a rather different individual right— namely, the right to respect as a person, which allegedly requires respect for cultural membership by virtue of its contribution to personhood. Respect for people's cultural membership demands the acknowledgment of their rights to political arrangements for protecting and expressing it, including statehood. Yet respect for personhood does not *entail* respect for cultural membership unless one is a person only through one's cultural identity. This, it has been held, is the German view—"I am essentially a German, and I am a man through my being a German"—whereas "on the French side, I am a man by nature and a Frenchman by accident."[33] It is a view, in other words, which reflects an aspect of some cultures and not others and has to do in part with their differential ranking of values. But in that case it cannot coherently be used to defend statehood for cultures which reject it and, hence, cannot be used as a general defense of statehood for cultural nations. Even if this objection could be overcome, the second step in the argument would be open to criticism, for it is not clear that respect for cultures demands *political* recognition.[34] Here it is important not to confuse demands for expression, such as we encountered in the preceding argument and which have nothing essentially to do with personhood, with demands for recognition which do. For it is as something of value that persons are entitled to respect, and recognition of what it is that makes them the persons they are is a way of showing respect. Yet though people may be entitled to respect by virtue of their cultural membership, it does not follow that they are entitled to any specific *form* of respect—for example, the granting of statehood. All that ought to be claimed is that whatever form of respect should be shown should be shown equally. It would follow that, if some cultural groups are granted statehood, others should be given it, assuming that the former were properly allowed it in respect of their culture. But this is what is in question. I conclude that an argument from respect is ineffective.

Both of the foregoing arguments concern the rights of individuals, not of a group characterized by its culture. A further argument starts with the rights of such a group and is, in some other respects, similar to the preceding argument. It is that a cultural group has a right to self-realization, which in turn requires political independence.[35] Self-realization involves the application of a culture to the activities of modern life—technological, economic, and so forth—without which it will become impoverished, losing its expressive power and becoming unsatisfying to the individuals who identify themselves in terms of it. Political independence can both help to prevent this and, in itself, open an avenue to cultural self-realization within the political sphere. Failure to grant political recognition demeans the culture and its members. It is, however, the group which has the right to it; and individuals are harmed, not wronged, by its refusal, since their identities presuppose the existence of the group. If the group is to be thought of as a community, then the argument is a societal one.

Does this make it immune from the criticisms leveled at the preceding argument? I do not know that it does. The idea of self-realization is an aspect of Romanticism[36] and, in particular, of the German Romanticism which J. G. von Herder represents. The subsequent development of this idea in Germany, although it distorts Herder, is not encouraging. But is there any principled reason to object to it *as* a development of the idea of self-realization? There would be only if we had an independent understanding of what self-realization meant—an understanding which was external to a culture and which could impose limits on what was a proper cultural expression and what was not. I do not think we do. What counts as the self-realization of a particular culture depends, I suggest, on the culture itself. Misguided as he may have been, de Valera did not see that the self-realization of a Gaelic Irish culture required adaptation to technological and commercial developments: It required instead a check on them. Similarly, there is no reason why a cultural group should not view political independence as inessential to its self-realization,[37] nor, less comfortingly, why it should not embark on an imperial self-realization. In short, cultural self-realization does not produce any obvious criterion for national statehood.

It is worth noting that the first and third of these arguments from the rights of individuals and groups support a right of independent statehood via a claim to *self*-government. So does the argument, considered at the end of the last chapter, which invokes the right of a cultural group to control its own culture. The argument from the right to respect, however, does not. Political recognition of cultural identity is all that is required by this argument, and this recognition could be accomplished through being governed independently but by others. Control of one's own culture obviously requires self-government, whereas it is hard to see how independent statehood could conduce to cultural expression or self-realization unless it was under the control of the cultural group.[38] Self-government is here, as in some other nationalist arguments, a reason for independence rather than the substance of a separate claim. But in that case, one must be thinking of the nation as the kind of group which *can* exercise control over its culture, whether as a cultural association or whatever. As such, it would be required to have a conception of its cultural identity as well as mere cultural distinctiveness. It is these conceptions, if anything, which must serve to resolve problems of the individuation of cultures, although, as we have seen, there is no principled reason to expect such self-identifications to avoid conflicting claims.

The entitlement arguments we have considered may not themselves succeed in establishing rights to statehood. It could be maintained, however, that in conjunction with aptness considerations they do so, or even that aptness considerations alone secure the desired conclusion. Here the argument is that those who share a state must normally share the same laws. But sharing the same laws is practicable, it is further claimed, only if the people to whom they are applied have basically the same value culture. So a group with a shared value culture is apt for statehood, and other aggregations of people are not. This argument has some force, but not enough to secure its conclusion, understood in a non-question-begging sense. There are areas, notoriously that of sexual morality, in which legislation is difficult if it is to apply to groups with diverse cultural attitudes. While the liberal attempt to minimize legislation in such circumstances can go some way toward reducing the problem, it is unlikely to remove it completely in, for example, the regulation of family responsibilities. But this difficulty would show at most that in those areas where legislation is necessary some correspondence between the values of cultural groups is required, not that a common culture is. Indeed, it may be suggested that where there is a common culture with firmly entrenched values the legal framework of a state is not necessary, for, conversely, "[t]he evidence . . . suggests that cultural and economic heterogeneity is associated with a state-like political structure. Centralised authority and an administrative organisation seem to be necessary to accommodate culturally diverse groups within a single political system."[39] Or so it seems to anthropologists writing about the formation of polities in Africa and drawing conclusions which are the opposite of those required by the aptness argument I have presented.

A weaker aptness argument claims, not that all those within the same state may need to have the same values, but that those with radically different values cannot share the same state. Claims of this sort have often been the basis for demands for independent statehood, as, for example, in Mohammed Ali Jinnah's case for a Pakistan independent of India:

> It is a dream that Hindus and Muslims can ever evolve a common nationality. . . . Hindus and Muslims have two different religious philosophies, social customs, literatures. They neither intermarry, nor even interdine. Indeed they belong to different civilisations which are based mainly on conflicting ideas and conceptions. . . . The Muslims are not a minority as the word is commonly understood. . . . Muslims are a nation according to any definition of the term, and they must have their homelands, their territory and their state.[40]

The argument here is that conflicting values inevitably lead to conflict, which will make the social cohesion required for shared statehood impossible. Suppose that in this case it were true. The difficulty is in generalizing the point to enable us to individuate nations. The criterion implied seems to be that of whether a group has a value system which conflicts with the value system of others to the extent of ruling out social intercourse with them. But first, it is quite unclear that the world can be divided up into such groups, each of which is apt for separate statehood; and second, it is arguable that only something less than the sort of social intercourse envisaged by Jinnah is required for shared statehood. At most, Jinnah's argument establishes that, in the particular circumstances where the allocation of statehood is in question, possible conflicts of value should be considered. This is well short of providing a criterion for a national right to statehood.

There is a very general difficulty with all these arguments for separate statehood from the existence of different value cultures. What supposedly

makes separate statehood necessary also makes it impossible to demarcate. In the absence of a system of clearly bounded value cultures, each of
which exhibits a pluralistic tolerance of the others, there is no way of arbi-
trating between competing claims to statehood. Thus liberal values, as we
have seen earlier, lay down different criteria of nationhood from those of,
for example, Muslim nationalists. But an adequate nationalist theory
must provide uniform criteria for justifiable statehood which can resolve
conflicts. The versions of value culture nationalism we have so far investigated signally fail to do so.

The Value of Community

In order to pick out a group as a nation by the criterion of a common culture, we should need to be able to identify distinct cultural systems. That,
I have argued, is not always possible, nor is it necessary if the requirements of shared statehood are to be fulfilled; at most, *some* shared values
may be necessary to achieve this end. Yet in order to qualify for a right to
statehood, a group must have values of a sort which make it desirable for
the group to enjoy statehood. On the face of it, this requirement rules out
any cultural case for national statehood, since whether a group happens
to have values of a sort suitable for statehood does not seem to characterize it as a group of a certain kind. But national rights, I have argued, are
rights that a group has by virtue of the kind of group it is, not by virtue of
what is desirable for it in the circumstances it is in. And these circumstances might arguably be that the group has, at a certain time, values of a
sort that should be fostered. This consideration would provide a way to
allocate states to groups—indeed, considerations of the same sort played
a part in decolonialization—but it would not be a way of allocating them
to nations.

Suppose, however, that we were able to identify kinds of groups in accordance with their values, so that it was desirable that all groups of a certain normative kind had statehood. Then, since the values that qualify
them for statehood are the same, we would not be able to differentiate
groups through their distinctive values as under the type of value culture
nationalism we have so far considered. We shall need some other criterion, but a criterion which, together with the required values, may yield a
case for national statehood. In order to see how to construct such a case,
we may remind ourselves of the ambiguity of the phrase "the particular
way of life" of a group, which has been offered as a definition of culture.[41]
The ambiguity is that between the particular *manner* in which a life is
lived and the particular *life* that is lived in that manner. Groups can agree
in terms of their manner of life and yet be leading different lives, as I suggested in discussing economic criteria for nationhood. Let us suppose

that we can individuate groups leading common lives. Now we can distinguish some ways in which these common lives are lived from others, and we can do so on the basis of the values they incorporate. The view to be considered is that there are kinds of groups distinguished from non-national groups by the values that make their common lives worthwhile—that is, by the sort of culture they have. On this view it will, of course, be possible for there to be separate nations that have the same values but incorporate them into separate common lives. Nationalism of this type will be essentially societal.

What sort of culture might constitute nations in this way? There is, I think, a nationalist tradition[42] which sees it as involving a number of features necessary to the group constituting a community in the way that it does and contributing to the desirability of such a community, so that the right to statehood flows from the advantages of fostering it politically. First, it is a community in which there is a common purpose: the good of the community as a whole. Second, this purpose is determined by the group as a whole. Third, there is a formal equality between the members of the group in respect of their contribution to, determination of, and benefit from the common purpose. Three sorts of value characterize these features: first, concord and cooperation as against strife and competition; second, trust and solidarity as against suspicion and divisiveness; and third, fairness and equality as against exploitation and oppression. These values are, I suggest, essential to all nationalist thinking, since they provide a normative framework to membership of the nation and an ethical motivation for the national obligations which attend it. The assumption is that a community which incorporates them is better than one which does not—that it is better than one which lacks a common purpose and is inherently conflictual, which has a purpose determined sectionally and is riven by factionalism, or which systematically treats some members worse than others. It is the ethical preferability of the national community which grounds its right to statehood.

Two points of clarification are required here. First, since the nation is a kind of group, the incorporation of these values must be essential to what binds its members together into a community, not merely an accidental feature of a community at a given time. This requirement will allow for the falling away of the community from the realization of its constitutive values in some circumstances, so long as it aims at and is capable of realizing them by virtue of being the kind of community it is. The second point to observe is that the values attributed to a national community can be realized in many different styles, depending upon how it chooses to pursue its purposes. The need for this choice to be made by the group as a whole, for example, does not demand democratic procedures but, rather, only some method, plausible within the other criteria of nationhood which are operative, for determining the national will as against a sectional one. Nor does the required equality need to be social or economic, so long as each member of the nation, *qua* member, enjoys the same treatment, the same rights, the same obligations, and so forth. Yet these considerations are enough to rule out many communities from qualifying as nations.

Now it is evident that some shared cultural resources will be needed to realize these values, though not so many as to prevent what are recognizably different cultures from forming part of the same nation, because their members play their part in the same community constituted by these values. This kind of value-based nationalism can, in other words, be multicultural. Nor should the different styles in which the values are realized incline us to detect different cultures for different communities. For one thing, the style may change (especially when a community has its own state) in the absence of anything we would want to call an underlying cultural change. For another, the different styles are often part of an international repertoire which has little to do with home-grown cultures, despite the rhetorical attempts of nationalist politicians to make such connections.[43] The sharing of the cultural resources supposedly required by multicultural nationhood can be accomplished in various ways. Possession of a common *political* culture is obviously an important example, and civic nationalism is sometimes motivated by the thought that such a culture is necessary for multicultural nationhood. But other ways include communities within which different cultural groups form a *system*, each with its allotted place, but with a common agenda. It appears that the Hutu and the Tutsi, with their different agricultural and pastoral functions, formed just such a system prior to its deformation by Belgian colonialism. And other less systematic ways of achieving cultural harmonization are possible—for example, through a public culture of multiculturalism! There is no reason to suppose that such harmony is not possible at a given place and time just because people, perhaps misled by cultural nationalism, do not think that it is; though, on the other hand, evidence is needed that it *is* possible.

How are we to assess this kind of nationalism, which we might fairly, I think, call *communitarian nationalism?*[44] It cannot, as I said, get by with only a claim to a common national culture of the required type: Indeed, it needs a further criterion to determine the scope of the community incorporating this culture, and that, as we have seen, may not be easy to come by. But suppose it can be provided; what then? In this case, two kinds of criticism might be entertained. One is a moral one which, crucial as it is, raises too many general ethical questions to tackle here in any detail.[45] It is that, though national communities as characterized may be more desirable than those with which they are contrasted, they are, for all that, not desirable enough to ground a right to statehood. Two basic types of reason might be offered for this position. The first is that the values of nationalism are themselves too limited: Equality within the nation, for example, is too restricted an ethical goal by comparison with equality for all humankind. Political cosmopolitanism is to be preferred to nationalism because moral universalism is to be preferred to particularism. The second is that the benefits of the nation-state are outweighed by its disadvantages: External wars, for instance, are not worth the price of internal harmony. The explanation may be that the realization of nationalist values in a state inevitably gives rise to countervailing moral dangers—perhaps because these values are in themselves too beguiling to generate a balanced moral consciousness if overemphasized institutionally, or because they do not impose sufficient constraints upon a state for it to avoid moral horrors. Both possibilities are interesting, though insufficiently explored.[46]

The other kind of criticism of communitarian nationalism involves the claim, not that the alleged national community is less desirable than it seems on the face of it, but that it is not even possible. The values postulated for the national character may be aimed at, but their pursuit is delusory, for a community which realizes them is not attainable, or is not attainable in the form required by the criteria for constituting a community which the nationalist offers. There is both a pessimistic and an optimistic version of this criticism. The pessimistic one holds that social relationships, or at least relationships wider in scope than those of face-to-face groups, are inevitably competitive, divisive, and exploitative, as individuals and shifting groups pursue their own interests. States must be organized, then, in a way that recognizes this fact, not in a way that involves moral motivations which cannot be securely relied upon. This, I take it, is the classic objection to nationalism from the libertarian Right. The optimistic version holds that morally motivated social relationships of the required kind are possible, but that the criteria offered for individuating a single community do not pick out an environment in which such relationships can exist. In particular, it might be claimed, the pursuit of a common good does not do so, since the consequential relationships whose scope bounds the community are limited by considerations of self-interest incompatible with moral motivations. Values of the kind that the nationalist invokes are attainable only if such considerations are transcended. This is one way of expressing the classic Marxist objection to nationalism, which has, as one of its premises, that socialism in one country is impossible.

I have, for reasons of symmetry, awkwardly and perhaps distortedly expressed the Marxist criticism in an unhistorical way, in that I make no mention of the particular form of economic relationships—namely, capitalist ones—which characterize the world of the modern state to which a right is claimed. But this criticism implies the fortuitousness of the scope of communities on the criteria offered, their dependence upon changing circumstance, which is incompatible with a nationalist picture of relatively enduring national communities. If they really are constituted by the incorporation of certain values, then such an incorporation must not, I insisted, be an accidental and ephemeral feature: It must have to do with what makes them the same throughout history. In the next section we shall investigate the historical requirements of nationhood; but to conclude this one we might note an objection, not to communitarian nationalism as such, but to its applicability at the present stage of world history.

The objection is one I touched on in discussing economic nationalism. It is that there might once have been nations in the communitarian nationalist sense—bounded communities incorporating nationalist values—but that now there are not and cannot be. For one thing, mentioned earlier, the globalization of economic relations prevents communities from being individuated by their economic bounds, and no others to take their place have emerged. But for another, in an era of world capitalism, large-scale social relationships within states cannot be constituted by such values as cooperation, solidarity, and equality, except in special circumstances—for example, where a whole group is persecuted and has to resist. The conditions for nationhood are therefore lacking. Even if the communitarian nationalist case for statehood is a good one, it lacks a contemporary application to any putatively national group. There is, I believe, sufficient force in this objection to shift the onus of proof upon advocates of nationalism. One move they may make is to represent contemporary obstacles to the realization of nationalist values as merely transient factors affecting groups whose persistence through time is characterized by their incorporation of these values. History is employed to embalm the nation against disintegration and oblivion. In de Valera's "dream" speech, three thousand years of it is deemed adequate proof against the ravages of modernity in Ireland. But what can history really do for nationalists?

Summary

In contrast to the language culture dealt with in the previous chapter, I have here discussed value culture—a culture identified in terms of distinctive values—as what is constitutive of nationhood. I consider four types of argument for a right to statehood on the basis of a group's possession of its own value culture. The first seeks to preserve the values enshrined *in* that culture; the second, to preserve the value *of* it. Both are susceptible to the criticism that the relevant values may not be worth preserving. They are incidental to particular groups, not definitive of a kind of group with a right to statehood. The third type of argument responds to such criticism by asserting a right to statehood in order to preserve cultural *rights;* but none of its various versions seems to secure the desired conclusion. The fourth type sidesteps the criticism by declaring that only those groups with shared values *can* enjoy shared statehood successfully, Yet this contention is both doubtful and inadequate.

The chapter therefore concludes by examining not distinctive values but values common to all putative national communities, distinguished from each other by their separate national lives. Such communitarian nationalism, as we may call it, is intellectually and ethically attractive. However, it founders, I suggest, on the conditions of contemporary life. Perhaps communities of the sort characterized would have a good claim to statehood if they existed; but arguably they do not.

Chapter Nine

History and Destiny

"A Tradition National"

"It is generally said that a common history and tradition, a common sense of the past, is one of the essential ingredients of successful nationalism. If that were true, the new United States would have been in a bad fix, for she had very little history of her own."[1] Nations need histories, but why do they need them and what will suffice as a national history? The authors of the preceding passage go on to cite various ways in which the American requirement was met—that is, by reference to (1) a comparison of the Founding Fathers to Romulus and Remus or Hengist and Horsa; (2) the evocation of Inca and Aztec civilizations; (3) the history of the struggle among Spain, France, and England for North America; (4) Longfellow's *Hiawatha*; and (5) Nathaniel Hawthorne's novels of Puritan New England. But these are very different sorts of history and seem to answer to very different needs. Such variety is not surprising since, as we shall see, history plays a different role in different kinds of nationalism, however intermingled these may be in actual practice.

The most important role for history is to help individuate nations. On some accounts, for example, it is not just that the members of a nation have some feature which distinguishes them from others and which is thought to be crucial. It is that they have continued to possess the same feature as their predecessors in membership. This can hold true of many features—language, customs, character, or whatever. The history of a nation supposedly constituted by them is simply the record of their continuance. It is to be discovered as evidence of nationhood, but nationhood is independent of the knowledge of or belief in it. This is the typical use of history in realistically conceived nonsocietal nationalisms. History *adds* nothing to the criterion of nationhood offered; it merely guarantees its long-term application through processes of transmission appropriate to the feature in question. A different case is represented by descent. "The kernel of the historical awareness of the Baltic peoples," writes one historian, "is the fact that they are directly descended from the original inhabitants of these countries."[2] What allegedly makes people a nation here is a supposed history of unmixed descent from the earliest indigonous occu pants. Having such a history is criterial of membership—in this case, in order to distinguish the Baltic peoples from others, principally Germans and Russians, who also occupied the Baltic lands from medieval times. Their different history is precisely what disqualifies them. But history plays an uncomplicated role of transmitting qualifying features from one time-slice of a nation to the next.

It is not a history in this sense that the Latvians were said to lack by an eighteenth-century Baltic German observer: "Those who know our 'nationals' have long since lost all hope for the Latvian people. It is a still-born nation. The Latvians have no national past and no history, they cannot have a future."[3] What history is, in the rich sense intended, we shall come to in a moment. But might not the Latvians have demurred at these comments and replied that they had a history precisely of occupation, and of the cultural oppression such comments confidently voice? This is, we might say, a history of a people's experience, and a history of the experience to which people are fated—shared and communicated between them—makes of them "a community of fate," in the words of the Austro-Marxist Otto Bauer.[4] On Bauer's conception, the nation is "a community of character"—that is, a culturally interactive group of people with shared characteristics bound together into it by their community of fate. History explains the features which distinguish members of the nation from others; yet it explains them not just by furnishing a set of common causes but also by furnishing causes which members of a nation can recognize as common because they are able to share their reactions to them with each other. This is a much more complex role for history to perform than the mere transmission of national features. History is something which a people confront together and which thereby shapes them, but it is still not something they need have any sense of *as* history, rather than as the particular temporal circumstances whose succession is history.

Bauer's view is a realist but societal one. A nation is identified through the relationships of its members—in particular, their communicative relationships made possible by a common language culture. Yet these communicative relationships are not themselves sufficient for nationhood. They must be employed in the formation of the shared reactions to experience which make the group a community of fate. These reactions manifest themselves in a "community of cultural tradition,"[5] which contributes to producing a national character. But such "inherited qualities" of the nation "are nothing other than the sedimentation of its past, its *history frozen*, so to speak."[6] Bauer expressed his theory in terms of a chain of causes, which seems to leave unclear which factors are crucial in the individuation of nations. Is it, for example, the difference between their national characters that distinguishes the Irish from the English, or the difference between the histories which shaped these characters? The answer should perhaps be that only what is a reaction to historical experiences counts as a national characteristic and only what brings into play national characteristics is national history. A nation is a group whose members are repeatedly placed in the same circumstances as one another, and who are able to recognize and respond to these circumstances as the same, through their capacity for communication with one another. Bauer would have seen this response as essentially involving the formation or actuation of social relationships within the group and, in this way, as a collective response.

History appears to function here as a test of the *reality* of putative nations. What makes certain culturally mediated relationships constitutive of a national community is that they are themselves shaped collectively in response to historical circumstances which, taken together, form the group's history. By this criterion some groups will really be national, and others will not because their relationships are not shaped in the right way or not shaped in response to the right train of events. The two requirements go together; for only a group that can respond collectively has a history, and only a group whose members are subjected to the same sequence of experiences can respond collectively to it. What counts as the history of a group, furthermore, is what is sedimented in the national character which such collective responses produce, and which, in its turn, fashions a collective response. A nation is a *kind* of group because of its members' national character, but this is only a reflection of the group's response to changing circumstances.

Bauer's theory is a complex and suggestive one, although one is indeed hard-pressed to distinguish causal from constitutive factors in it in a way that makes clear how it is to be applied in practice so as to individuate nations. Yet its basic premise is simple and compelling: A nation's history is what befalls and leaves a mark on it, and only a group with a history in this sense can be a nation. Bauer tacitly acknowledged, however, that having such a history does not entitle a group to statehood. He told a story to explain "why people find it natural and sensible that each nation and always only one nation should form a political polity"[7] in classic Marxist terms, which do indeed draw on the aptness of putative national groups for fixing state boundaries. But he also defended the multinational Austrian state of his day against nationalist attacks. One might add that, since it is a common language culture which is needed for history to make a nation of a people, it is unclear that Bauer's theory can escape the weaknesses of the language culture criterion noted earlier. In particular, it is not clear that his historical realism can escape social constructionist criticisms. What is more, the community that constitutes the nation is not necessarily, so far as one can see, a community with a common good. It therefore cannot benefit from the ethical advantages of such a community in arguments for statehood.

There are two ways in which Bauer's conception of history might be enriched, and these, if desired, can be combined. The first is to make a nation's history a history of what it *does* rather than of what befalls it. It is in this sense, I suspect, that Baltic Germans viewed the Latvians as lacking a history. But to have a history of action, two things are necessary: first, a corporate organization capable of initiating action and, second, continuity in this organization. By this criterion, it is through their participation in the collective actions initiated by such an organization that people at different times count as members of the same nation. The Zulus, for example,[8] are commonly distinguished as a nation from the other Bantu people of South Africa by the fact that their successive clan leaders succeeded in conducting a series of military campaigns against other indigenous groups, rebellions against colonial rule, and so on. While the Zulu clan itself originally totaled only a few hundred, those who were subsequently identified and came to identify themselves as Zulus numbered in the hundreds of thousands. Their supposed national identity depended not on descent, whatever their pretensions to it, but on involvement in a history of collective action. Some version of political nationalism is, despite appearances to the contrary, required to support the claims to statehood based on such a history[9]—claims which quite recently nearly wrecked the peaceful achievement of majority rule in South Africa.

A history of action is likely to be made part of a history richer in a second way than on Bauer's conception—namely, in being a temporal sequence of events such that the group is in some sense conscious of some past members of the sequence. We can distinguish here between an episodic and a serial consciousness—between a grasp of episodes in the past and a grasp of them as forming a series; and this is important in connection with another distinction—that between a collective and an individual awareness of the past. If only collective awareness is required, then a group may be said to have a history if its present cultural productions bear, and are taken to bear, the traces of times past. Such productions incorporate what one might call a folk memory of the group's past. A host of customs, traditions, turns of phrase, place-names, folk songs, and stories point back to a past, grasped indistinctly and disjointedly. English mothers who teach their children

Old King Cole was a merry old soul and a merry old soul was he.
He called for his pipe and he called for his bowl and he called for his fiddlers three.

have no sense of anachronism in thus speaking of Coel Hen, the accred-
ited ancestor of the Welsh kings and possibly a Roman governor of the
northern legions in Britain. Individually they need have no knowledge of
this personage in order to recite the verse, which reaches back into their
country's ancient past. But historical consciousness of this sort is episodic
only; no connected narrative can be spun out of the disparate cultural materials that make up a collective consciousness of the nation.

Folk memory, as I have characterized it, is genuine memory, for it bears
traces of the past. Invented traditions and baseless legends do not count.
Folk memory may suffice to underpin the identity over time of a supposed nation. It can scarcely suffice to individuate one. The cultural productions we employ incorporate too many folk memories from too many
diverse sources for that. Coel Hen, as we noted, has given rise to folk
memories of both the English and the Welsh, although these are taken to
be distinct nations. Perhaps he was a Roman, though classical forebears
play no role in current conceptions of Welsh or Englishness.[10] It was not
always thus.

> Books may be burn'd, and Monuments may lie
> Demolished, thy works and mine may die:
> But a Tradition National, alive
> While is that Nation, will in force survive.[11]

So wrote a Welsh epigrammatist on the historical tradition attesting that
Brutus, great grandson of Aeneas, founder of Rome, was the first king of
the British people. That tradition seems no longer to be a living part of either Welsh or English history. Memories may also die, but the identities of
nations cannot be made contingent upon them. History must yield a
greater determinacy if it is to individuate nations.

In fact, the same problem arises if we turn from collective to individual
awareness of the past. There are simply too many ways of telling the
story. Yet a serial consciousness may be formed precisely to individuate a
nation, to tell a story which includes the events in *its* history and which
excludes those in another's. But the facts seldom or never determine what
is to be included and what excluded. They leave room for choice and con-
sequently for contestation. Russians trace their history back through Rus,
the medieval polity that was centered on Kiev. But Kiev is in the Ukraine,
thus making a clear distinction between Russians and Ukrainians impossible on this narration—a narration which must be rejected by Ukrainians
who wish to emphasize their difference from the Russians.[12] Similar difficulties attend the distinction between Polish and Lithuanian identities in
view of the union of these peoples in the medieval Grand Duchy.[13] Historical facts cannot serve to individuate them in accordance with realist

principles. Rather, a history is constructed in order to individuate them, although facts evidently constrain their individuation.

Yet the construction of a history may not be intended principally to individuate a nation. It may be consequential upon an individuation already made, which in itself may depend upon other choices—though the fact that choices are being made may, of course, be hidden, even from those making them. Whether the English, for example, are to think of themselves as the descendants of Anglo-Saxon invaders or as successors to the British inhabitants depends upon choices about the nature of English identity. Which history is told depends upon the criterion that is currently being used to individuate the English, with repercussions for who is to be included now and who is not. In such cases, history follows the individuation of nations by other means. But why should we care who were included at some previous time by our preferred criterion?

Here a history of action is particularly important.

> The nation, like the individual, is the fruit of a long past spent in toil, sacrifice and devotion. Ancestor worship is of all forms the most justifiable, since our ancestors have made us what we are. A heroic past, great men and glory—I mean real glory—these should be the capital of our company when we come to found a national idea. To share the glories of the past, and a common will in the present; to have done great deeds together, and to desire to do more—these are the essential conditions of a people's being.[14]

In this passage, Ernest Renan links his voluntarist conception of the nation to its history. Evidently history cannot determine what the nation constituted voluntaristically shall be. But it can tell prospective members what they are joining and why they should. That the history is constructed is of no account, for what they join is determined by the members. They decide what the nation should be regarded as having done, just as they decide what it should do. They decide the former on the basis of the latter. What looks like the continuation of a predetermined pattern is the finding of a pattern in the past that fits the intentions of the present.

What is an essential part of voluntarism, however, is also a possible aspect of other nationalisms. We care about who in the past were included in the nation which our particular nationalism identifies because we want to know what they have done and, thus, what we might do. But here facts may constrain some nationalisms more than they need trouble voluntarism. The "heroic past" may be viewed realistically as something given and as thereby setting an agenda which the nation cannot simply decide to shirk: "Because our forebears have toiled and spilt their blood to build and defend the nation, we who are born into it inherit an obligation to continue their work, which we discharge partly towards our contemporaries and partly towards our descendants."[15] This idea, which may be presented as a mere gloss on the historical continuity of the nation, in fact represents a very specific conception of it—one in which the past is important in providing a content for the national obligations of the present. It is clear that if this is the point of a national history, then debates about it are equally debates about what these obligations are. That this is an entirely optional view of nationalism can be seen from the fact that one can take a different view of national obligations. It might be thought, for example, that a grasp of what these are springs naturally from the possession of the national character, shaped perhaps by history, so that *reflection* upon history is unnecessary; or that these obligations are discovered from reflection upon the present interests of the national community or upon its values or whatever. Certain sorts of nationalism can quite easily dispense with this use of history; others will typically turn to it. Indeed, such a use cannot be necessary to the generation of national obligations, for some putative nations lack the kind of history required for it.

National Myths

The Latvians, with no history of political organization, lacked a history of action too. This is, no doubt, what Baltic German denials of their historicity referred to. It is in the absence of such a history, it has been suggested, that Latvians resorted to myth. In 1888 Andrejs Pumpurs produced the epic *Lacplesis*, derived from folk stories but incorporating historical events relating to the early history of Latvia.[16] One hundred years later, as pressure for independence from the Soviet Union mounted, it was turned into a rock opera. Lacplesis himself, literally "Bear Tearer," is a figure of heroic strength and courage, but a quite unbelievable one. His mother is a bear and as a result he is born with bear's ears, an embarrassment in a national hero that came to be disguised by earmuffs in modern representations. What, we may ask, is the point of a myth of this kind, and how does it differ from national history?

The question is important, since it is commonly noticed that national histories retain not only an *optional* understanding of the past but an erroneous one as well. "To forget and—I will venture to say—to get one's history wrong," wrote Renan famously, "are essential factors in the making of a nation."[17] But surely, it will be replied, this fact fatally undermines the claims of nations based upon such history. Is it not as if myths of origin such as the Lacplesis epic were taken seriously? And worse; for the obliviousness and error of which Renan wrote are known or suspected by nationalists. Must we not agree with García Lorca in despising "the man who sacrifices himself for an abstract nationalist idea only to love his country with a bandage over his eyes"?[18]

Whether national history needs to be true depends on what use is made of it, and this in turn depends upon the kind of nationalism that is employing this history. It is not in general true that "historical accuracy is not important from the point of view of constituting the nation."[19] If a nation is conceived of as constituted by descent, for example, then the historical story of descent must be true. But history must also be true on an account which individuates a nation by the character of its members and identifies that character as national because of the history which has shaped it. Causal processes must be real to have real effects. Similarly, where a nation is individuated by the origins and continuity of its cultural productions, rather than by their current character, the history provided for them must be true. And it must be true, too, where a criterion of continuous collective action is employed. No doubt other cases could be produced to illustrate this general point: Facts about the past can be constitutive or partly constitutive of nationhood on some conceptions of it. Yet in none of the cases mentioned do members of the nation need an individual consciousness of that history. If it were needed, must this history be true?

Again, we have to consider the history which is regarded as individuating a nation, as it might be on certain culturalist conceptions. It might, for example, be held that it is language *and* history which individuate national groups, perhaps because language alone is insufficient in light of the existence of groups speaking the same language but with distinct histories.[20] Each group's history may then be held to be part of a common culture which binds its members together into a group with a shared understanding of their situation. It is not immediately obvious why, on this contextualist account of historical culture, truth should be important, any more than, say, the classificatory systems in a language should be scientifically respectable. What must be the case is that the history is *resilient*. Confrontations with the facts must not disturb the shared story to such an extent that the group ceases to possess a common understanding. This may happen with far-fetched narratives. The long-standing history of the English as an Anglo-Saxon people, for example, has almost completely vanished as a result of nineteenth-century ethnographic criticism[21] (not to mention the embarrassment of Teutonic origins in two world wars against Germany). Little is left in its place. True histories are, other things being equal, more resilient than false ones; but whether facts do disturb false stories depends on whether their audiences have a concern for truth.

Often they do not. In the many cases when the repetition of a narrative has been undertaken precisely to reinforce a shared understanding, its factual basis is of less significance than its effect. It may be traitorous to dispute it. A national history is here treated more like an article of faith than a belief susceptible to confirmation or disconfirmation by factual evidence. It is surprising that so many recent theorists[22] consider this ritual respectable. Their defense is that such a delusive history may support valuable social relationships. This effect goes beyond the mere perpetuation of a cultural group to the sustaining of a community. Whether such a community is, other things being equal, a valuable type of community will depend upon many factors. But its reliance upon a false or even one-sided story of its past scarcely seems to be a point in its favor. This state of affairs must raise doubts about whether the relationships involved are in themselves sufficiently worthwhile for the participants to have a reason to continue in them which is independent of their false beliefs. If the false beliefs are necessary in principle[23] for the continuation of the community, then there cannot be sufficient reasons deriving from its value; whereas if they are not necessary, then they play no essential part in the community's constitution but, rather, are simply dispensable adjuncts to those features of history or whatever which supposedly do pick it out as the national community it is.

Consider next the case where the nation is to be identified voluntaristically. Is it unimportant, as Renan implied, if the history its members choose to associate themselves with is false? It might be suggested that all that matters is that the history be useful in sustaining the association. This would explain why forgetting inconvenient facts is so important. For to the extent to which members remember only stories of concord and collective action, rather than conflict and sectionalism, they will tend to act in a way that fosters concord and collectivity: The beliefs about the association derived from history will become self-confirming.[24] If we assume that the reasons for entering the association are the furthering of members' interests, then this justification of false beliefs is successful only to the extent to which the association sustained by them does serve those interests. Yet it is vulnerable to the classic Marxist suggestion that the obscuring of conflict and sectionalism works precisely to disguise the fact that there are in actuality no shared interests between all members of the putative national association. Conversely, the forgetting of, for example, common interests between Catholics and Presbyterians in eighteenth-century Ireland works to conceal the possibility of common interests in Ulster today. Indeed, it is hard to see why the facts should ever need to be disguised if action in the clear-sighted pursuit of interests is to be undertaken successfully.

We have moved from considering the role of history in individuating nations to examining its other purposes—in particular, the focusing of loyalties. Two ways in which history might work here need to be sharply distinguished.[25] First, history might fix the content of national obligations, specifying the task which we allegedly inherit. Second, it might motivate us in the performance of these obligations. The first requires that the history by which we determine our obligations should be true. We can no more incur obligations from a supposititious past than we can incur them from a fictitious relative.[26] The second, however, does not require that the national history be true. It is, though, often assumed[27] that this history must be believed if it is to influence conduct. The extent to which it must is questionable. Fictional stories of heroism on behalf of the nation may seem to have the same effect as factual ones. Probably more time is spent reading them than reading history, so that the Harmsworth Press could justifiably boast that its British comics "served as useful recruiting agencies for the armed forces."[28] If fiction can have such effects, why should not myth?

Myths used to be treated merely as false histories. This error may now be less often made, and those peoples who employ myths are seldom credited with such absurd beliefs as, for example, that bears can give birth to boys with bears' ears. Yet it is almost equally erroneous to treat false history as if it were myth, and to tolerate it as having a similar function. A myth may incorporate history, true or false, but it is precisely *not* narrated as having the status of an ordinary factual record, nor, therefore, as a self-deceiving substitute for one.

> It is not concerned so much with the succession of events as with the moral significance of situations, and is hence often allegorical or symbolic in form. It is not incapsulated, as history is, but is a re-enactment fusing present and past. It tends to be timeless, placed in thought beyond, or above, historical time; and where it is firmly placed in historical time, it is also, nevertheless, timeless in that it could have happened at any time, the archetypal not being bound to time and space.[29]

Evans-Pritchard's anthropological characterization of myth can serve us well. It brings out the affinity between myths proper, like the Lacplesis epic, and mythic uses of history—uses in which the historical character of the material is inessential and where, in consequence, its historical truth is not an issue. What is at issue is its "moral significance," its truth with respect to value.

It is easy to oversimplify the point of national myths, and to see them either merely as arousing patriotic emotions and motivating manifestations of loyalty or as setting moral examples. This is to make the point of myths look either nonrational or moralistic and hence insufficiently specific to the nation in question. When Lacplesis overcomes monsters guarding the scrolls which contain the ancient wisdom of Latvia in a castle sunk beneath a lake, he sets an example, but not an obviously moral one, nor one that is crudely inflammatory, since cool reflection is required as to what a contemporary emulation of his act might be. The landscape of the myth fixes the action firmly in Latvia and evokes feelings, by no means uncomplicated ones, of involvement in the place. But it is national values that the epic is designed to inculcate—in particular, of veneration for traditional wisdom and of the resolution required to wrest it from alien appropriation. What precisely these values are may emerge only from their mythic expression and from that pursuit of them which counts as an active understanding of the myth. This, I suggest, is the mythic use of national history. It sets before us national values that only this history can convey in their specificity and relevance to national life.

History, under this mythic conception, is necessary for a group to have the kind of worthwhile distinctiveness which generates an argument for statehood. It is a part, an indispensable part, of their value culture. This conception yields a different account of how a national history might generate obligations from that considered earlier, which detected a plan of work in the nation's actual past that needed to be continued. The mythic conception sees only the repeated, and perhaps imagined, realization of national values, which there is an obligation to realize that is no different now than it was then. This account escapes the objection[30] that the nation's work might not be worth continuing if it realizes nothing of value. That the nation's values may be contestable is a different issue.

On the mythic conception, too, a national history may be only episodic, not serial as when it supposedly follows a plan.[31] This feature differentiates its role in instantiating values from another which was touched on earlier—namely, providing members of the nation with a narrative in terms of which they can have a shared understanding of their lives. If this shared understanding is to be worthwhile, I have suggested, the narrative needs to be resilient in the face of rational criticism. And for this to be the case, a national history must be largely true and credible in the serial account of events it offers. A group with such a history has the kind of claim to state protection that language culture has.

These sorts of history can be combined, just as value and language of culture can. But there is a significant tension between them. The imperatives of myth can easily conflict with the requirements of history, as noted by the Irish nationalist poet George Russell (AE):

> *We would no Irish sign efface,*
> *But yet our lips would gladlier hail*
> *The first born of the Coming Race*
> *Than the last splendour of the Gael.*
> *No blazoned banner we unfold—*
> *One charge alone we give to youth,*
> *Against the sceptred myth to hold*
> *The golden heresy of truth.*[32]

The mythic history of Gaelic Ireland, though powerfully evocative of national values, provides too rigid a framework for an adequate understanding of contemporary communal realities; its ethical coherence is ill-suited to capture a way of life mediated by a complex mix of cultures. So long as these sorts of history are recognized for what they are and segregated, all may be well. It has been held, however, that "the serious study of Irish history" is incompatible with being "a Fenian or an Orangeman"[00]—perhaps because Fenians and Orangemen ride roughshod over the distinction. To pass off myth as narrative history, even when the myth is set in historical time, is to invite intellectual and political disaster. Yet perhaps the very notion of a national history makes this inescapable. For is a satisfactory shared understanding of peoples' lives possible within the confines of a supposedly national narrative? Or is the notion of a *national* history itself dictated by the need to possess a myth rather than merely a narrative? These are, at the very least, open questions. What is not open to question is the importance of national history. "Loss of the past," wrote Simone Weil, "is the supreme human tragedy. . . . [I]t is above all to avoid this loss that people will put up a desperate resistance to being conquered."[34] But what they fear to lose is a continuity that has more to do with the persistence of national myths than with the unfolding of a restricted narrative.

Tradition and Mission

There is a rather different way from those already considered in which a nation's history may be thought to make the nation what it is and to establish its value. It is by giving it, in a word, tradition. *Traditional nationalism*,[35] as I shall term it, identifies the nation as a community held together by relationships which depend upon traditional norms. In seventeenth- and eighteenth-century England, for example, these norms were conceived of as the laws and liberties of the Anglo-Saxons, as the customs of the people enshrined in common law and traditional usage.[36] It is by regulating their relationships in accordance with some such body of tradition that a people is identifiable as a distinct society. This view is in direct opposition to the Hobbesian one that it is by being under common government that people form a nation, for such a view opposes traditional English society to the state instituted by the Norman Conquest. The consequential "Norman Yoke"[37] constantly threatened to unsettle traditional relationships and to replace them with ones which lacked their value.

That value was guaranteed by their antiquity. Edmund Burke, the classic exponent of traditional nationalism, explained the matter as follows:

> A nation is not an idea only of local extent, and individual momentary aggregation; but it is an idea of continuity, which extends in time as well as in numbers and in space. And this is a choice not of one day, or one set of people, not a tumultuary and giddy choice; it is a deliberate election of the ages and of generations; it is a constitution made by what is ten thousand times

better than choice, it is made by the peculiar circumstances, occasions, tempers, dispositions, and moral, civil, and social habitudes of the people, which disclose themselves only in a long space of time.[38]

The continuous adaptation of a society to circumstances over time is what makes it a worthwhile society, for it thereby develops a particular flexibility and robustness in the face of the new. A society which lacks such a history or which ignores it cannot have this kind of value. Burke went so far as to say that, given time, a people always acts rightly.[39] The comparison and contrast with Rousseau could scarcely be more striking. For Rousseau, it was the "general will" of the people that is always right;[40] but the general will is arrived at on the basis of a rational and disinterested calculation as to what would serve the common good and thereby sustain the community of which it is definitive. This line of thought presupposes that the common good can be discerned and pursued quite independent of society's traditional ways of life, which is exactly what Burke disputed. Only through the following out of traditions can society prosper; only within this framework can people have a clear sense of what it is to act rightly.

If such faith in the past were justified, traditional nationalism would have a strong argument for statehood, since it would be able to claim that a continuing society existed by virtue of customs which a state could enforce, and, what is more, that this society provided the only secure setting for its members to act morally. Yet such faith will strike many as quite unfounded. Burke attacked the French Revolution on the grounds that France, like England, had a constitution which checked the excesses of royal power. This is exactly what the revolutionaries denied,[41] and their denial illustrates the difficulties in Burke's position. Only if a society develops free from the distorting influence of those with powerful sectional interests can its traditional institutions be regarded as serving the common good. Yet few if any societies develop in this way. Thus Gerrard Winstanley, leader of the Diggers in the English Civil War, concluded that as a result of the Norman Yoke "the best laws that England have are yokes and manacles, tying one sort of people to be slaves to another."[42] In fact, Burke conceded that the story of English laws being of ancient origin might be incorrect, but that did not trouble him:

> If the lawyers mistake in some particulars, it proves my position still the more strongly; because it demonstrates the powerful prepossession towards antiquity, with which the minds of all our lawyers and legislators, and of all the people whom they wish to influence, have always been filled; and the stationary policy of this kingdom in considering their most sacred rights and franchises as an *inheritance*.[43]

But this gives the game away. Unless the common law really has evolved as the story describes, it cannot confer the advantages of accumulated adaptation to changing circumstance, and any traditional nationalism based upon it collapses.[44]

To look to tradition is to look backward. To look to a mission is to look forward. But for all that, tradition and mission cannot be *contrasted* as grounds of nationhood, for it can be argued that a nation's mission is precisely to carry forward its traditions. Or its tradition may be to pursue a mission, as in the conception of Ireland as a land of saints and scholars. Nevertheless, a group may be thought to constitute a nation precisely because it has a certain sort of mission—in particular, one for which statehood is required. The mission may or may not involve the pursuit of distinctive national values. What distinguishes this conception from that which characterizes nations in terms of their pursuit of values is that the mission is viewed as a specific task rather than as the general realization of values.[45] The model for what we may call *missionary nationalism* is provided by the Jews in their role as the chosen people, with a special mission to worship God and to keep his commandments. What makes a group with a mission one people need not be that the members have a common purpose or that they form a community whose constitutive relationships are shaped for the carrying out of such a purpose. Rather, it may be that they are of common descent, live in the same territory, or whatever. But what makes them a *nation* is supposedly that they have or should have this purpose, or lead or should lead a common life tending to its attainment, for it is this which gives them a claim to statehood.

Yet how might it do so? We need to distinguish here between the view that a nation has a mission from the view that it has a *destiny*.[46] The historic destiny of a nation which leads it to statehood and to the fulfillment of its role in world history is, I take it, not constituted by its members' individual or collective purposes, and, hence, it cannot miscarry as a result of their failure to achieve them. Just as a nation's history is what fate has made it, so its destiny is what it is fated to become. Destiny, thus conceived, can confer no rights or duties, though it can bless some actions, and doom others. What all this might come to, short of a politically destructive fatalism, is quite unclear. It is otherwise with national missions, which, if only we knew them, could guide our actions. For example, it was commonly believed in the nineteenth century that God had committed to some nations "a solemn trust of principles and territory . . . and when false to the trust . . . He has swept them away and chosen Him other instrumentalities."[47] Giuseppe Mazzini shared this view, but generalized and desacrilized it to accord a specific mission to every nation: "Humanity is a great army moving to the conquest of unknown lands, against powerful and wary enemies. The Peoples are the different corps and divisions of that army. Each has a post entrusted to it; each a special operation to perform; and the common victory depends on the exactness with which the different operations are carried out."[48] Mazzini was unilluminating as to what the missions entrusted to each nation are. They will not help us to identify individual nations unless we know. But he was right to ascribe them to *all* nations, for otherwise no *general* criterion of nationhood would be provided. Unfortunately, those who lack faith in divine providence will need convincing that such national missions exist at all.

That is not the case if groups announce the goals which they are committed to achieve, as for example a revolutionary nation does. It proclaims liberty, equality, and fraternity, say, and sets itself the task of building a society which instantiates them. This account could be generalized, such that we regard a putative nation's mission as the achievement of a society which realizes certain values. Then a nation will not be just a group with certain values (for this characterization may well not differentiate one nation from another or serve to fix the bounds of statehood) but a group which can be seen as working collectively toward realizing such values in the sort of society it aims to be. In principle, it could be argued, this is something we could discover even when the national mission was unannounced. In practice it might be more difficult. Herder's belief that the mission of the Slavs was to fulfill the idea of goodness (whereas that of the Germans was to realize truth) took little account of the separatist tendencies of those like the Slovaks who were to be corralled by it into a Panslav political community.[49] But if this conception of a nation's mission can be made to work, it moves us from the mysterious notion of what the group should do to the observable one of what it does. Yet in doing so, it removes the prima facie support for independent statehood that nations with a mission have. For, although Herder carefully selected national missions which avoid this criticism, what people *do* do may not warrant the benefit of statehood that what they *should* do deserves. Again, we seem to be plunged back into the case-by-case adjudication which defeats any general argument from nationhood.

The only way to avoid this conclusion would be to find some general characterization of national missions which conferred on nations the right to statehood. And one way to do this would be to see nationalist projects as essentially progressive and emancipatory, implicitly if not explicitly dedicated to building societies more liberal, more equal, and more fraternal than their predecessors. Or if this is not taken to be the right project for a group that aspires to statehood, then some other project can be selected—the creation of a homogeneous culture, say. But it is evident that such an approach will take us nowhere beyond the terrain that we have already trodden. Each of these projects merely incorporates a particular form of nationalism whose strengths and weaknesses it has been the present book's purpose to explore. The fact that these nationalisms are taken up into the collective endeavors of supposedly national groups does nothing to affect their moral standing.

Summary

This final chapter has attempted to assay the role of national history in different types of nationalism, particularly that of individuating nations. National history can be a record of a nation's experience, which supposedly makes of it a community, or a record of its actions, which implies its political existence as a corporate body. Yet the difficulties of individuating histories are as great as those of individuating nations. In an effort to resolve them, nationalists often resort to voluntarist criteria. Here, as in other cultural nationalisms, the truth of the national history may not be important. Yet, in considering a group's right to statehood, false history may be disqualificatory. It is not, however, to be confused with myth, or the mythic use of history, which may have a respectable role in national culture—albeit a perilous one. A principal form of value culture nationalism stresses the importance of tradition in the formation of a national community; yet it is the communal relationships themselves, not their origins, which determine the desirability of such a community. The same may be said of nationalisms based, instead, on the idea of a national mission. Only optimism about the nationalist project itself could turn aside such a conclusion.

Conclusion

Recent philosophical works on nationalism have typically each presented a single account of the nation and defended, on this basis, its claim to independent statehood. This is, of course, exactly what my own theory of nationhood predicts that they would do. The constitutive principle of nationalism requires it of them. But I have attempted to do something both more and less ambitious: more ambitious in that I have offered a wide variety of accounts of the nation and assessed the claims for statehood consequential on them; less, in that I have not plumped for a preferred account and gone to the limits to defend it. In particular, I have not attempted to assemble a composite account of the nation from the various elements I have unraveled and whose separate strengths I have attempted to assay. Should I have done so? I do not think so. There are, of course, legitimate compounds in which it is clear how the elements work together to ground a putative right to statehood. We have looked at a good many of these forms of nationalism—political voluntarism; cultural nationalism, which identifies a community through its history; and several others. But the more recent and more theoretically motivated assemblages of which I speak are not, I think, of such a character. Rather, they borrow elements from different kinds of nationalism to put together arguments for national statehood on the basis of a group's having a variety of seemingly independent features. I do not think that such assemblages are ever stronger than their parts, though I do not know how to prove it.

Certainly, in a political argument for self-determination, a variety of considerations may be marshaled in support of it which might outweigh the reasons against it that stem from its possible adverse effects. That people have a common culture, desire a separate state, and form a viable economic unit, for example, might all be adduced in such an argument, alongside the claim that they constitute a nation. But it is often unclear how such considerations are supposed to work together to ground this claim, and, in particular, how they underpin a *right* to statehood, as against the political desirability in the prevailing circumstances of conceding it. However, it is one thing to pick out a determinate kind of group with a right to statehood and, hence, by the constitutive principle, to recognize a nation; and quite another to concede self-determination on the current balance of political considerations. Overlooking this distinction can result, I believe, in misbegotten endeavors to weld together inconsistent elements in the hope of benefiting from both.

Thus attempts to combine subjectivist with nonsubjectivist accounts[1] seem bound to lead to disaster, for either it is, say, their belief that they share certain characteristics which constitutes people as a nation, or it is the shared characteristics themselves which do so; it cannot be both, for there is no apparent way in which the arguments for statehood from the one kind of consideration could be propped up by arguments from the other. The reason is that, if their shared characteristics are necessary but insufficient for the right, then their belief in them cannot make good the deficiency, for it is irrelevant to the moral desirability (as against the likelihood) of people with such characteristics attaining statehood. Conversely, if their shared sense of identity is by itself inadequate to render statehood desirable for such a group, then the mere fact of their common identity cannot make it so.[2] Either each kind of consideration is adequate on its own for the right to statehood or neither is.

Such an argument need cut no ice with those who view the reasons for conceding statehood as purely pragmatic, since what is in question here is not what is morally desirable for a certain kind of group but, rather, what is expedient in certain circumstances. But to present nationalist claims in such pragmatic terms is grossly misleading. It obscures the nature of the conflicts between different sorts of nationalism—liberal and ethnic ones, say— which occur even *within* particular nationalist movements.

It is, I have suggested, the presupposition underlying this pervasive struggle of different nationalisms that needs to be coolly scrutinized, even if we cannot avoid joining in the more local debates in which it issues. The presupposition in question is, of course, that there is a *kind* of group which has, *ceteris paribus*, a right to statehood—namely, the nation. I do not know how to examine this presupposition except by taking the various accounts of nationhood that have been offered and assessing their claims, as I have done here. But nor do I know how anyone could argue for the presupposition in general terms, without advancing some particular account. And yet it is hard to see why, stripped of any particular national dress, it should be credible. Why should there be *any* such kind of group, rather than merely groups in particular circumstances with the variously grounded claims to statehood which spring from them?

The view that there *is* this kind of group stems, I suggest, from a combination of two assumptions which characterize modernity. One is that the political organization of the entire world should form a unitary system— the state system—such that people everywhere should ideally be grouped into the same sort of political communities in accordance with the same principles. What lies behind this assumption is, I further suggest, a second one, namely, that only one form of political organization—the state—can be justified on the basis of what people are really like. The differences in different types of nationalism are ultimately differences about human nature. But that there are truths about human nature to ground nationalist claims, as to ground other ethical assertions, is simply an assumption. It is, one might say, the fundamental assumption of modern philosophy.

I can illustrate this point by comparing, for example, the naturalist and the voluntarist accounts of nationhood. Both are characteristically modern, but they draw on different strands in modern thought. Voluntarism sees people as essentially rational calculators, able to compute the arrangements that are most advantageous to them and to enter into agreements with each other on this basis. Because they are placed in broadly similar situations everywhere, their solutions will be correspondingly similar and a uniform system of states will emerge as a result. The naturalist view, by contrast, sees human beings as an animal species constrained in its behavior by natural regularities.[3] Their similarities of political organization are simply a reflection of the fact that they form a single species rather than several. One can multiply examples. These two alone serve, however, to indicate why nationalist disputes are so intractable. They are deeply rooted in competing traditions of philosophical thinking.[4] Metaphysics is, indeed, the intellectual battleground of nations, as significant for the fact that it draws certain soi disant nations together into agreement and harmony as for the fact that it divides others and leads them into discord.

My own study here has barely scratched the surface of these issues. That is one reason why its findings have been so provisional. Yet there are two possible conclusions suggested by it. One, which I favor, is that there are no good cases for statehood based on the character of kinds of groups, and I shall return to the consequences of this in a moment. While I have commended as serious contenders a form of economic nationalism and communitarian nationalism more generally, I have expressed reservations about their internal cogency. But even more damaging, I believe, are doubts as to their applicability to a world of globalized economies, and of human relationships dominated by the market rather than by collective solidarity. It is an irony, though an understandable one, that nationalisms of this sort should search most frantically for an adequate political expression in such a world.

The other possible conclusion is that there are too many good cases for statehood. There are too many, it may be felt, because while no one type of argument for statehood is better than the rest, a number are strong. For several different arguments might all seem to draw plausibly on different aspects of human nature to yield reasonably desirable forms of political organization. The problem, of course, is that these results do not yield a criterion for deciding *between* the conflicting claims of nations which incorporate these sometimes competing accounts, and then no harmonious rights to statehood can be conceded. In these circumstances there would be no reason to determine national claims according to a uniform formula. Ethically, one would just have to accept their irresolubility and do what one could to secure mutual tolerance and accommodation. It is just the same where *no* cogent case for a right to statehood for a certain kind of group is granted. There, too, we must look at the moral character of the groups in question and decide which has the stronger case, though sometimes there may be no clear answer. This is not to rule out all generalizations. The sorts of nationalism I have tended to favor over others are, it seems to me, the nationalisms of groups with a healthier moral complexion in general. But what is generally true may not be so in specific cases.

There is, I suspect, a tendency to make these sorts of moral judgments anyway. Thus those political philosophers who reject what they call nationalism in favor of statist principles of political organization tend to prefer what I call the political nationalism of established states to the nationalisms of their rivals. They find, for example, virtues of order combined with plurality in the former that may be lacking in the latter. I, however, tend toward the view that there are, in many cases, discernibly separate communities below the level of the state whose relationships are regulated by ethical principles more valuable than the law-governed relations of purely political groupings. These, I believe, often have good claims to independent statehood. Yet they have them not for generalizable nationalist reasons but because they promise something better for their members than what they currently have. And sometimes the same may be true for larger groups than for those that fall under a single state, as well as for smaller ones. Indeed, I tend toward the view that groups motivated by *resistant* nationalism often, though of course not always, have better moral claims than politically well-established ones. For their demands for justice evince a concern for the realization of moral values which their entrenched opponents may have lost sight of.

The important objective in such cases is to assess the claims of each group on their individual merits in the particular circumstances it is in. To espouse any specific type of nationalism, I believe, tends to obscure these, and to substitute facile doctrinaire pronouncements for reasoned conclusions sensitive to the particularities of the situation. To abandon the principle of nationalism makes good political sense. It may even lead us to question the assumption that there should be a world system of similarly constituted states at all. Perhaps particular circumstances should yield more individualized political solutions. However, a caveat is in order. Nationalism argues for a *moral* right to statehood. If it is abandoned, a moral support for claims should not be jettisoned along with it in favor of policies of pure pragmatism and *realpolitik*. If nationalism is abandoned, then the principles whereby morality can be retained in determining political organization will require quite fresh consideration.

As will have become apparent, my own ethical sympathies lie with forms of communitarianism which respect the cultural diversity of people sharing a common life. The conditions of economic life now make cultural homogeneity possible only as a result of repression or the cultural imperialism of those who dominate global markets. The assumption of an equivalence between a common culture and a shared community which jointly underpin a nation-state is no longer tenable. The challenge is to find forms of political organization which are at once liberal enough to foster cultural pluralism, yet able to nurture a shared commitment to a common good rooted in the realities of mutual interdependence. But the diverse nature of such dependencies, as well as the variety of cultural formations, implies that no single system of political institutions should be expected to emerge. It is, I suggest, because the state system itself is no longer adequate to the complex facts of cultural and communal life that even the most plausible nationalisms fail, and with them the fantastical dream of a single world order which reflects popular loyalties, not coercive power.

Notes

Introduction

1. A useful collection is J. Hutchinson and A. Smith (eds.), *Nationalism* (Oxford: Oxford University Press, 1994).

2. See, especially, Yael Tamir, *Liberal Nationalism* (Princeton: Princeton University Press, 1993); David Miller, *On Nationality* (Oxford: Oxford University Press, 1995); and Margaret Canovan, *Nationhood and Political Theory* (Cheltenham: Edward Elgar, 1996).

3. R. E. Goodin and P. Pettit (ed.), *A Companion to Contemporary Political Philosophy* (Oxford: Blackwell, 1993), p. 3.

4. Cf. Michael Billig, *Banal Nationalism* (London: Sage, 1995).

5. See, for example, Canovan's *Nationhood and Political Theory.*

Chapter One

1. From Kipling's poem entitled "For All We Have and Are," reprinted in English Association, *England: An Anthology* (London: Macmillan, 1944), p. 119; with an Introduction by Harold Nicolson.

2. Ibid., p. x.

3. See, for example, Anthony Giddens, *Power, Property and the State,* Vol. 1: *A Contemporary Critique of Historical Materialism* (London: Macmillan, 1981), p. 116; Montserrat Guiberneau, *Nationalisms: The Nation-State and Nationalism in the Twentieth Century* (Cambridge: Polity, 1996), p. 43.

4. As in one sense of the word by Stanley Benn, "Nationalism," in P. Edwards (ed.), *Encyclopaedia of Philosophy,* Vol. 5 (Cromwell: Collier & Macmillan, 1967), p. 442.

5. The contrast also holds for Maurizio Viroli, but for the quite different reason that he misconstrues patriotism as a contrasting *doctrine.* See Viroli, *For Love of Country: An Essay on Patriotism and Nationalism* (Oxford: Oxford University Press, 1995).

6. See Stephen Nathanson, "In Defence of Moderate Patriotism," *Ethics* 99 (1989); Alastair MacIntyre, "Is Patriotism a Virtue?" in M. Daly (ed.), *Communitarianism: A New Public Ethics* (Belmont: Wadsworth, 1994), pp. 304–318.

7. See Viroli, *For Love of Country,* especially p. 124.

8. Such as are described by M. Billig in *Banal Nationalism* (London: Sage, 1995).

9. This point is grasped by Peter Alter, who *infers* nationalist ideology from practices, rather than, like Billig, equating it with them. See Alter's *Nationalism* (London: Edward Arnold, 1994), p. 4, and Billig's *Banal Nationalism*, p. 154.

10. The disagreement *would* be a factual matter if both sides agreed on a cultural criterion, say, but disagreed as to what culture was shared.

11. Many authors consider this doctrine central to nationalism. See, for example, Anthony Smith, *Nations and Nationalism in a Global Era* (Cambridge: Polity, 1995), p. 56.

12. In this connection, see Liah Greenfeld, *Nationalism: Five Roads to Modernity* (Cambridge, Mass.: Harvard University Press, 1992), chapter 1. However, the emergence of a British nation should, perhaps, be distinguished from that of an English one, as Linda Colley argues in *Britons: Forging the Nation 1707–1837* (New Haven: Yale University Press, 1992).

13. The Welsh example is complicated, however; see Eric Hobsbawm, *Nations and Nationalism Since 1780: Programme, Myth, Reality* (Cambridge: Cambridge University Press, 1992), especially p. 117.

14. See, for example, Yael Tamir, *Liberal Nationalism* (Princeton: Princeton University Press, 1993), p. 67.

15. From Archibald Macleish's "American Letter," quoted in Harold Nicolson, *Friday Mornings 1941–1944* (London: Constable, 1944), p. 11.

16. Ibid.

17. Pace Walker Connor argued that "whatever the American people are . . . they are not a nation in the pristine sense of the word." See Connor, "A Nation Is a Nation, Is an Ethnic Group, Is a . . . ," in J. Hutchinson and A. Smith (eds.), *Nationalism* (Oxford: Oxford University Press, 1994), p. 38.

18. See, for example, Benedict Anderson, *Imagined Communities* (London: Verso, 1991), p. 6; Hobsbawm, *Nations and Nationalism Since 1780*, pp. 18–19.

19. This unresolved diversity is apparent in, for example, John Hall's "Nationalisms Classified and Explained," in S. Percival (ed.), *Notions of Nationalism* (Budapest: Central European University Press, 1995).

20. The term was apparently introduced in its modern sense by Johann Gottfried von Herder in 1774. See Altier, *Nationalism*, p. 3.

21. See Aira Kemiläinen, *Nationalism: Problems Concerning the Word, The Concept and Classification* (Jyväsklyä, Finland: Kustantajat, 1964), chapter 2.

22. William Shakespeare, *The Merchant of Venice*, act 1, scene 3.

23. George Eliot, *Daniel Deronda*, ed. T. Cave (Harmondsworth: Penguin, 1995), p. 803. (Originally published in 1876.)

24. Sean O'Faolain, "Foreign Affairs," in his *Foreign Affairs and Other Stories* (Harmondsworth: Penguin, 1978), pp. 108–109; emphasis added.

25. Nationality in this sense is often equated with citizenship—for example, by D. D. Raphael, *Problems of Political Philosophy* (London: Macmillan, 1976), p. 40.

26. There are some complexities in the case of federations and the like which need to be allowed for but do not affect this argument.

27. I mean *scientific* in the broad sense of systematic and theory-oriented, although in a narrower sense anthropologists may not apply this term to their work.

28. This conclusion is not, I think, contentious even among so-called primordialists who do not believe the *nation* is a modern phenomenon. That the *concept*

of nation is modern does not imply that the phenomenon is. What is contentious is whether the phenomenon of the nation is itself modern, as so-called modernists believe, or whether the nation is a group of a kind that has long existed, antedating the state system, as primordialists think. See John Hutchinson, *Modern Nationalism* (London: Fontana, 1994), chapter 1.

29. Charles R. Beitz, *Political Theory and International Relations* (Princeton: Princeton University Press, 1979), pp. 106–107.

30. Notwithstanding complications concerning dual nationality.

31. Hugh Seton-Watson, *Nations and States: An Enquiry into the Origin of Nations and the Politics of Nationalism* (Boulder: Westview Press, 1977), p. 5.

32. The argument I refer to here is that of John Charvet. See his "What Is Nationality, and Is There a Moral Right to National Self-Determination?" in S. Caney, D. George, and P. Jones (eds.), *National Rights, International Obligations* (Boulder: Westview Press, 1996), p. 59.

33. Indeed, a nominalist element often enters anthropologists' accounts, which hold that a nation must be a group of people calling themselves by the same name. See, for example, Lucy Mair, *Primitive Government* (Harmondsworth: Penguin, 1962), p. 15.

34. Cf. Hobsbawm's "working assumption," in *Nations and Nationalism Since 1780*, p. 8.

35. Max Weber, quoted in H. H. Gerth and C. Wright Mills (eds.), *From Max Weber* (London: Routledge, 1970), p. 174. (This book is an anthology of Weber's work.)

36. Ibid., p. 172.

37. Ibid., p. 179.

38. Ibid., p. 176.

39. Ibid., p. 172.

40. Though some deny the importance of this condition; see, for example, Brian Barry, "Nationalism," in D. Miller (ed.), *The Blackwell Encyclopaedia of Political Thought* (Oxford: Blackwell, 1991), p. 353. Barry holds that "making the demand for independent statehood the defining characteristic of a nationalist movement is to mistake the effect for the cause" (p. 353). But this statement seems to confuse the justification of the claim—namely, that the nation represents its members' "material and cultural interests"—with what makes it nationalist—namely, the right it claims.

41. Thus David Miller believes that talk of claims is more appropriate than talk of rights. See Miller, *On Nationality* (Oxford: Oxford University Press, 1995), p. 80 But see also the criticism by Brendan O'Leary, "Insufficiently Liberal and Insufficiently Nationalist," *Nations and Nationalism* 2 (1996), pp. 446–447.

42. This is how Ernest Gellner formulates his principle of nationalism in *Nations and Nationalism* (Oxford: Blackwell, 1983), p. 1.

43. The pursuit of autonomy is not a general feature, contrary to the view of Anthony Smith in *National Identity* (Harmondsworth: Penguin, 1991), p. 74. It is important to appreciate the fact that independent and self-government do not come to the same thing: A group can be governed independent of others but not by its own members, or it can govern itself but not independent of others. Indeed, while *any* group might be expected to desire self-government, independent gov-

ernment will normally be desired only on the grounds of some difference, usually a national one. If the difference concerns, for example, what the group *wants* for itself, then independent government will probably require self-government; but if it simply involves, say, a different legal system, then it need not.

44. See my "Prolegomena to an Ethics of Secession," in M. Wright (ed.), *Morality and International Relations: Concepts and Issues* (Aldershot: Avebury, 1996).

45. According to some kinds of nationalism, a certain form of federation *will* lead to the replacement of its constituent nations by a single one, as when the nations give up their right of secession; but for other kinds, this is not a right that nations *can* legitimately relinquish.

Chapter Two

1. Reprinted in Frank O'Connor (ed.), *A Book of Ireland* (London: Collins, 1959), p. 120.

2. One commentator who claims this is Anthony Smith. See his *Nations and Nationalisms in a Global Era* (Cambridge: Polity, 1995), p. 149.

3. Simon Caney is right to assert that valuing loyalty does not *imply* the imputation of obligations, but he seems unaware of the centrality of this imputation for nationalists. See his "Individuals, Nations and Obligations," in S. Caney, D. George, and P. Jones (eds.), *National Rights, International Obligations* (Boulder: Westview Press, 1996), p. 121.

4. For further discussion of this point, see Caney, "Individuals, Nations and Obligations"; D. Miller, *On Nationality* (Oxford: Oxford University Press, 1995), chapter 3.

5. Miller, *On Nationality*, p. 23.

6. See Michael Freeman, "Nation, State and Cosmopolis," *Journal of Applied Philosophy* 11 (1994), p. 84.

7. Elizabeth Bowen, *The Last September* (Harmondsworth: Penguin, 1983), pp. 91–92. (Originally published in 1929.)

8. This latter account is not Bowen's own, which draws a contrast between the "inherited loyalty (or at least adherence) to Britain" of the Anglo-Irish and "their own temperamental Irishness" (H. Lee [ed.], *The Mulberry Tree: Writings of Elizabeth Bowen* [London: Virago, 1986], p. 125.) I personally do not see such "temperamental Irishness" in the novel itself.

9. This is not to deny that nations may also be thought of as communities, but through features other than those that make them nations.

10. Even if the obligations are incurred only within the social relations.

11. This is true even in the contractualist accounts we shall consider later, for entering the contract automatically produces the social relations of nationhood.

12. Though in such cases there may be non-nationals with the appropriate qualifications who differ from nationals only by virtue of their nonmembership.

13. Sometimes a right to shared statehood seems simply to be *assumed* to follow from a right to independence. For if a people's right to be governed with others is based on their having some property F not shared by others, then *ex hypothesi* there is no further point of difference among them which gives them a right to *more* than one state. Yet that they have no right to more than one state does not at

all obviously imply that they have a right to *just* one. Or to put it differently, that Fs should be governed together does not obviously imply that they should be governed *all* together.

14 However, not *all* aggregative nationalisms fail to generate the right to shared statehood. Allegiance, for instance, may generate the right to a single state since those similar in their allegiance are so because their allegiance is to a common object. Conversely, societal nationalisms generate this right only if there is something about the relationships which renders political division undesirable— as when, for example, a single community is formed.

15. This quote appears in R. Coles, *The Middle Americans* (Boston: Little, Brown, 1971), p. 43; and the issue is discussed by Richard D. Alba, *Ethnic Identity: The Transformation of White America* (New Haven: Yale University Press, 1990), pp. 37–38. Alba distinguishes ancestry from identity, which he views as self-ascribed.

16. This last example may seem insignificant. But in Ulster, to "dig with the wrong foot" means to be a member of the other ethno-religious group.

17. "Other things," in this case, include the fact that the nation has not opted for shared statehood with others.

18. William Trevor, "The Distant Past," in his *Collected Stories* (Harmondsworth: Penguin, 1993), p. 355.

19. Technically speaking, in the latter case we have an intentional relation rather than a real relation. For a discussion of both the political and pre-political approaches, see my "Prolegomena to an Ethics of Secession," in M. Wright (ed.), *Morality and International Relations* (Aldershot: Avebury, 1996), p. 61.

20. Act 3 of *The Playboy of the Western World*, in Synge's *Plays, Poems and Prose* (London: Dent, 1958), p. 155. (In actuality, at the first performance the play did not reach act 3).

21. Thomas Davis, quoted in F.S.C. Lyons, *Culture and Anarchy in Ireland 1890–1939* (Oxford: Oxford University Press, 1979), p. 32.

22. D. P. Moran, quoted in Declan Kiberd, *Inventing Ireland: The Literature of the Modern Nation* (London: Cape, 1995), p. 174.

23. Mícheál MacLiammóir, Introduction to Synge's *Plays, Poems and Prose*.

24. Flann O'Brien, quoted in A. Warner, *A Guide to Anglo-Irish Literature* (Dublin: Gill and MacMillan, 1981), p. 161.

25. See, for example, Anthony Smith, *National Identity* (Harmondsworth: Penguin, 1991), chapter 2.

26. From W. B. Yeats's "Under Ben Bulben," in his *Collected Poems* (London: Macmillan, 1950), p. 400.

27. See, for example, Smith, *Nations and Nationalism in a Liberal Era*, p. 54; Miller, *On Nationality*, p. 22.

28. Max Weber, quoted in H. H. Gerth and C. Wright Mills (eds.), *From Max Weber* (London: Routledge, 1970), p. 176.

29. Eldridge Cleaver, *Post-Prison Writings and Speeches* (London: Panther, 1972), pp. 84, 90.

30. For a discussion of these differences in treatment, see T. H. Eriksen, *Ethnicity and Nationalism: Anthropological Perspectives* (London: Pluto, 1993), pp. 139–141.

31. Closed, that is, in Weber's sense of the word; see J. Rex, *Race and Ethnicity* (Buckingham: Open University Press, 1986), p. 8.

32. This is Miller's phrase; see his *On Nationality,* p. 23.

33. This point illustrates the more modest truth behind Miller's story of inherited obligations. (See Notes 5 and 6.)

34. See Miller, *On Nationality,* pp. 83–85.

35. Though note again that something less than a state may suffice.

36. This is Weber's celebrated definition, cited in Gerth and Mills (eds.), *From Max Weber,* p. 78.

37. Whether colonies are *states* in the sense that they possess an "international personality" is a question contested by lawyers. See D. W. Greig, *International Law* (London: Butterworth, 1970), pp. 80, 142–143. Note that the fact that they are not self-governing does not imply that they are not relevantly separate polities.

38. Under the Ottoman *millet* system, different cultural groups had different obligations. But this is precisely why the Ottoman Empire could scarcely be regarded as a modern state. Ataturk's secularization of Turkey established in principle the political equality that the Empire lacked.

39. Cf. the classification offered by Caney in "Individuals, Nations and Obligations," p. 120.

40. "Euskadi" is the term that Basques use for their homeland; "Padania" was coined by the Northern League to refer to an extended Lombardy. Independence is claimed for both territories.

Chapter Three

1. Joseph [Giuseppe] Mazzini, *The Duties of Man and Other Essays* (London: Dent, 1907), p. 52. (Originally published in 1858.)

2. See E. Kedourie, *Nationalism* (London: Hutchinson, 1960), p. 106. What Mazzini usually stressed as natural, however, were a nation's territorial boundaries.

3. Daniel Defoe, "The True Born Englishman," in C. Williams (ed.), *A New Book of English Verse* (London: Gollancz, 1935), pp. 424–428.

4. Or lineage, as Michael Banton calls it in his *Racial Theories* (London: Cambridge University Press, 1987), chapter 1. I am assuming unilineal descent: See Lucy Mair, *Introduction to Social Anthropology* (Oxford: Oxford University Press, 1965), pp. 67–68.

5. William Beinart, *Twentieth-Century South Africa* (Oxford: Oxford University Press, 1994), pp. 93, 92.

6. Max Weber, quoted in H. H. Gerth and C. Wright Mills (eds.), *From Max Weber* (London: Routledge, 1970), pp. 179, 176.

7. P. L. van den Berghe, *The Ethnic Phenomenon* (Oxford: Elsevier, 1981), p. 62.

8. Ibid., p. 27.

9. If it is suggested that we recognize people as genetically similar by cultural markers because they were so related in our evolutionary past, then it should be replied that we do not *need* an evolutionary explanation of why we get on well with them if they speak our language and so on. In this connection, H. S. Chamberlain got it right: "[W]hoever behaves as a Teuton is a Teuton[,] whatever his racial origin." Quoted in W. L. Shirer, *The Rise and Fall of the Third Reich* (London: Secker & Warburg, 1973), p. 106.

10. See Banton, *Racial Theories,* chapter 2.

11. David T. Goldberg, *Racist Culture* (London: Routledge, 1993), p. 87.

12. I mean the view that there are broad inherited differences between peoples relevant to the way they should be treated. Benedict Anderson *contrasts* racism and nationalism, owing to the overly narrow view that "nationalism thinks in terms of historical destinies, while racism dreams of eternal contaminations." (See Anderson, *Imagined Communities* [London: Verso, 1991], p. 149.) Hitler's Germany demonstrated, however, that these two lines of thought are compatible.

13. See Raymond Firth, *Human Types* (London: Nelson, 1938), p. 16. Note that even this modest notion of race is problematic and contested, not least because the principles of classification by phenotypical features are unclear and classification by genotypical differences is not well correlated with them (see Robert Miles, *Racism* [London: Routledge, 1989], pp. 32–40).

14. Robert McNeil, quoted in P. Gordon and F. Klug, *New Right, New Racism* (London: Searchlight, 1986), p. 14.

15. Roger Scruton, *The Meaning of Conservatism* (Harmondsworth: Penguin, 1980), p. 68.

16. Ralph Waldo Emerson, *English Traits, Representative Men and Other Essays* (London: Dent, 1908), p. 67. (Originally published in 1856.)

17. Emerson, *English Traits*, p. 25. Emerson misunderstands, I believe, Defoe's use of the term "race" discussed earlier.

18. Somerset Maugham, *A Writer's Notebook* (London: Heinemann, 1951), p. 142; notebook entry made in 1917.

19. L. Hagendoorn and H. Linssen, "National Characteristics and National Stereotypes," in R. F. Farnen (ed.), *Nationalism, Ethnicity and Identity* (New Brunswick, N.J.: Transaction, 1994), pp. 118, 122. The authors of this study fail to draw the conclusion I suggest, instead raising the question, "Are the external observers right, are the internal observers right, or neither of the two?" (p. 123). For a discussion of some American examples, see M. C. Waters, *Ethnic Options: Choosing Identities in America* (Berkeley: University of California Press, 1990), pp. 138–144.

20. British Conservative politician Norman Tebbit's test for English national identity was support for the national team, which even long-settled West Indian, Indian, and Pakistani immigrants failed to display.

21. F. M. Barnard (ed.), *J. G. Herder on Social and Political Culture* (Cambridge: Cambridge University Press, 1969), p. 324.

22. Ibid.

23. I failed to grasp this point in my "The Concept of a National Community," *Philosophical Forum* 28 (1996–1997), pp.153–156.

24. *J. G. Herder on Social and Political Culture*, pp. 324–325.

25. Herbert Spencer, *Man Versus the State* (London: Watts, 1940), p. 54. (Originally published in 1884.)

26. E. R. Service, *Primitive Social Organization: An Evolutionary Perspective* (New York: Random House, 1962), p. 51.

27. See my "Family Values and the Nation State," in G. Jagger and C. Wright (eds.), *Changing Family Values* (London: Routledge, 1998).

28. *J. G. Herder on Social and Political Culture*, p. 324.

29. Ibid.

30. Indeed, many theorists claim that this, or the related claim that supreme loyalty is *due* to the nation, is essential to or even definitive of any nationalism. See, for example, Peter Alter, *Nationalism* (London: Edward Arnold, 1994), pp. 4–5.

31. W. B. Yeats, *Explorations* (London: Macmillan, 1962), p. 118.

32. Arthur Griffith, quoted in E. Cullingford, *Yeats, Ireland and Fascism* (London: Macmillan, 1981), p. 56.

33. Patrick Pearse, quoted in ibid., p. 88.

34. Bertrand Russell, *Freedom and Organisation 1814–1914* (London: Allen & Unwin, 1934), p. 394.

35. The "gregarious instinct" has been a commonplace of evolutionary psychology since Francis Galton's *Inquiries into Human Faculty and Its Development* (London: Dent, 1951), pp. 47–57. (Originally published in 1883.)

36. This view is embraced as a Humean one by David Miller in *On Nationality* (Oxford: Oxford University Press, 1995), p. 58, fn. 11.

37. For a discussion along these lines, see S. Caney, "Individuals, Nations and Obligations," in S. Caney, D. George, and P. Jones (eds.), *National Rights, International Obligations* (Boulder: Westview Press, 1996), p. 124.

38. Christopher Lasch, *A Haven in a Heartless World* (New York: Basic Books, 1977).

39. In this connection, see Hugh LaFollette, *Personal Relationships* (Oxford: Blackwell, 1996), p. 5.

40. Including continuity beyond my death, a point often made by nationalists following Johann Fichte. See Caney, "Individuals, Nations and Obligations," pp. 131 and 137, fn. 34.

41. *Pace* Andrew Oldenquist, "Loyalties," *Journal of Philosophy* 79 (1982), pp. 186–187.

42. See, for example, Miller, *On Nationality*, pp. 65–73.

43. In this sense the family model is sometimes held to characterize *all* nationalism. See, for example, Ross Poole, *Morality and Modernity* (London: Routledge, 1991), pp. 100–105.

44. Edmund Burke, *Reflections on the Revolution in France* (Harmondsworth: Penguin, 1986), pp. 119–120. (Originally published in 1790.)

45. See, for example, Marilyn Friedman, "Feminism and Modern Friendship: Dislocating the Community," *Ethics* 99 (1989), pp. 275–290.

46. For a still-relevant discussion of this issue, see Tom Nairn, *The Left Against Europe?* (Harmondsworth: Penguin, 1973).

47. *J. G. Herder on Social and Political Culture*, p. 324.

48. Anthony Quinton, *The Politics of Imperfection* (London: Faber, 1978), p. 16.

49. Herbert Spencer, "The Social Organism," *Essays Scientific, Political and Speculative*, Vol. 1 (London: Williams & Northgate, 1901), p. 306.

50. Ibid., pp. 297, 295.

51. Ibid., pp. 273–274.

52. Ibid., p. 288.

53. Karl Popper, *The Open Society and Its Enemies*, Vol. 1 (London: Routledge, 1966), pp. 173, 174.

54. Ibid., p. 9.

55. Zygmunt Bauman, *Postmodern Ethics* (Oxford: Blackwell, 1993), p. 230.

56. This is one feature of the modernist/primordialist debate, but it is distinct from the question of whether modern nations are based on premodern ethnic communities.

Chapter Four

1. Contrary to the self-definitional view.

2. W. B. Yeats, quoted in F.S.C. Lyons, *Culture and Anarchy in Ireland 1890–1939* (Oxford: Oxford University Press, 1979), p. 49.

3. Declan Kiberd, *Inventing Ireland: The Literature of the Modern Nation* (London: Cape, 1995), p. 289; original emphasis.

4. Though, historically, subjectivism precedes naturalism.

5. Frantz Fanon, *The Wretched of the Earth* (Harmondsworth: Penguin, 1967), pp. 170–171.

6. H. H. Gerth and C. Wright Mills (eds.), *From Max Weber* (London: Routledge, 1970), p. 176.

7. D. Miller, "In Defence of Nationality," in P. Gilbert and P. Gregory (eds.), *Nations, Cultures and Markets* (Aldershot: Avebury, 1994), p. 22.

8. F. M. Barnard (ed.), *J. G. Herder on Social and Political Culture* (Cambridge: Cambridge University Press, 1969), p. 324.

9. From William Cowper's "England, with All Thy Faults," in English Association, *England: An Anthology* (London: Macmillan, 1944), p. 141.

10. L. Greenfeld, *Nationalism: Five Roads to Modernity* (Cambridge, Mass.: Harvard University Press, 1992), p. 487.

11. From Lord Byron's "England! With All Thy Faults," English Association, *England: An Anthology* (London: Macmillan, 1944), pp. 172–173.

12. R. M. MacIver, *The Modern State* (Oxford: Oxford University Press, 1926), p. 124.

13. This example, though not the interpretation offered here, is discussed by Albert Boime in *Art and the French Commune* (Princeton: Princeton University Press, 1995), pp. 102–107.

14. The English translation is "Speak of it never, think of it always." Gambetta's quote appears in H.A.L. Fisher, *A History of Europe* (London: Edward Arnold, 1936), p. 1002.

15. René Descartes, *Meditations*, 2nd meditation (1641; many editions).

16. This view is not representative of nominalism, for under nominalism (a) people who consider themselves to form a nation do not need to think of their thoughts as what makes them so; (b) there is *no* essence to the nation; and (c) it is belief rather than the entertaining of thoughts that is involved.

17. Ernest Renan, "What Is a Nation?" reprinted in A. Zimmern, *Modern Political Doctrines* (London: Oxford University Press, 1931), p. 203. (Originally published in 1882.)

18. This point needs a small qualification to be plausible—namely, that the desire must be nonreactive rather than one arising from the circumstances that people are in.

19. Renan, "What Is a Nation?" p. 194. (In Alsace, of course, German was spoken.)

20. Ibid., p. 198.

21. See A. J. Grant and H. Temperley, *Europe in the Nineteenth Century* (London: Longmans, 1929), p. 354.

22. Heinrich von Treitschke, quoted in P. A. Gagnon, *France Since 1789* (New York: Harper & Row, 1964), p. 203.

23. John Stuart Mill, *On Liberty, Representative Government, The Subjection of Women* (London: Oxford University Press, 1912), pp. 380–381. I interpret Mill's talk of what people "should be free to do" in terms of what rights they have, though it needs to be remembered that his overall justification is utilitarian. These utilitarian considerations inform much of Mill's argumentation concerning the borders of states, and I have ignored them here.

24. Note that in this sense a group right is not necessarily the right of a community, contrary to the assumption of Michael Hartney. See his "Some Confusions Concerning Collective Rights," in W. Kymlicka (ed.), *The Rights of Minority Cultures* (Oxford: Oxford University Press, 1995), p. 203.

25. Mill, *On Liberty, Representative Government, The Subjection of Women*, p. 382.

26. As apparently by Harry Beran in *The Consent Theory of Political Obligation* (Beckenham: Croom Helm, 1987), pp. 37–38.

27. Beran treats this argument as a separate one in *Consent Theory*, pp. 39–42.

28. Ibid., pp. 38–39.

29. Renan, "What Is a Nation?" p. 204.

30. This point is made forcibly by Beran in *Consent Theory*, p. 37.

31. Mill, *On Liberty, Representative Government, The Subjection of Women*, p. 385.

32. *Pace*, for example, Micheline R. Ishay, *Internationalism and Its Betrayal* (Minneapolis: University of Minnesota Press, 1995), especially part 2.

33. Or civic: The terms are interchangeable here.

34. Ivor Jennings, *The Approach to Self-Government* (Cambridge: Cambridge University Press, 1956), p. 56.

35. Made by Beran, *Consent Theory*, pp. 40–41. Note, however, that Beran refers here to a way of demarcating not *nations* but groups with rights of secession.

36. Which may just be their desire to associate. The argument here is not viciously circular, since this circumstance would make a nation a group of people who desired to associate for its own sake, by contrast with desiring it from shared interests, for instance.

37. Renan, however, speaks of *continuing* a life in common, perhaps suggesting that he has an actual association in mind.

38. Anthony Ashley Cooper, Earl of Shaftesbury, *Characteristics of Men, Manners, Opinions, Times* (Gloucester, Mass.: Smith, 1963), p. 248. (Originally published in 1711.)

39. John Locke, *Two Treatises of Government* (Cambridge: Cambridge University Press, 1960), 2nd Treatise, §95. (Originally published in 1698.)

40. An example would be a unitary multinational state in which the nationals of one sector were employed as troops to put down dissent in another.

Chapter Five

1. George Washington, quoted in C. Chesterton, *A History of the United States* (London: Dent, 1940), pp. 324–325.

2. Louis Dumont denies that Locke thought of the political agreement as a contract per se rather than as a trust. See Dumont, *Essays on Individualism* (Chicago: University of Chicago Press, 1986), p. 75.

3. Note that, by the terms of the constitutive principle, all membership features involve a covert reference to some state to which they supposedly confer a right. But political nationalism differs from nationalism generally in two respects: (a) there must be an actual or desired state, whereas there can be a right with neither; and (b) there must be a *specific* state referred to in characterizing membership, whereas the right may simply be to *some* state (its specificity provided by features of members other than those that make them a nation).

4. As I myself have done previously. See my "Prolegomena to an Ethics of Secession," in M. Wright (ed.), *Morality and International Relations* (Aldershot: Avebury, 1996), p. 61.

5. Because other conditions for national society may be lacking, for example, shared will.

6. Henry Sidgwick, *Elements of Politics* (London: Macmillan, 1891), p. 621.

7. Perhaps a trade-off could be found between security and freedom, but it would not ground a right of *national* secession; rather, it would ground only a right to secession as what was best in the circumstances.

8. Thomas Hobbes, *Leviathan* (London: Dent, 1962), chapter 17. (Originally published in 1651.)

9. Ibid., chapter 13.

10. Ibid.

11. Ibid., chapter 30.

12. For a discussion of this assumption, see Hedley Bull, *The Anarchical Society* (London: Macmillan, 1977), pp. 46–51.

13. Hobbes, *Leviathan*, chapter 13.

14. See David George, "The Right of National Self-Determination," *History of European Ideas* 16 (1993), pp. 507–513.

15. I treat political corporatism as a form of societal nationalism, since the relations of members to the state can be regarded as a species of relationship between them.

16. See Hobbes, *Leviathan*, chapter 17.

17. Notably Eugene Kamenka, "Political Nationalism: The Evolution of the Idea," in E. Kamenka (ed.), *Nationalism* (London: Edward Arnold, 1976).

18. See David Miller, *On Nationality* (Oxford: Oxford University Press, 1994), pp. 88–90.

19. In this connection, see my *Terrorism, Security and Nationality* (London: Routledge, 1994), pp. 28–33.

20. George Washington, quoted in Chesterton, *A History of the United States*, p. 327.

21. Ibid.

22. See, for example, Cornelia Navari, "Civic Republicanism and Self-Determination," in M. Wright (ed.), *Morality and International Relations* (Aldershot: Avebury, 1996), p. 80.

23. Hobbes, *Leviathan*, chapter 21.

24. For discussion of these details, see Chandran Kukathas, "Liberty," in R. E. Goodin and P. Pettit (eds.), *Companion to Contemporary Political Philosophy* (Oxford: Blackwell, 1993), pp. 542–545.

25. John Stuart Mill, *Utilitarianism* (1863; many editions), chapter 4.

26. Equality and fraternity are the other values which spring immediately to mind. But equality in the republican sense can be regarded as a condition on membership of the state, and fraternity may be regarded as the civil friendship required in the pursuit of values, rather than as an independent value.

27. From Percy Bysshe Shelley's "A New National Anthem" (1819), reprinted in J. Lucas, *England and Englishness* (London: Hogarth Press, 1990), p. 129.

28. From Shelley's "Sonnet: England in 1819," reprinted in ibid., p. 124.

29. Gerrard Winstanley, quoted in L. Greenfeld, *Nationalism: Five Routes to Modernity* (Cambridge, Mass.: Harvard University Press, 1992), p. 75.

30. Rather than love of the land, with which republican writers contrast it. In this connection, see Andrew Oldfield, *Citizenship and Community: Civic Republicanism and the Modern World* (London: Routledge, 1990), p. 53.

31. See Oldfield, *Citizenship and Community*, pp. 20–24.

32. For a development of this point, see Margaret Canovan, *Nationhood and Political Theory* (Cheltenham: Edward Elgar, 1996), pp. 92–97.

33. This distinction is still alive in P. F. Strawson, "Social Morality and the Individual Ideal," *Philosophy* 26(1961), pp. 1–17.

34. Clermont Tonnerre (1791), quoted in G. Kates, "Jews into Frenchmen: Nationality and Representation in Revolutionary France," *Social Research* 56 (1989), p. 229.

35. Hobbes, *Leviathan*, chapter 42.

36. Ibid., chapter 43.

37. Indeed, this is the line that some republicans themselves began to follow, especially those involved in devising the checks and balances of the American Constitution which were intended to dispense with ethical motivations; see Iain Hampshire-Monk, *A History of Modern Political Thought* (Oxford: Blackwell, 1992), pp. 210–212.

38. See, for example, Kamenka, "Political Nationalism," p. 7.

39. Abbé Sieyès, quoted in J.R. Llobera, *The God of Modernity* (Oxford: Berg, 1994), pp. 183–184.

40. Abbé Sieyès, quoted in P. Alter, *Nationalism* (London: Edward Arnold, 1994), p. 40.

41. Benito Mussolini, *The Political and Social Doctrine of Fascism* (1932), reprinted in A. Zimmern, *Modern Political Doctrines* (London: Oxford University Press, 1931), p. 38.

42. Jean Jacques Rousseau, *Social Contract*, edited by E. Barker (London: Oxford University Press, 1947), book 2, chapter 3, p. 274. (Originally published in 1762.)

43. Ibid., pp. 291–292.

44. I am not claiming that Rousseau himself would have held to these positions consistently and unqualifiedly, much less that his work tends to their possible totalitarian consequences.

45. Michael Ignatieff, *Blood and Belonging: Journeys into the New Nationalism* (London: Vintage, 1994), p. 3.

46. Benito Mussolini, *The Doctrine of Fascism* (1936), reprinted in K. B. Webb (ed.), *Sourcebook of Opinion on Human Values* (Hadleigh: Tower Bridge, 1951), p. 114.

47. E. M. Forster, *Two Cheers for Democracy* (Harmondsworth: Penguin, 1965), pp. 76–77.

Chapter Six

1. See A. Sutherland, *Gypsies: The Hidden Americans* (London: Tavistock, 1975), p. 132.

2. See J. Okely, *The Traveller Gypsies* (Cambridge: Cambridge University Press, 1983), chapter 10.

3. Sir Henry Maine, *Ancient Law* (London: Dent, 1959), p. 76. (Originally published in 1861.)

4. See Lucy Mair, *Primitive Government* (Harmondsworth: Penguin, 1962), pp. 11–16.

5. Note that John Armstrong identifies two sorts of political community: a territorial one arising from sedentarism and a genealogical one arising from nomadism. See Armstrong, *Nations Before Nationalism* (Chapel Hill: University of Carolina Press, 1982).

6. R. Segal, *Whose Jerusalem? The Conflicts of Israel* (Harmondsworth: Penguin, 1973), p. 123. It is therefore false to say that a "nation must have a homeland," *pace* D. Miller in *On Nationality* (Oxford: Oxford University Press, 1995), p. 24.

7. This requirement is intended to allow for adjacent islands and occasional enclaves.

8. Benedict Anderson, *Imagined Communities* (London: Verso, 1991), p. 19. For a discussion of the distinction between frontiers and borders, see Anthony Giddens, *The Nation State and Violence* (Cambridge: Polity, 1985), pp. 83–90.

9. As opposed to occupancy by *these people*, which is what the desirability-based claim regards as generating the right. The distinction is not always sharp: Occupancy by people leading a common life can be regarded either as a kind of occupancy or as occupancy by a group of a certain kind.

10. F. M. Barnard (ed.), *J. G. Herder on Social and Political Culture* (Cambridge: Cambridge University Press, 1969), p. 324.

11. J. G. Herder, quoted in R. R. Ergang, *Herder and the Foundations of German Nationalism* (New York: Columbia University Press, 1931), p. 90.

12. Ibid., p. 91.

13. See *J. G. Herder on Social and Political Culture*, pp. 294–295.

14. Robert Ardrey, *The Territorial Imperative* (London: Collins, 1967), p. 191.

15. Ibid., pp. 252–253.

16. Quoted in T. C. McLuhan, *Touch the Earth* (New York: Simon and Schuster, 1971), p. 15.

17. Quoted in ibid., p. 56.

18. Quoted in J. Tully, *Strange Multiplicity: Constitutionalism in an Age of Diversity* (Cambridge: Cambridge University Press, 1995), p. 76.

19. From W. B. Yeats's "The Dreaming of the Bones," reprinted in F. O'Connor, *A Book of Ireland* (London: Collins, 1959), pp. 81–82.

20. Harold Nicolson, *England: An Anthology* (London: Macmillan, 1944), p. vi.

21. From Laurence Binyon's "Inheritance," reprinted in Nicolson, *England: An Anthology*, p. 4. Nicolson's comment also appears in ibid., p. vii.

22. Ernest Gellner, "Introduction," S. Periwal (ed.), *Notions of Nationalism* (Budapest: Central European University Press, 1995), p. 4.

23. From Edward Thomas's "Adlestrop," reprinted in S.P.M. Mais (ed.), *A Cluster of Grapes* (London: Heinemann, 1941), p. 71. This is a wartime anthology similar to *England: An Anthology*.

24. That is, the similarities are specified *as* the similarities of those living in England, not independent of it.

25. Such as is deliberately repudiated in England: "The country is so lovely: the man-made England is so vile." See D. H. Lawrence, *Selected Essays* (Harmondsworth: Penguin, 1950), p. 119. (The essay in question was originally published in 1936.)

26. See J. F. McMillan, "La France Profonde, Modernity and National Identity, " in J. House (ed.), *Landscapes of France* (London: South Bank Centre, 1995), pp. 52–59.

27. From Frances Cornford's "Cambridgeshire," reprinted in English Association, *England: An Anthology* (London: Macmillan, 1944), p. 32.

28. George Gissing, *The Private Papers of Henry Ryecroft* (London: Constable, 1928), p. 149. (Originally published in 1903.)

29. Sir Walter Scott, "Lay of the Last Minstrel," reprinted in G. F. Maine (ed.), *A Book of Scotland* (London: Collins, 1950), p. 23.

30. Richard Price (1789), quoted in M. Viroli, *For Love of Country* (Oxford: Oxford University Press, 1995), p. 97.

31. John Newton, quoted in W. Stafford, "Religion and the Doctrine of Nationalism in England at the Time of the French Revolution and Napoleonic Wars," in S. Mews (ed.), *Religion and National Identity* (Oxford: Blackwell, 1982), p. 383.

32. David Miller, "In Defence of Nationality," in P. Gilbert and P. Gregory (eds.), *Nations, Cultures and Markets* (Aldershot: Avebury, 1994), p. 16.

33. From Patrick Kavanagh's *The Great Hunger* (London: Macgibbon and Kee, 1966), p. 21.

34. See Viroli, *For Love of Country*, pp. 29–40.

35. Quoted in O. MacDonagh, *States of Mind* (London: Allen & Unwin, 1983), p. 15.

36. Joseph [Giuseppe] Mazzini, *The Duties of Man* (London: Dent, 1907), p. 52.

37. Abraham Lincoln, quoted in Liah Greenfeld, *Nationalism: Five Roads to Modernity* (Cambridge, Mass.: Harvard University Press, 1992), p. 445.

38. Lincoln, quoted in McLuhan, *Touch the Earth*, p. 54.

39. John Locke, *Two Treatises of Government* (Cambridge: Cambridge University Press, 1960), 2nd Treatise, §192. (Originally published in 1698.)

40. Will Kymlicka, *Multicultural Citizenship* (Oxford: Oxford University Press, 1995), p. 220.

41. David Hume, *A Treatise of Human Nature*, edited by L. A. Selby Bigge (Oxford: Oxford University Press, 1978), book 3, part 2, section 3. (Originally published in 1739–1740.)

42. Thomas Baldwin, "The Territorial State," in H. Gross and R. Harrison (eds.), *Jurisprudence: Cambridge Essays* (Oxford: Oxford University Press, 1992), p. 222.

43. Locke, *Two Treatises of Government*, 2nd Treatise, §95.

44. Ibid., 2nd Treatise, §3.

45. See M. K. Dudley and K. K. Agard, *A Call for Hawaiian Sovereignty* (Honolulu: Na Kane O Ka Malo Press, 1990), especially chapters 4–7.

46. See D. N. Buckley, *James Fintan Lalor: Radical* (Cork: Cork University Press, 1990). The connection between land and nationalism in the seminal Irish case is discussed by Philip Bull in *Land, Politics and Nationalism* (Dublin: Gill and McMillan, 1996)

47. Thomas Hobbes, *Leviathan* (London: Dent, 1962), chapter 24. (Originally published in 1651.)

48. Ibid.

49. Hillel Steiner, "Territorial Justice," in S. Caney, D. George, and P. Jones (eds.), *National Rights, International Obligations* (Boulder: Westview Press, 1996), p. 144.

50. Locke, *Two Treatises of Government*, 2nd Treatise, §38.

51. Ibid., 2nd Treatise, §26.

52. Ibid., 2nd Treatise, §32.

53. Ibid., 2nd Treatise, §27.

54. Ibid., 2nd Treatise, §43.

55. Ibid., 2nd Treatise, §28.

56. Ibid., 2nd Treatise, §42.

57. Ronald Storrs, *Orientations* (London: Nicholson & Watson, 1945), p. 351, fn. 5.

58. Locke, *Two Treatises of Government*, 2nd Treatise, §41.

59. Bertrand Russell, *Freedom and Organisation 1814–1914* (London: Allen & Unwin, 1934), p. 394. Contrast with Gustave de Molinari's (1845) statement that "the division of humanity into autonomous nations is essentially economic," quoted in E. Hobsbawm, *Nations and Nationalism Since 1780* (Cambridge: Cambridge University Press, 1992), p. 28.

60. See, for example, Ernest Gellner, *Nations and Nationalism* (Oxford: Blackwell, 1983).

61. For a discussion of this point, see Onora O'Neill, "Justice and Boundaries," in C. Brown (ed.), *Political Restructuring in Europe: Ethical Perspectives* (London: Routledge, 1994).

62. Joel Barlow, quoted in D. Simpson's "Destiny Made Manifest," in H. K. Babha (ed.), *Nation and Narration* (London: Routledge, 1990), p. 188.

63. Christina Rossetti, "Goblin Market," in her *Poems* (London: Macmillan, 1897), pp. 1–20. (Originally published in 1862.)

64. Rosa Luxemburg, quoted in H. B. Davis (ed.), *The National Question: Selected Writings by Rosa Luxemburg* (New York: Monthly Review Press, 1976), pp. 135–136.

65. Antonio Gramsci, quoted and discussed in Ephraim Nimni, *Marxism and Nationalism* (London: Pluto, 1991), p. 96.

66. Ibid., p. 102.

67. Ibid., p. 105.

Chapter Seven

1. Karl W. Deutsch, "Peoples, Nations and Communication," in D. Potter and P. Sarre (eds.), *Dimensions of Society* (London: Hodder and Stoughton, 1974), p. 128.

2. Ibid., p. 132.

3. Ibid., p. 138.

4. Ibid., pp. 137–138.

5. Johann Gottlieb Fichte, quoted in R. R. Ergang, *Herder and the Foundations of German Nationalism* (New York: Columbia University Press, 1931), p. 173.

6. Thomas Macaulay, quoted in A. Bamgbose, *Language and the Nation* (Edinburgh: Edinburgh University Press, 1991), p. 6.

7. In this connection, see E. A. Walker, *The British Empire: Its Structure and Spirit* (London: Oxford University Press, 1943), p. 152.

8. E. M. Forster, *A Passage to India* (Harmondsworth: Penguin, 1961), p. 9. (Originally published in 1924.)

9. Macaulay, quoted in K. Singh, "India," in K. Bradley (ed.), *The Living Commonwealth* (London: Huchinson, 1961), p. 217.

10. Richard Hoggart, "A Question of Time," in Hoggart (ed.), *Speaking to Each Other*, Vol. 2 (London: Chatto, 1970), p. 195. Not everyone perceived this typicality at the time of *Passage's* publication. For instance, T. E. Lawrence wrote to Forster, "You surpass the Englishman and you surpass the Indian, and are neither: and yet there is nothing inhuman . . . in your picture." See D. Garnett (ed.), *Selected Letters of T. E. Lawrence* (London: Cape, 1941), p. 209.

11. John Fiske, *Power Plays, Power Works* (London: Verso, 1993), p. 154.

12. Hoggart, "A Question of Time," pp. 196–197.

13. See Edward Said, *Culture and Imperialism* (London: Vintage, 1994), pp. 241–250.

14. Forster, *A Passage to India*, p. 135.

15. Hoggart, "A Question of Time," p. 198.

16. By Sir Henry Newbolt in *The Teaching of English in England* (London: His Majesty's Stationery Office [HMSO], 1926), p. 15.

17. See T. H. Eriksen, *Ethnicity and Nationalism* (London: Pluto, 1993), pp. 38–39, 102–104.

18. For an extended discussion of this phenomenon, see Julia Kristeva, *Strangers to Ourselves* (New York: Columbia University Press, 1991).

19. Forster, *Passage to India*, p. 317.

20. Jan Penrose, "Essential Constructions? The Cultural Basis of Nationalist Movements," *Nations and Nationalism* 1 (1995), p. 394. Penrose derives this account from Raymond Williams.

21. In this case, members of the same nation would be only to a limited degree the same kind of people, in the sense of having the same cultural characteristics.

22. A cultural imperialist cannot in principle be a cultural nationalist since the former seeks to extend culture across the boundaries of the state whereas the latter seeks to extend the boundaries of the state to comprehend culture.

23. Eriksen, *Ethnicity and Nationalism*, p. 103.

24. More particularly, the version expounded by Yael Tamir in *Liberal Nationalism* (Princeton: Princeton University Press, 1993), especially chapter 3.

25. Tamir, *Liberal Nationalism*, pp. 87–90, 135.

26. *Pace* John Hutchinson, *Modern Nationalism* (London: Fontana, 1994), pp. 39–47. Hutchinson holds that cultural nationalism is not necessarily political in its definition. But this stance confuses rights to statehood with intentions to exercise it.

27. Charles Wentworth Dilke, quoted in L. L. Snyder (ed.), *The Dynamics of Nationalism* (Princeton: Van Nostrand, 1964), p. 90.

28. In *Terrorism, Security and Nationality* (London: Routledge, 1994), I associate this "mould" or "form" model with voluntarism in a way that I now reject. (See p. 114 of that volume.)

29. William Butler Yeats, quoted in R F Foster, *Paddy and Mr. Punch* (London: Allen and Unwin, 1993), pp. 304–305.

30. This conception is, so far as I can see, the one preferred by Tamir.

31. See D. Young, *Scotland* (London: Cassell, 1971), chapter 11. An analogous question regarding the relationship of Dutch and Flemish is discussed in J. Blommaert, *Nations and Nationalism* 2 (1996), pp. 235–256. And for some interesting African parallels, see Bamgbose, *Language and the Nation*, p. 15.

32. Will Kymlicka, *Liberalism, Community and Culture* (Oxford: Oxford University Press, 1989), pp. 166, 165. Tamir fails to appreciate the force of this point in her criticism of Kymlicka in *Liberal Nationalism*, p. 38.

33. This point seems to be implied by Kymlicka in *Liberalism, Community and Culture*, p. 135; though see p. 179, fn. 2, for some caveats.

34. See Kymlicka, *Liberalism, Community and Culture*, pp. 175–177.

35. Ibid., p. 177.

36. Jan Hofmeyr, quoted in B. Williams, *Cecil Rhodes* (London: Constable, 1938), p. 60.

37. *Pace* Charles Taylor. See his criticism of Kymlicka in *Multiculturalism* (Princeton: Princeton University Press, 1994), pp. 40–41, fn. 16.

38. Ernest Gellner, quoted in A. D. Smith, *The Ethnic Revival* (Cambridge: Cambridge University Press, 1981), p. 47.

39. Johann Gottlieb Fichte, *Addresses to the German Nation*, reprinted in A. Zimmern, *Modern Political Doctrines* (London: Oxford University Press, 1931), pp. 168–170. (Originally published in 1808.) For an interesting discussion, see Hans Sluga, *Heidegger's Crisis* (Cambridge, Mass.: Harvard University Press, 1993), pp. 34–41.

40. *Pace* Tamir, who criticizes Kymlicka for creating "a tie between the right to a culture and the innate nature of membership, thus unjustifiably depriving, for instance, converts." See Tamir's *Liberal Nationalism*, p. 38.

41. See Kymlicka's discussion of "civic" nationalism in *Multicultural Citizenship* (Oxford: Oxford University Press, 1995), pp. 24 and 200, fn. 15.

42. Identity was supposedly threatened by "cosmopolitanism," identified in Fichte's day with the French and later, murderously, with the Jews. Although Fichte discounted the previous ancestry of those who continue to speak an "original language" (*Addresses to the German Nation*, p. 170), it is not clear that we can make sense of the idea that they speak their original language without identifying them through race or descent.

43. Fichte, *Addresses to the German Nation*, p. 173.

44. Ibid., pp. 170, 171.

45. National literature may not always be relevant, but I cite it here because it is exemplary of other aspects of a language culture.

46. René Wellek and Austin Warren, *Theory of Literature* (Harmondsworth: Penguin, 1973), p. 52.

47. A. Warner, *A Guide to Anglo-Irish Literature* (Dublin: Gill and Macmillan, 1981), pp. 205–206.

48. J. Hildebidle, *Five Irish Writers* (Cambridge, Mass.: Harvard University Press, 1989), p. 8.

49. Elizabeth Bowen, quoted in V. Glendinning, *Elizabeth Bowen: Portrait of a Writer* (Harmondsworth: Penguin, 1989), p. 8.

50. Sean O'Faolain, quoted in ibid., p. 120.

51. *The Last September* was originally published in 1929, but my page references are to the Penguin edition of 1983. This and other novels by Bowen are discussed by Foster in *Paddy and Mr. Punch,* pp. 102–122; and by myself in "The Idea of a National Literature," in A. Baumeister and J. Horton (eds.), *Literature and the Political Imagination* (London: Routledge, 1996), pp. 198–217.

52. Oscar Wilde, quoted in H. M. Hyde, *Oscar Wilde* (London: Methuen, 1976), p. 69.

53. From act 3 of "Lady Windermere's Fan" (1892), in Oscar Wilde's *Plays* (Harmondsworth: Penguin, 1954), p. 55.

54. Wilde, quoted in Frank Harris, *Oscar Wilde* (New York: Brentano, 1918), p. 75.

55. Bowen, *The Last September*, p. 125.

56. Ibid., p. 93.

57. This is Wolfe Tone's phrase. See D. G. Boyce, *Nationalism in Ireland* (London: Croom Helm, 1982), p. 128.

58. Edith Somerville and Martin Ross, *Some Experiences of an Irish RM* (London: Sphere, 1987), p. 107. (Originally published in 1889.)

59. Frank O'Connor, quoted in Warner, *A Guide to Anglo-Irish Literature*, p. 60.

60. Anthony Cronin, quoted in ibid., p. 8.

61. And it does this without implying that we choose our cultures. Individually we do not; we make them collectively, so that individuals alone cannot determine their culture. Note that people must think of the national culture they construct for themselves as *important* to them. Otherwise, this kind of cultural voluntarism will collapse into an untenable nominalism obviously incapable of supporting a claim to statehood.

Chapter Eight

1. Eamon de Valera, quoted in M. Moynihan (ed.), *Speeches and Statements of Eamon de Valera 1917–1973* (Dublin: Gill and Macmillan, 1980), p. 466.

2. Irish speakers in de Valera's day could commonly recall two hundred lines of poetry composed six centuries earlier. See P. J. Dowling, *The Hedge Schools of Ireland* (Cork: Mercier, 1968), p. 12.

3. See J. Patterson, *Exploring Maori Values* (Palmerston North, New Zealand: Dunmore Press, 1992), chapter 1.

4. Ibid., p. 184.

5. Johann Gottlieb Fichte, *Addresses to the German Nation* (1808), reprinted in A. Zimmern, *Modern Political Doctrines* (London: Oxford University Press, 1931), p. 170.

6. Ibid., p. 171.

7. F. R. Leavis, *The Common Pursuit* (Harmondsworth: Penguin, 1962), p. 188.

8. Ibid., p. 208.

9. See F. R. Leavis, *Revaluation* (Harmondsworth: Penguin, 1972), chapter 2.

10. Andrew Miller, *Contemporary Cultural Theory* (London: UCL Press, 1994), p. 35. For a more considered account, see C. Baldick, *The Social Mission of English 1848–1932* (Oxford: Oxford University Press, 1983).

11. Kymlicka distinguishes the "character" of a culture which includes values from the culture itself. For further discussion of this point, see his *Liberalism, Community and Culture* (Oxford: Oxford University Press, 1989), chapter 8.

12. Heinrich von Treitschke, quoted in L. Greenfeld, *Nationalism* (Cambridge, Mass.: Harvard University Press, 1992), pp. 377–378.

13. From Matthew Arnold's "To the Hungarian Nation," in *The Poems of Matthew Arnold 1840–1866* (London: Dent, 1908), p. 37.

14. Ayn Rand, *The Virtue of Selfishness* (New York: Signet, 1964), pp. 86, 129.

15. E. M. Forster, *Two Cheers for Democracy* (Harmondsworth: Penguin, 1965), p. 41.

16. Ibid.

17. *Protestant Telegraph* (1971), quoted in J. D. Cash, *Identity, Ideology and Conflict* (Oxford: Oxford University Press, 1996), p. 82.

18. See, for example, Elie Kedourie, *Nationalism* (London: Hutchinson, 1966), chapter 6.

19. Thomas Kiernan, *The Arabs* (London: Sphere, 1975), p. 200.

20. For discussions of liberal attitudes toward illiberal cultures, see W. Kymlicka, *Multicultural Citizenship* (Oxford: Oxford University Press, 1995), chapter 8; and D. Philpott, "In Defense of Self-Determination," *Ethics* 105 (1995), pp. 371–375.

21. See, for example, David Bell, *Communitarianism and Its Critics* (Oxford: Oxford University Press, 1993), chapter 2.

22. Cf. Bell, *Communitarianism*, pp. 133–134.

23. John Gray, *Berlin* (London: Fontana, 1995), p. 118.This quotation appears in a passage characterizing Isaiah Berlin's value pluralism.

24. Though its value has sometimes been thought of as derived from the fact that "civilisation progresses by differentiation as well as by assimilation of interests and character." See C. Delisle Burns, *Political Ideals* (Oxford: Oxford University Press, 1919), p. 194.

25. For example, Kymlicka says that "I am using 'a culture' as synonymous with 'a nation' or 'a people'—that is as an intergenerational community, more or less institutionally complete, occupying a given territory or homeland, sharing a distinct language and history." See his *Multicultural Citizenship*, p. 18.

26. Stuart Hampshire, "Nationalism," in E. and A. Margalit (eds.), *Isaiah Berlin: A Celebration* (London: Hogarth Press, 1991), p. 128.

27. This seems to be Miller's position. See his *On Nationality* (Oxford: Oxford University Press, 1995), pp. 86–88.

28. A. Margalit and J. Raz, "National Self-Determination," in J. Raz (ed.), *Ethics in the Public Domain* (Oxford: Oxford University Press, 1994), p. 117.

29. Kymlicka, *Multicultural Citizenship*, p. 86. It should be said that Kymlicka's conclusions do not straightforwardly support nationalism.

30. See J. Tomari, "Kymlicka, Liberalism and Respect for Cultural Minorities," *Ethics* 105 (1995), pp. 580–603.

31. Miller, *On Nationality*, p. 87.

32. Advanced by Neil MacCormick in "Nation and Nationalism," *Legal Right and Social Democracy* (Oxford: Oxford University Press, 1982).

33. Louis Dumont, *Essays in Individualism* (Chicago: University of Chicago Press, 1986), pp. 131, 130.

34. For some general criticisms of this point, see David George, "The Ethics of Self-Determination," in P. Gilbert and P. Gregory (eds.), *Nations, Cultures and Markets* (Aldershot: Avebury, 1994).

35. See Charles Taylor, *Reconciling the Solitudes* (Montreal and Kingston, Canada: McGill-Queens University Press, 1993), pp. 47–53.

36. As Taylor emphasizes, in ibid.

37. To this extent J. Hutchinson is right (see his *Modern Nationalism* [London: Fontana, 1994], chapter 2). But this is just why such groups are *not* nations; for, as noted in Chapter 7, Hutchinson holds that cultural nationalism is not necessarily political in its definition—a stance which I dispute.

38. Indeed, Taylor presents his arguments as supporting self-government, which he acknowledges need not be democratic. See his *Reconciling the Solitudes*, p. 51.

39. M. Fortes and E. E. Evans-Pritchard, *African Political Systems* (Oxford: Oxford University Press, 1940), p. 9.

40. Mohammed Ali Jinnah, quoted in N. Mansergh (ed.), *Documents and Speeches on British Commonwealth Affairs 1931–52*, Vol. 11 (London: Oxford University Press, 1953), pp. 609–612.

41. See Jan Penrose, "Essential Constructions," *Nations and Nationalism* 1 (1995), p. 394.

42. It is in this tradition that Miller stands; see his *On Nationality*, chapters 2–3.

43. An example was the enterprise of the English commended by Mrs. Thatcher. See Bhikhu Parekh, "National Identity and the Ontological Regeneration of Britain," in P. Gilbert and P. Gregory (eds.), *Nations, Cultures and Markets* (Aldershot: Avebury, 1994), pp. 93–108.

44. For discussions of the relation between nationalism and communitarianism, see John O'Neill, "Should Communitarians Be Nationalists?" *Journal of Applied Philosophy* 11 (1994), pp. 135–143; and David Archard, "Should Nationalists Be Communitarians?" *Journal of Applied Philosophy* 13 (1996), pp. 215–220.

45. For an extended discussion of these questions, see Miller, *On Nationality*, chapter 3.

46. It is noteworthy that Brian Barry seems to draw on both in his criticism of Miller, in "Nationalism Versus Liberalism?" *Nations and Nationalism* 2 (1996), pp. 430–435.

Chapter Nine

1. A. Nevins and H. S. Commager, *A Pocket History of the United States* (New York: Simon & Schuster, 1981), p. 151.

2. G. van Pistolkors, quoted in J. Hiden and P. Salmon, *The Baltic Nations and Europe* (London: Longmans, 1991), p. 91.

3. Pastor Georg Brasche, quoted in A. Lieven, *The Baltic Revolution* (New Haven: Yale University Press, 1993), p. 118.

4. Otto Bauer, *The Nationalities Question and Social Democracy* (1907), reprinted in S. Woolf (ed.), *Nationalism in Europe: 1815 to the Present* (London: Routledge, 1996), p. 71. (Note that "fate" here is often translated as "destiny.")

5. Ibid., p. 67.

6. Ibid., p. 61.

7. Ibid., p. 79.

8. Soo D. R. Morris, *The Washing of the Spears* (London: Cape, 1965), pp. 40–67.

9. And the denial of it to what, following Hegel, are called "unhistorical nations." See Hegel's *Philosophy of Mind*, translated by William Wallace (Oxford: Oxford University Press, 1971), p. 279.

10. See G. A. Williams, "When Was Wales?" in S. Woolf (ed.), *Nationalism in Europe: 1815 to the Present* (London: Routledge, 1996), pp. 193–195.

11. John Owen (c. 1560–1622), in D. M. and E. M. Lloyd (eds.), *A Book of Wales* (London: Collins, 1953), p. 261.

12. See D. Saunders, "What Makes a Nation a Nation? Ukrainians Since 1600," *Ethnic Studies* 10 (1993), p. 116.

13. See Lieven, *Baltic Revolution*, p. 163.

14. Ernest Renan, "What Is a Nation?" in A. Zimmern, *Modern Political Doctrines* (London: Oxford University Press, 1931), p. 203.

15. David Miller, *On Nationality* (Oxford: Oxford University Press, 1995), p. 23. For criticism of his position as discussed here, see Michael Freeman, "Nation-State and Cosmopolis," *Journal of Applied Philosophy* 11 (1994), p. 84.

16. See Lieven, *Baltic Revolution*, pp. 118–123.

17. Renan, "What Is a Nation?" p. 190.

18. García Lorca, quoted in E. Honig, *García Lorca* (London: Editions Poetry, 1945), p. 26. Lorca was, of course, shot by Fascists.

19. David Miller, "The Ethical Significance of Nationality," *Ethics* 98 (1988), p. 656, n. 21. Miller distinguishes ethnicity from nationality to disallow ethnic criteria for nationality, but his doing so does not allow for other essentially historical nationalisms.

20. Kymlicka, however, seems to require *both* to be distinct. In this connection, see his *Liberalism, Community and Culture* (Oxford: Oxford University Press, 1989), chapter 8.

21. For example, that of E. A. Freeman by Grant Allen; see M. D. Biddiss (ed.), *Images of Race* (Leicester: Leicester University Press, 1979), pp. 205–256.

22. See, for example, Miller, *On Nationality*, pp. 35–39; and David Archard, "Myths, Lies and Historical Truth," *Political Studies* 43 (1995), pp. 472–481.

23. As against necessary in practice—for example, as a result of a psychological need to reinforce reasons.

24. Cf. Archard, "Myths, Lies and Historical Truth," pp. 475–477.

25. As they are not by Miller; cf. his *On Nationality*, pp. 23 and 36–39.

26. Cf. Charles Jones, "Revenge of the Philosophical Mole," *Journal of Applied Philosophy* 13 (1996), pp. 78–79.

27. As by both Archard in "Myths, Lies and Historical Truth" and Miller in *On Nationality*.

28. See Bob Dixon, *Catching Them Young*, Vol. 2 (London: Pluto, 1977), p. 89.

29. E. E. Evans-Pritchard, "Anthropology and History," *Essays in Social Anthropology* (London: Faber, 1962), p. 53.

30. Made, for example, by Freeman in "Nation-State and Cosmopolis," p. 84.

31. Thus, as Anthony Smith notes, golden ages which exhibit national values may be discontinuous from their present—as, for example, in Egypt and Greece. See Smith, "Memory and Modernity," *Nations and Nationalism* 2 (1996), p. 383.

32. From George Russell's "On Behalf of Some Irishmen Not Followers of Tradition," in B. Kennelly (ed.), *Penguin Book of Irish Verse* (Harmondsworth: Penguin, 1981), p. 314. ("AE" is Russell's pen name.)

33. E. J. Hobsbawm, *Nations and Nationalism Since 1780* (Cambridge: Cambridge University Press, 1992), p. 13.

34. Simone Weil, *The Need for Roots* (London: Routledge, 1952), p. 114.

35. This phrase is used by Carlton Hayes in *The Historical Evolution of Modern Nationalism* (New York: Macmillan, 1931), p. 88.

36. See J. G. A. Pocock, "Burke and the Ancient Constitution," in J. Lively and A. Reeve (eds.), *Modern Political Theory from Hobbes to Marx* (London: Routledge, 1988), pp. 159–182.

37. See Christopher Hill, *The Century of Revolution* (Edinburgh: Nelson, 1962), pp. 176–177.

38. Edmund Burke, "Reform of Representation in the House of Commons" (1785), quoted in G. H. Sabine, *A History of Political Theory* (London: Harrap, 1963), p. 609.

39. Ibid.

40. Jean-Jacques Rousseau, *Social Contract*, book 2, chapter 3.

41. See A. Cobban, *Historians and the Causes of the French Revolution* (London: Historical Association, 1958), pp. 3–7.

42. Gerrard Winstanley, quoted in Hill, *Century of Revolution*, p. 177.

43. Edmund Burke, *Reflections on the Revolution in France* (Harmondsworth: Penguin, 1986), p. 118. (Originally published in 1790.)

44. It might be objected that the tradition to be defended is "based on the understanding that moral principles and virtuous exemplars from history must be interpreted and applied" and that this is done within a "socially embedded argument about the good of the community." (See Daniel Bell, *Communitarianism and Its Critics* [Oxford: Oxford University Press, 1993], p. 126.) The difficulty here is to understand how tradition can be essential to determining the common good, rather than something invoked within some societies and not others.

45. Though the task can be the realization of distinctive values. See H. H. Gerth and C. Wright Mills (eds.), *From Max Weber* (London: Routledge, 1970), p. 176.

46. This distinction is overlooked by Margaret Canovan. See her *Nationhood and Political Theory* (Cheltenham: Edward Elgar, 1996), p. 8.

47. Charles B. Boynton, quoted in R. Cawardine, "The Know-Nothing Party, the Protestant Evangelical Community and American National Identity." in S. Mews (ed.), *Religion and National Identity* (Oxford: Blackwell, 1982), p. 450. The idea derives from Herder via Schleirmacher; see R. R. Ergang, *Herder and the Foundations of German Nationalism* (New York: Columbia University Press, 1931), p. 250.

48. Joseph [Giuseppe] Mazzini, *Duties of Man* (London: Dent, 1907), p. 55.

49. See Eugen Steiner, *The Slovak Dilemma* (Cambridge: Cambridge University Press, 1973), chapter 1.

Conclusion

1. I am thinking particularly of Y. Tamir's *Liberal Nationalism* (Princeton: Princeton University Press, 1993) and D. Miller's *On Nationality* (Oxford: Oxford University Press, 1995).

2. It could be retorted that a true identity belief is a better basis for statehood than a deluded one. No doubt; but still left obscure is the question of how true identity beliefs could generate the right to it.

3. This is not to underestimate the extent to which naturalistic nationalisms draw on older traditions of thought in their *rhetoric*.

4. Jonathan Rée has perceived the importance of this point more clearly than most recent theorists. See, for example, Rée, "Internationality," *Radical Philosophy* 60 (1992), pp. 3–11.

Index

"Adlestrop" (Thomas), 97–98
Africa, 59, 147, 150
Aggregative accounts, 22, 26, 27, 28,
    179(n14)
    and national communities, 32–33, 36
    See also Nonsocietal accounts
Alba, Richard D., 179(n15)
Alien rule, 26
Alsace Lorraine, 62, 68, 69
Alter, Peter, 176(n9)
Amazons, 27
American nationalism, 7
Americas
    indigenous people of, 101, 105, 106
Ancestry, 179(n15)
Anderson, Benedict, 181(n12)
Anglo-Saxons, 165
Anthropologists
    and concept of nation, 10–11,
        176(n27)
    and nominalism, 177(n33)
    and race, 42–43, 181(n13)
    and territorial nationalism, 91
Aptness consideration, 40, 42, 44, 71,
    146–147
Armstrong, John, 187(n5)
Arnold, Matthew, 136
Ataturk, Kemal, 180(n38)
Australia, 102
Auto-stereotype, 45

Baghdad Caliphate, 138
Baltic Germans, 157, 160
Baltic states, 21, 155
Banton, Michael, 180(n4)
Bantus, 157
Barry, Brian, 177(n40), 194(n46)
Bauer, Otto, 155–157

Belgian colonialism, 150
Beliefs, 5–6
    and naturalism, 61–62
Benn, Stanley, 175(n4)
Beran, Harry, 184(n35), 184(nn26, 27)
Berlin, Isaiah, 193(n23)
Billig, M., 176(n9)
Binyon, Lawrence, 97, 98–99
Black nationalism, 8, 33
Bowen, Elizabeth, 22–23, 128–130,
    178(n8)
British nationalism, 7, 176(n12)
Bunyan, John, 134
Burke, Edmund, 53, 165–166
Byron, Lord, 60–61

Canada, 121
Canadian nationalism, 7
Caney, Simon, 178(n3), 180(n39),
    182(n37)
Canovan, Margaret, 196(n46)
Catholics, 31, 137–138, 162
Character, national, 44–45, 46, 156
Charvet, John, 177(n32)
Chicano nationalism, 8
Citizenship, 21, 84–85, 176(n25)
Civic nationalism, 3, 75. See also
    Political nationalism
Civil association, 70–74, 78, 103
Cleaver, Eldridge, 33–34, 36
Closed-container model, 126–127
Collective voluntarism, 87
Colley, Linda, 176(n12)
Colonialism, 58–59, 116, 150, 180(n37)
Communication. See Language
Communication model, 115
Communicative relationships, 155
Communitarianism, 174